Getting Started
WITH
MULTIMEDIA

Calleen Coorough

Skagit Valley College

THE DRYDEN PRESS
HARCOURT BRACE COLLEGE PUBLISHERS

Fort Worth   Philadelphia   San Diego   New York   Orlando   Austin   San Antonio
Toronto   Montreal   London   Sydney   Tokyo

PUBLISHER	*George Provol*
EXECUTIVE EDITOR	*Wesley Lawton*
DEVELOPMENTAL EDITOR	*Larry Crowder*
PRODUCT MANAGER	*Federico Arrietta*
PROJECT EDITOR	*John Haakenson*
ART DIRECTOR	*Scott Baker*
PRODUCTION MANAGER	*Darryl King*
ELECTRONIC PUBLISHING COORDINATOR	*Cathy Spitzenberger*
PERMISSIONS EDITOR	*Adele Krause*

ISBN: 0-03-023671-1

Library of Congress Catalog Card Number: 98-070996

Address for Editorial Correspondence:
The Dryden Press, 301 Commerce Street, Suite 3700, Fort Worth, TX 76102

Address for Orders:
The Dryden Press, 6277 Sea Harbor Drive, Orlando, FL 32887-6777. 1-800-782-4479

Website address:
http://www.hbcollege.com

The Dryden Press, Dryden, and the Dryden Press Logo are registered trademarks of Harcourt Brace & Company.

Harcourt Brace College Publishers may provide complimentary instructional aids and supplements or supplement packages to those adopters qualified under our adoption policy. Please contact your sales representative for more information. If as an adopter or potential user you receive supplements you do not need, please return them to your sales representative or send them to:

Attention: Returns Department, Troy Warehouse, 465 South Lincoln Drive, Troy, MO 63379

Printed in the United States of America
8 9 0 1 2 3 4 5 6 7 048 10 9 8 7 6 5 4 3 2 1

The Dryden Press
Harcourt Brace College Publishers

The Dryden Press Series in Information Systems

Coorough
Getting Started with Multimedia

Fenrich
Practical Guidelines for Creating Instructional Multimedia Applications

Fuller/Manning
Getting Started with the Internet

Gordon and Gordon
Information Systems: A Management Approach

Gray, King, McLean, and Watson
Management of Information Systems
Second Edition

Harrington
Database Management for Microcomputers: Design and Implementation
Second Edition

Harris
Systems Analysis and Design: A Project Approach

Head
An Introduction to Programming with QuickBASIC

Larsen/Marold
Using Microsoft Works 4.0 for Windows 95: An Introduction to Computing

Laudon and Laudon
Information Systems and the Internet: A Problem-Solving Approach
Fourth Edition

Laudon and Laudon
Information Systems: A Problem-Solving Approach
(A CD-ROM interactive version)

Licker
Management Information Systems: A Strategic Leadership Approach

Lorents and Morgan
Database Systems: Concepts, Management, Applications

Martin
Discovering Microsoft Office 97

Martin/Parker
PC Concepts

Mason
Using Microsoft Access 97 in Business

Mason
Using Microsoft Excel 97 in Business

McKeown
Living with Computers
Fifth Edition

McKeown
Working with Computers
Second Edition

Morley
Getting Started with Computers

Morley
Getting Started: Web Page Design with Microsoft FrontPage 97

Parker
Understanding Computers: Today and Tomorrow
98 Edition

Parker
Understanding Networking and the Internet

Spear
Introduction to Computer Programming in Visual Basic 4.0

Spear
Visual Basic 3.0: A Brief Introduction
Visual Basic 4.0: A Brief Introduction

Sullivan
The New Computer User
Second Edition

Martin and Parker
Mastering Today's Software Series

Texts available in any combination of the following:

Disk Operating System 5.0 (DOS 5.0)
Disk Operating System 6.0 (DOS 6.0)
Windows 3.1
Windows 95
Microsoft Office 97
Microsoft Office for Windows 95 Professional Edition
WordPerfect 5.1
WordPerfect 5.2 for Windows
WordPerfect 6.0 for DOS
WordPerfect 6.0 for Windows
WordPerfect 6.1 for Windows
Corel WordPerfect 7.0 for Windows 95
Word 6.0 for Windows
Word 7.0 for Windows 95
Word 97
Lotus 1-2-3 (2.2/2.3)
Lotus 1-2-3 (2.4)
Lotus 1-2-3 for Windows (4.01)

Lotus 1-2-3 for Windows (5.0)
Lotus 1-2-3 97
Excel 5.0 for Windows
Excel 7.0 for Windows 95
Excel 97
Quattro Pro 4.0
Quattro Pro 6.0 for Windows
dBASE III PLUS
dBASE IV (1.5/2.0)
dBASE 5 for Windows
Paradox 4.0
Paradox 5.0 for Windows
Access 2.0 for Windows
Access 7.0 for Windows 95
Access 97
PowerPoint 7.0 for Windows 95
PowerPoint 97
A Beginner's Guide to BASIC
A Beginner's Guide to QBASIC
Netscape Communicator

The Harcourt Brace College Outline Series

Kreitzberg
Introduction to Fortran

Interactive multimedia is a burgeoning field. Consumers are demanding a wide array of interactive products and services including reference materials, games, virtual communities, digital periodicals, kiosks, edutainment, and computer-based training products.

In addition, the Internet has evolved from a text-based network to a powerful multimedia delivery system. According to the March 1997 issue of *Career Opportunities News,* Websites grew 600 percent last year. With the added growth of Intranets and Extranets, this percentage will continue to increase. As a result, the market for multimedia products will continue to grow and expand.

This explosion of activity and interest in interactive multimedia technologies offers incredible opportunities for individuals interested in learning more about multimedia.

Last year, five of the 20 Hot Track Jobs listed in *US News* were multimedia related.

This explosion in interactive multimedia technologies also offers incredible opportunities for institutions of higher learning. Many colleges are incorporating multimedia training into their computer information systems and technology programs. As evidence of this trend, the Northwest Center for Emerging Technologies (NWCET) and the Regional Advanced Technology Education consortium (RATEC) have included Interactive Digital Media Specialist as one of the eight career clusters for which they have created SCANS (Secretary's Commission on Achieving Necessary Skills, U.S. Department of Labor) skill standards. These standards will be a major thrust of curriculum development throughout the United States.

All of this interest in multimedia and demand for people with multimedia skills creates a huge need for curriculum. It is my hope that this textbook will serve as the fundamental resource for an introductory multimedia course. The primary focus of this book is on multimedia concepts, terminology, trends, media elements, design, and emerging hardware and software used to create and distribute interactive multimedia applications. There are tips and illustrations scattered throughout the book, and end-of-chapter questions and exercises that help students solidify the knowledge and skills they have acquired as they conclude each chapter.

At the end of the textbook, you will find a comprehensive Glossary and Index, as well as a Reference List of suggested multimedia books and Websites. In addition, you'll find a CD-ROM complete with demo copies of software applications and hundreds of sample media elements.

From the Dryden Press Web site at www.dryden.com/infosys/coorough, you'll find additional curriculum materials and updates on online courses and testing.

Acknowledgments

This book is first and foremost dedicated to my husband, Barclay Berry, for his knowledge and unending enthusiasm of technology, his pervasive support and endurance, and his extensive help with the figures in this book.

I would like to thank my friends for continuously reminding me to "recreate" and my parents for always encouraging me.

I appreciate the many helpful suggestions from the following reviewers: Min Liu, The University of Texas, Austin; Kathy Marold, Metropolitan State College;

Liz Hammond-Kaarremaa, Malaspina University–College; and Carolyn Rude-Parkins, University of Louisville.

I would also like to thank the team at Dryden Press for its hard work, support, and creative ideas: Wesley Lawton, executive editor; Federico Arrietta, product manager; Larry Crowder, developmental editor; Annette Bratcher, editorial coordinator; John Haakenson, project editor; Darryl King, production manager; Scott Baker, art director; Cathy Spitzenberger, electronic publishing coordinator; and Adele Krause, art and literary rights editor.

CONTENTS IN BRIEF

CONTENTS

Chapter 7 - Multimedia Authoring   209

Chapter 8 - Multimedia and the Internet   235

Introduction to Multimedia

UPON COMPLETION OF THIS CHAPTER, YOU WILL BE ABLE TO:

1. Define multimedia and interactive multimedia
2. Explain the difference between linear and non-linear multimedia
3. Briefly describe the evolution of multimedia
4. Define and explain the importance of digitizing media elements
5. Describe the different ways people learn and explain how to balance multimedia elements to teach or inspire effectively
6. List and briefly describe the five most commonly used multimedia elements
7. Define hypertext, hotword, and hypermedia. Explain how they are used in multimedia applications
8. Define clip art
9. Describe three different ways of obtaining digital photographs
10. Define animation and give an example of how it is incorporated into multimedia applications
11. Define audio and describe two different techniques used to capture sound
12. Describe one of the primary obstacles encountered when trying to deliver video files and explain how this obstacle can be overcome
13. List and describe the different applications for multimedia
14. Define immersion virtual reality and describe several uses of this technology
15. Identify some of the tools used to create lower-end virtual reality on the Web
16. Identify several multimedia career opportunities

Introduction

Welcome to the wonderful world of interactive multimedia!

Multimedia applications are all around you. Whether you know it or not, chances are you see or interact with one or more multimedia applications daily. If you watch television, surf the Internet, play video games, personalize an electronic greeting card, or withdraw money from your local ATM, you are viewing or using a multimedia application. Our society depends on information, and multimedia is an effective way to present it. By providing a more user-friendly interface, multimedia makes information more accessible to the multitudes.

What Is Multimedia?

At the most basic level, **multimedia** means using more than one media element. It refers to the integration of text, graphics, animation, sound, and video. This integration is primarily accomplished through the use of the computer.

When we incorporate multiple media into an application, more of our senses are activated. Consequently, one of the reasons we use multimedia is to give life to flat information. Multimedia encourages users to embrace, internalize, and glean more from information because they can attack the information from multiple directions. In other words, users of multimedia applications have an opportunity to read about information, but they can also see it and hear it. As you will soon see, even smell and touch have a place in multimedia applications.

At the next level, we add interactivity to multimedia. **Interactive multimedia** allows the user to respond directly to and control any or all of these media. Users of interactive multimedia become active participants in an application instead of passive recipients of information. It is interactivity that gives multimedia range

FIGURE 1.1

We use multimedia applications every day.

FIGURE 1.2

Interactive multimedia allows the user to respond to or control the application.

and depth because it requires creativity on the part of both authors and users. It also frees users by giving them choices.

Categories of Multimedia

Interactive multimedia applications fall into two categories. Some are linear, while others are non-linear. With **linear media**, users start at the beginning and progress through a set sequence of events until they reach the end. Most digital slide shows and plays would be examples of linear media. **Non-linear media** leaves the order of events to the discretion of the user. An interactive CD-ROM encyclopedia would be an example of non-linear media. There is no predefined order; users can enter or exit at any point and at any time.

The Evolution of Multimedia

Multimedia is not new. We have been working with multiple media for quite some time. As a society, we are very accustomed to viewing and working with multiple media. We are used to seeing text combined with graphics and photographs. We are used to hearing music and sound with animated video game characters. Movies with sound replaced silent movies more than 50 years ago, and even silent movies incorporated multiple media by using video and text captions together.

Though working with multiple media is not new, the growth of computer-based multimedia has definitely exploded over the past few years. There are many

FIGURE 1.3

This non-linear multimedia encyclopedia program lets you see animations, hear sounds, and jump from topic to topic.

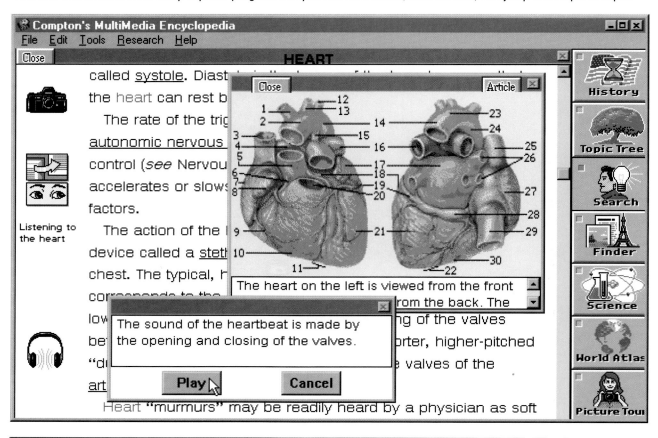

reasons for this growth. Computer processing power and technology have improved, making it easier and more fun to work with media elements on the computer. People throughout many industries have found new and beneficial ways of using multimedia applications, thereby creating a demand for multimedia technology. The growth of the Web has spurred the growth of multimedia as more and more multimedia applications are being designed for the Internet and the World Wide Web. Undoubtedly, this growth in multimedia will continue at an exponential rate as the technology continues to improve and people find more reasons to use it.

Past

Because multimedia is the combination of text, graphics, animation, sound, and video, its history ultimately stretches back to the first sounds, language, drawings, cartoons, radios, and motion pictures. To explore the history of multimedia by exploring the history of each of these multimedia elements independently would require an interactive multimedia CD-ROM of its own. This is obviously beyond the scope of this book. And though it is helpful and worthwhile to have a background in each of these elements, knowing the history of each is not crucial to understanding multimedia. The important point to remember is that working with multiple media is not new, but working with computer-based multiple media is.

FIGURE 1.4

Multimedia has been around for a long time. However, computer-based digital multimedia is relatively new.

FIGURE 1.5

Growth in multimedia is directly related to growth in the Internet.

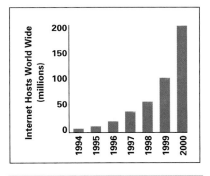

FIGURE 1.6

Digitized media elements have been converted to a series of 0's and 1's that can be interpreted by the computer.

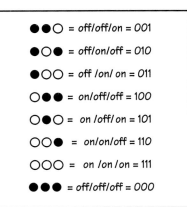

Present

Working with media elements that have been **digitized** is fairly new, at least in the grand scheme of media. When media elements have been digitized, it means they have been captured as a series of 0's and 1's and can now be interpreted by the computer. This means people can now transmit media elements across phone lines, developers can create and modify elements in ways they never dreamed possible, and users can interact and control these media elements for greater personalization.

As a result of digitized media elements, a variety of uses for multimedia have been created within a multitude of industries. Consequently, we are surrounded by multimedia applications. Today, most of these applications consist primarily of elements that involve our eyes and ears, but this too is changing.

Future

In the future, multimedia will afford transition into an environment that easily involves all of our senses. In addition, it will provide us with more opportunities and options to control our environment, whether it be for entertainment, research, education, or conducting business. Multimedia will continue to evolve into an extremely rich and powerful information environment that can be easily shared across networks.

Multimedia is growing at an exponential rate. According to the Information Workstation Group, multimedia will evolve into a $30 billion industry with the top three applications being entertainment ($9.1 billion), publishing ($4.7 billion), and education/training ($4.3 billion).

Why Multimedia?

Each of us learns differently, and each of us is inspired by something different. When we use multimedia, we are able to tap into these differences. For example, some people are very visual. They learn or are inspired by reading, seeing, or visualizing. Others are quite auditory and learn best by listening. Finally, there are kinesthetic learners who learn by doing.

Though most of us have a preferred learning style, for all of us, learning is enhanced when each of these learning styles is accommodated. In fact, research shows that people remember only 20 percent of what they see and 30 percent of what they hear. When they see it and hear it, they remember 50 percent. When they see it, hear it, and interact with it, they remember 80 percent. That's a big difference, and certainly a good rationale supporting the tremendous growth of multimedia, as well as justification for using it.

The importance of interactive multimedia can be summed up in the Chinese proverb, "Tell me and I will forget; show me and I may remember; involve me and I will understand."

FIGURE 1.7

Virtual reality programs like this one incorporate multimedia elements that provide a multisensory experience.

FIGURE 1.8

Learning is enhanced when a variety of learning styles are addressed.

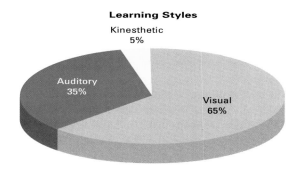

Learning Styles

Kinesthetic
5%

Auditory
35%

Visual
65%

One of the best ways to convey content is to use a variety of media to reinforce *one* idea. In other words, we use multiple media to direct the user's attention to one concept or idea. At the same time, we have to be careful not to overwhelm the user by trying to use multiple media to convey *multiple* ideas all at the same time. Finding the right balance and relationship between the media elements is critical.

FIGURE 1.9

Balance is critical in designing effective multimedia applications. The Western Washington University Web page does a nice job of balancing graphics and text.

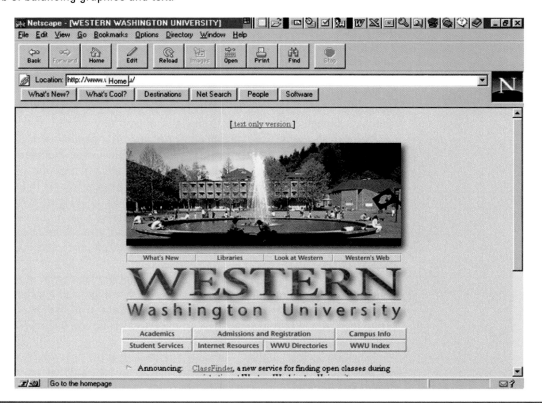

Let's take a quick glance at the key multimedia elements. Each of these elements will be discussed in greater depth throughout this textbook, but this should give you a feel for the most common elements used in multimedia applications.

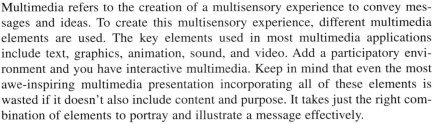

Multimedia Elements

Multimedia refers to the creation of a multisensory experience to convey messages and ideas. To create this multisensory experience, different multimedia elements are used. The key elements used in most multimedia applications include text, graphics, animation, sound, and video. Add a participatory environment and you have interactive multimedia. Keep in mind that even the most awe-inspiring multimedia presentation incorporating all of these elements is wasted if it doesn't also include content and purpose. It takes just the right combination of elements to portray and illustrate a message effectively.

Balance is key. A well-designed multimedia application appeals to more than one sense. It is important to give users enough stimulation to peak their interest without overwhelming them. If balance is achieved, retention and understanding are enhanced. If balance is off, users will either become bored or confused.

Don't overwhelm the reader by using too many multimedia elements.

Text

In the past, content was disseminated primarily via text. Though additional elements have been added, text remains vital to multimedia applications. This is because text is still an effective way to communicate. In multimedia, text is used as headlines, subtitles, and captions. In addition to supplying content, text is used to give directions and communicate information, text-based menus and buttons help guide users through the multimedia application, and electronic books, magazines, and reference materials still rely on text to inform and educate.

Text doesn't have to be boring. Emphasis can be added by varying the font style, size, or color. Special effects and drop shadows that give the feeling of three dimensions can be added using tools like Microsoft WordArt. In fact, three-dimensional, animated text can also be created using modeling and animation programs. There really are no limits because text can be treated like any other graphic element.

Text can also serve as a link that allows the user to expand the existing text and learn more about a topic. **Hypertext** is text that allows you nonlinear access to information. In other words, hypertext links automatically transport you to related information without requiring you to get to that information by following a set path. These links are similar to a cross-reference. By clicking on a **hotword** or link, you have access to information on the topics you are most interested in exploring. Hypertext is very common on the World Wide Web as well as CD-ROM reference materials such as Microsoft Encarta, an interactive encyclopedia on CD-ROM.

Hypertext gives you immediate access to an entire macrocosm of related and connected information. Once you have used hypertext and had a wealth of information at your fingertips, reverting back to linear text can be quite dull. Therefore, in addition to standard text, hypertext also plays a significant role in multimedia applications.

When designing with text, there are several key terms with which you should be familiar. First, you should be aware that there are different types of fonts. **TrueType fonts** are fairly consistent from computer screen to computer screen and

FIGURE 1.10

A variety of special effects can be applied to text to make it more interesting.

FIGURE 1.11

Hypertext and hypergraphics are common on CD-ROM reference materials.

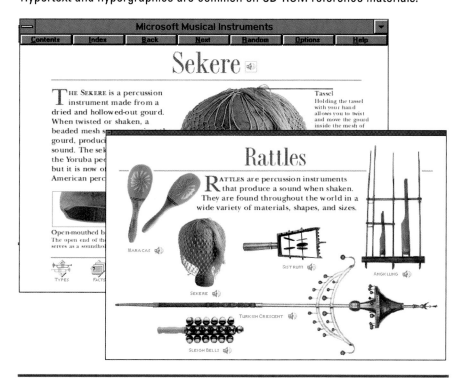

Convert text to a bitmapped graphic to maintain consistency and obtain a certain degree of insurance that your font will appear as you would like it to regardless of the viewer's monitor, printer, and installed applications.

from printer to printer. TrueType fonts come with the application software. **Printer fonts** are fonts that are specific to the printer or printers connected to the computer. Because the type of printer connected to computers significantly differs, printer fonts may not be available from one computer to another. **Screen fonts** depend on the monitor and may not appear the same from one computer to another.

Other terms you should be familiar with are **serif** and **sans serif.** Serif fonts have feet or tails as illustrated in Figure 1.12. Sans serif fonts do not have feet. Because our eyes have become accustomed to reading serif fonts and using the little feet to track, you should use serif fonts for larger bodies of texts. Sans serif fonts should be used for headings, titles, and callouts because they are more likely to draw attention. Because much of our text in multimedia applications is often quite short, sans serif fonts are used quite extensively in multimedia applications.

The last two terms have to do with spacing. **Kerning** is the term used to specify the amount of space between characters. **Leading** is the amount of space between lines of text. Kerning and leading are dependent upon the font size and the use of the text, and both are important in making text readable.

From a design perspective, when you use text in multimedia applications, keep the following guidelines in mind:

- Convert text to bitmapped graphics to ensure that the fonts you wish to appear in the project will look the same on the user's monitor.
- Align headings and bodies of text at the left to make it easier for readers to follow.
- Use text colors that provide a strong contrast against the background.
- Use serif fonts for large bodies of text and sans serif fonts for titles, headings, and callouts.
- Make sure the text is a readable size. Use a 12-point font size and 18-point leading.
- Keep blocks of text shorter than 60 characters.

Graphics

Because most people are quite visual, **graphics,** 2D and 3D images, are crucial to multimedia development. In fact, multimedia applications are predominantly

FIGURE 1.12

Serif fonts are best for body text while sans serif fonts should be used as titles and headings.

Serif fonts:
This is a sample of New Baskerville in an 11-point size.
This is a sample of Garamond in an 11-point size.
This is a sample of Palatino in an 11-point size.
This is a sample of Times New Roman in an 11-point size.

Sans-serif fonts:
This is a sample of Univers in an 11-point size.
This is a sample of Avant Garde in an 11-point size.
This is a sample of Helvetica in an 11-point size.
This is a sample of Gill Sans in an 11-point size.

graphic. Because they play such a critical role, balancing graphics is essential. When designing a multimedia application, it is important not to get carried away with graphics. Adding just the right graphic and just the right number of graphics may help the user learn and retain more information in less time and with less effort. Adding inappropriate graphics or bombarding the user with too many graphics will most likely be counterproductive.

Graphics that fit most any need are quite easy to find. Commercially prepared drawings called **clip art** come packaged with many application programs. Clip art is also sold on disk and CD-ROM, or you can download it from the Internet. In addition, you can create your own graphics by using a draw or paint program. These programs will be further discussed in Chapter 3.

Charts, another type of graphic, can convey a great deal of information in a very limited space. It might take pages of text to describe an idea that can be better illustrated through the use of a single **pie chart** or **bar graph.**

Photographs can also be used to enhance multimedia applications. Photographs can be digitized through a **color scanner** or taken directly with a **digital camera.** We will talk more about this equipment in Chapter 2. Collections of digital photographs called **stock photography** are also available on CD-ROM or can be downloaded from the Internet. Sometimes these photographs are free, but many times a fee is charged to use the photo or purchase the rights to the photo.

When a graphic or other multimedia object serves as a link to additional information about a topic, the link is called **hypermedia.**

Animation

Animation refers to graphic images that change or move. Animation can convey information, add visual interest, or draw attention to important information or links in a multimedia application. Animation is commonly used in advertising and marketing on the Web because the movement does grab the visitor's attention. By

FIGURE 1.13
Type size is measured in points.

24-point
18-point
12-point
10-point
8-point
6-point

Create and design graphics that are meaningful and consistent with your application.

FIGURE 1.14
Four methods of aligning paragraphs.

Centered text
is balanced between
margins.

Left-justified text has a ragged right margin. It is popular because it is easy to read.

Right-justified text has a ragged left margin and is rare because it is hard to read.

Justified text has even margins on both sides. Books and newspapers use justified text.

FIGURE 1.15
Clip art is also available for download from the Internet.

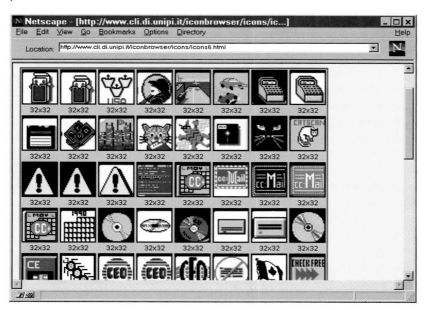

FIGURE 1.16

FIGURE 1.16
Collections of digital photographs are also available.

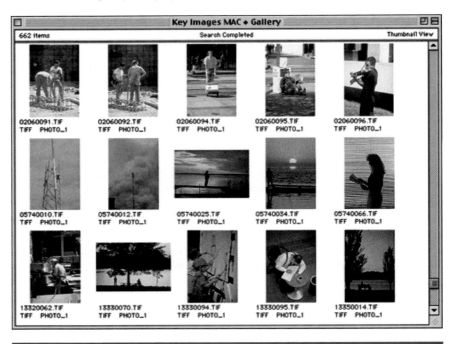

Choose your audio clips carefully. They are instrumental in setting the mood of any multimedia application.

illustrating proper techniques or explaining complex procedures, animation can also serve as an excellent learning aid in computer-based training programs.

Like clip art and stock photography, animated graphics are available for purchase on CD-ROM or they can be downloaded from the Internet. In addition, commercial software and shareware can be purchased or downloaded and used to create simple or complex animations.

Sound

By incorporating sound into a multimedia application, you require the user to make use of yet another sense. This enhances the experience and increases the likelihood of user understanding and enjoyment.

In multimedia applications, sound that has been digitized is called **audio.** Audio can be obtained by capturing sound into a personal computer using a microphone, CD-ROM, or other input device. It can also be played from a synthesizer, keyboard, or other musical instrument that is connected to the computer using a **MIDI (musical instrument digital interface) port.** In Chapter 5 we will discuss audio in greater detail.

FIGURE 1.17
When animated, this worm would appear to inch its way along.

Video

Video can do a great deal to enhance a presentation, illustrate a proper technique, or advertise a new product. **Video files** are photographic images played at speeds that make it appear as if the images are in full motion. Video files are incredibly large because a huge number of images are required to give the appearance of motion. Depending on the screen size of the video file, a single second of uncompressed video running at 30 frames per second may require more than 30 MB of storage space. In addition to storage, **bandwidth,** the amount of data a communication channel can carry, is also an obstacle to the delivery of video. Delivering video over the Internet is particularly challenging.

Despite these challenges, more and more multimedia applications, including multimedia applications disseminated via the Internet, include video. In order to be used effectively, however, video is often **compressed,** or reduced in size, for storage and transfer, and then **decompressed** for use. We will further discuss compression standards and techniques in Chapter 6. As computer resources continue to improve, the use of video in multimedia applications will also grow.

Multimedia Applications

From video games to computer-based training, multimedia offers a wide variety of applications to a wide variety of industries. The entertainment industry has been the primary creator and user of multimedia in the past. However, the recent surge of activity on the World Wide Web has caused multimedia creation tools to become more prevalent. This has opened the doors to multimedia production by

FIGURE 1.18

Multimedia files may need to be compressed for storage and transfer.

DATA COMPRESSION

Original text (98 characters):
The Internet has evolved from a text-based
network to a powerful multimedia delivery
system with world-wide reach.

Substitute one character for several characters:
ney = !
ed = @
as = #
er = $
wor = %
th = ^
ul = &

Compressed text (78 characters):
e^ Int$! h# evolv@ from a text-b#@ !%k to a
pow$f& m&tim@id deliv$y system wi^ %ld-wide reach.

a variety of users and has expanded the application of multimedia outside the world of entertainment.

The Internet and World Wide Web

A few years ago, just having a presence on the Web was considered exemplary, but to get a visitor to return to your Web page today, you may need more than good content. For this reason and because it is getting easier and easier to include multimedia on a Web page, multimedia applications are becoming more important on the World Wide Web. Graphics and animation convey information, reinforce content, and guide the user. Audio and video clips involve additional senses, thus improving understanding and giving depth to a flat page. Hyperlinks allow users access to resources from around the globe.

Software packages empower users to create Web pages with multimedia elements including games, interactive forms, electronic magazines, reference materials, sound, and more. As bandwidth issues pose less and less of a concern, the use of multimedia on the Web will continue to explode.

Computer-Based Training (CBT)

Computers are often used by companies or educational institutions to teach a certain set of skills. Although they have slightly different connotations, **computer-based training (CBT)** is also referred to as **computer-assisted instruction (CAI)** or **multimedia computer-assisted instruction (MCIA).** Companies use CBT to update the skills of current employees on a new series of procedures or to teach them how to operate new equipment. It is also used to train new employees on company policy.

Educational institutions find CBT useful in ensuring that students have achieved a certain level of mastery before they advance to the next level. Studies show that multimedia is effective in overall learning while at the same time reducing the time it takes to learn.

FIGURE 1.19

Multimedia enhances static Web pages.

FIGURE 1.20

Multimedia is used to create educational testing tools.

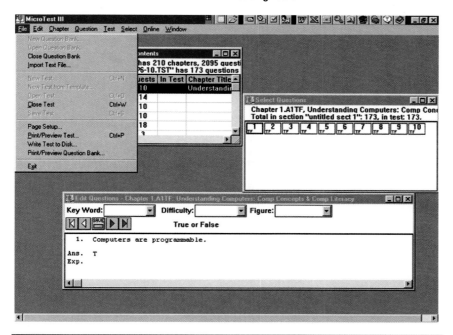

There are many advantages to computer-based training including:

- Open-entry/open exit—Students can begin training at any time and are finished when they have mastered the information. They do not have to depend on a trainer's schedule.

- Self-paced instruction—Students can advance at their own pace. They are neither held back nor advanced too quickly by other students. This feature is particularly appealing in the instruction of students who are physically challenged or learning disabled.

- Immediate feedback—Computer-based training programs provide immediate feedback offering positive reinforcement when students answer correctly, or further assistance when their answers are wrong.

- Assessment—Computer scoring automatically ensures that students have mastered the information before they are advanced to the next level.

- Simulated experiences—Simulations offer students an opportunity to practice real-world activities that may be too expensive or too dangerous to recreate for practice purposes.

Because multimedia applications appeal to a variety of learning styles by offering students an opportunity to experiment in a variety of learning environments, they tend to be more fun and less threatening than traditional learning.

Electronic Periodicals, References, and Books

Today, more and more newsletters, newspapers, magazines, books, encyclopedias and other reference materials are being offered in CD-ROM or online formats. These formats offer full multimedia features including full-text search, graphics, audio, and video. If you want to see an example, check out *The New York Times* at http://www.nytimes.com or *USA Today* at http://www.usatoday.com.

FIGURE 1.21

Like *USA Today,* most newspapers today supplement their publications with a Web site.

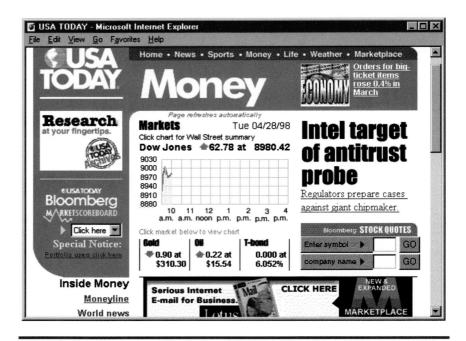

Many new terms have emerged from this area of multimedia. For example, two new terms are **zine** and **digizine.** A zine is a net-based document generally targeted to a very specific audience through e-mail. Zines offer viewers an opportunity to express anything they want. Digizines are print magazines that have been translated into a digital format. Digizines usually include access to an expanded set of information and often include more multimedia than most zines.

Obviously, there are many advantages to offering reference materials in a multimedia format.

- Cross-referencing—Multimedia reference materials provide hotlinks that allow the user immediate access to related information. This is particularly true if the reference is online because it gives the user access to other online resources around the globe.

- Expanded search capabilities—Access to search engines enables users to locate specific topics of interest.

- Multisensory experiences—By incorporating graphics, sound, animation, and video to provide information, the reference comes to life and is often more enjoyable and more memorable than text alone.

Because of these many advantages, more self-help and how-to guides are also being offered as interactive multimedia applications. Access to online counselors and psychologists both real and simulated are quite popular, as are guides to help you build a deck, repair your car, and plant a perennial garden.

There is a growing trend on the Internet toward **push technology.** Traditionally, if you are interested in a particular topic, you use a search engine and upload a request to the server where that information is stored. The server then downloads the requested information to your desktop. With push technology, you no longer have to make a request each time you want up-to-date information. Instead, you

FIGURE 1.22

A digizine is a print magazine that has been translated into a digital format.

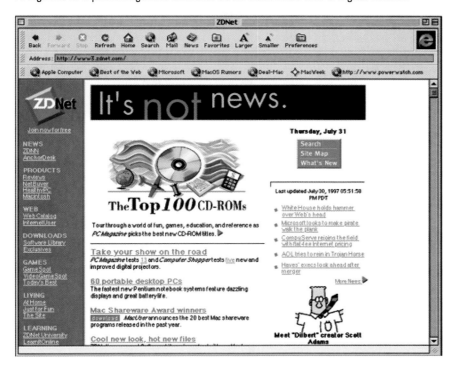

FIGURE 1.23

This Gardening Encyclopedia is an excellent guide to the perfect plants for your garden.

fill out a customized form in advance. On this form, you supply information to the server about your interests or needs. Whenever the server receives new information that you might be interested in viewing, it automatically sends it to you.

For a sample of one of the first technologies to use push technology, check out PointCast Network (PCN) http://www.pointcast.com. It offers customized news. You select the type of news you are most interested in viewing (weather, sports, headline news) and PointCast delivers it right to your desktop as you work. Marimba's Castanet is another new push technology that allows you to subscribe to different information channels.

Kiosks

Kiosks are free-standing interactive information stations usually installed in public places to answer customer or visitor questions. A kiosk is equipped with interactive software that responds to user requests. Users generally select options from menus using touch-screen monitors or keyboards.

Kiosks in airports, large hotels, shopping centers, museums, and libraries provide information on services and locations. Companies may use kiosks at trade shows to provide product, service, and other company details. Even educational institutions are using kiosks to allow students access to class schedules, registration, and transcript information.

Advertising and Marketing

Because multimedia is much more likely to grab attention than text alone, it is used extensively to advertise and market company products and services.

FIGURE 1.24

PointCast uses push technology to deliver the news you are most interested in knowing about.

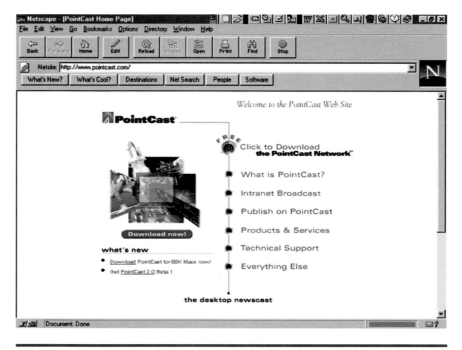

Television commercials employ **multimedia authoring software** to create unique, attention-getting advertisements with **animated text** and **morphed graphics.** On a more personal level, **presentation software** like Microsoft PowerPoint makes it extremely easy for sales associates to create top-quality **online slide shows** for marketing presentations. Advertising also pays for Web sites so that most of these sites remain free to users. Animated logos and banners advertising products, services, and links to other sites proliferate on the Web.

Virtual Shopping

Multimedia is changing the way we shop and buy. Record numbers of businesses are using the Internet and the World Wide Web to market their goods and services online. **Electronic catalogs** and **malls** offer users variations to shopping experiences that buyers are already quite accustomed to using. The Internet Mall is the world's largest online shopping mall. It has been around since 1994 and proudly boasts products and services from over 27,000 stores. From name brands to obscure specialty shops and legal services, there really is something for everyone at the Internet Mall. You can check it out at http://www.internet-mall.com. Addresses for additional shopping sites are listed at the end of this book.

At this time, the biggest shortcoming to online purchasing is security, or perceived problems with security. It's interesting that we will generously give our credit cards to waiters and waitresses who often keep them for 10–15 minutes, yet

FIGURE 1.25
A user-friendly multimedia interface makes it easy for users to surf the net with the click of a mouse.

FIGURE 1.26
Most search engines make money by allowing companies to advertise on their often-frequented sites.

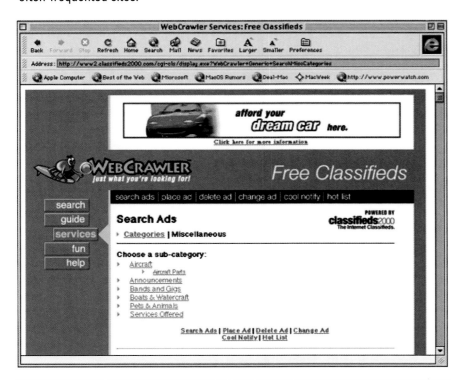

FIGURE 1.27

Online shopping malls proliferate on the Web.

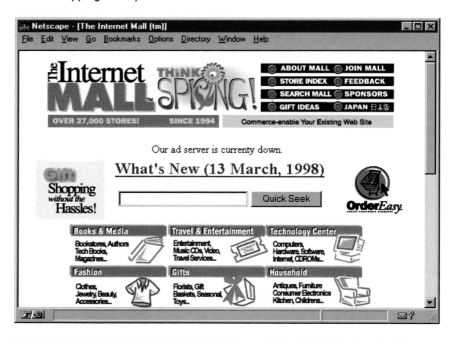

we aren't comfortable plugging those numbers into Web sites that undoubtedly offer more safeguards to security than even the finest hotel or restaurant. This too shall pass. As security improves, more and more people will feel comfortable ordering online using credit cards and **electronic cash (e-cash).** With electronic cash, buyers will "make a deposit" with a third party such as a bank. This party will then electronically pay the online vendor when the buyer authorizes a request that a vendor be paid.

The number of businesses marketing products and services online will continue to grow as more and more people learn about and have access to multimedia technologies and as purchasing products online becomes more secure and commonplace.

Entertainment and Games

Games are the most popular, and most varied, interactive entertainment product available. Games offer structured entertainment that simulates real or imaginary worlds in which characters are controlled, obstacles are encountered, and goals are achieved.

Though the purpose of most games is primarily entertainment, more and more interactive CD-ROMs and online games are designed to educate as well as entertain. This area of multimedia is referred to as **edutainment.** Titles designed for all age groups and for all purposes are quite common. Visit Educorp's site at http://www.educorp.com to see what's available.

Virtual Reality (VR)

Multimedia can also be used to create an artificial environment complete with 3D images that can be explored and manipulated. This computer-induced illusion of

FIGURE 1.28

As security improves, more and more people will purchase online.

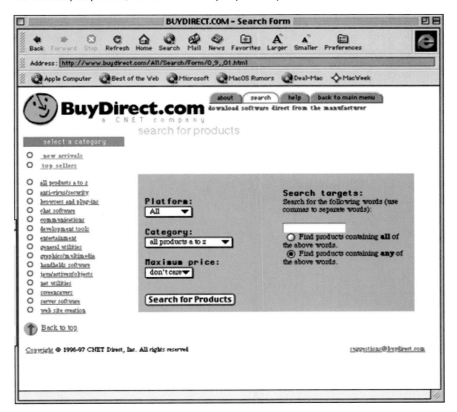

FIGURE 1.29

Some games are designed to educate and entertain.

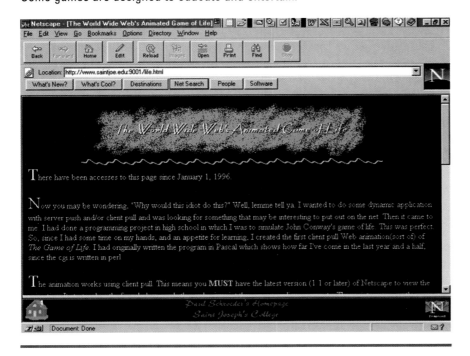

FIGURE 1.30

Multimedia titles designed for all purposes and all age groups are available from Educorp.

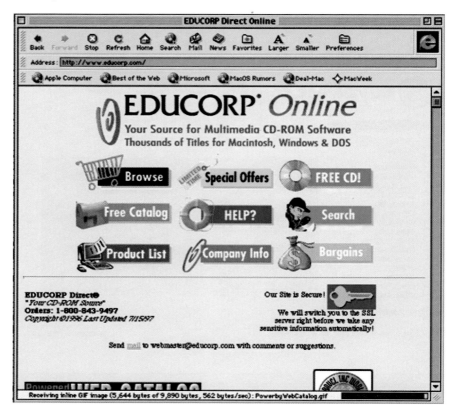

reality is called **virtual reality.** In order to fully experience this environment, users must wear special equipment including a headset, headphones, a suit, and gloves. The reality of this artificial environment is dependent upon the hardware and software used to create it. The hardware and software also determine how much users can interact with the environment. In order to make the experience even more lifelike, experts have recently added smell and touch into this environment.

The type of virtual reality that requires additional equipment is called **immersion virtual reality** and is most often encountered in electronic games and simulations. In games, special visors that simulate a computer-generated environment are worn. As you move, sensors recognize your movement and change your view of the environment based on your new position. Virtual reality came out of the military, where it was (and still is) used for simulations. In simulations, as with games, special sensors record your reactions in a simulated environment and require you to respond to special conditions.

There are many other practical applications of virtual reality. NASA has used virtual reality in space exploration. Virtual reality has also been effectively used by architects to create VR models of buildings that they can show clients before construction begins. Clients can "walk through" a building as it is being designed. Using VR, clients get a much better sense of what the building will look and feel like before they spend hundreds of thousands of dollars on construction. Similar applications have spilled over to the automobile and airplane manufacturing industries.

FIGURE 1.31

Virtual reality programs let you "see" and "feel" simulated objects when wearing a special glove and goggles.

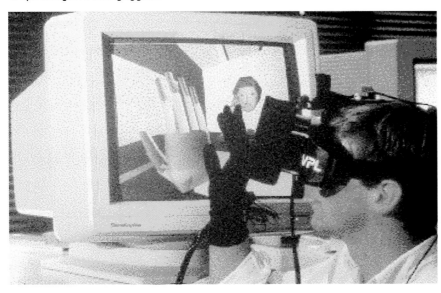

Today's doctors and surgeons are also using virtual reality. With this technology, they can practice a procedure until they have mastered it. Using virtual reality, they become proficient and confident before they even touch a real patient.

At this time, the biggest obstacle to widespread use of immersion virtual reality is the cumbersome and high-cost equipment needed to make it work. Like all computer-based technology, however, virtual reality continues to advance and the end to its advancement is nowhere in sight. Virtual reality will become common reality in the not-too-distant future, and the possibilities for using it in a variety of areas are endless. Who knows? In the near future, we may find ourselves active participants in action movies and love stories or practicing cultural mores with aliens in a simulated environment. *Star Trek*'s holodeck really isn't that farfetched.

FIGURE 1.32

This VR game allows you to view Europe from 8,000 feet while surviving multi-plane dogfights in your state-of-the-art biplane.

The virtual reality we have been talking about so far is high end. Lower-end virtual reality is available and more common. VR can be found on the Web where it is created using the **VRML (virtual reality modeling language)** or the **(QTVR) QuickTime VR** authoring tool. VRML enables Web page developers to create 3D objects that users can manipulate with a pointing device such as a mouse, trackball, or joystick, and QTVR allows developers to create 3D interactive environments for the Web. These environments include 3D objects and full panoramic views of objects and locations. To see some of these 3D interactive environments and find out more about the tools used to create them, you can visit Apple Computer's QuickTime City site at http://quicktime.apple.com/qt-city.

Careers in Multimedia

Though some people refer to multimedia as a separate industry, it is probably more accurate to say that many varied industries use multimedia technologies and techniques for different types of products and markets. Industries including film, advertising, games, publishing, and software have used multimedia as an established and fundamental technology for quite some time, although uses of multimedia in other industries is still emerging.

Consumers are demanding a wider variety of interactive multimedia products and services including Web pages, reference materials, games, virtual communities, digital periodicals, music, education, business, and training material. In order to respond to this demand, industry must employ people who can help them deliver the multimedia products consumers want.

Because more and more industries are discovering the value of and creative uses for multimedia, there are more and more multimedia-related jobs advertised

If you are interested in a career in multimedia, be prepared to be a life-long learner. Keep up with the latest and greatest technologies by reading trade journals and attending relevant conferences and seminars.

FIGURE 1.33

Multimedia products are generally created by teams of specialists.

each day. Opportunities for individuals with multimedia skills are plentiful and varied with starting and upper-level salaries for these jobs ranging from $30,000–$150,000 and up.

Regardless of the industry, creating a multimedia application is a team effort. Position titles and job duties vary, depending upon the industry and even within the same industry. Some of the more common titles and job duties of team members are listed below. Keep in mind that a project team will rarely include someone from every one of these potential positions. If a job duty is necessary to complete the project effectively, at times the same person will fill several positions within a project. For example, the audio specialist may also be responsible for the video on a project.

COMMON MULTIMEDIA CAREER TITLES AND RESPONSIBILITIES

- **Executive Producer**—The primary role of the executive producer is to move a project into and through production. This person will work with clients and is particularly active in the development and delivery stages of the application. The executive producer needs to have high-level communication skills and the ability to see the big picture.

- **Production Manager**—The production manager is responsible for forming a project, moving it into production, and overseeing its creation. This involves working with clients, developing original concepts, preparing budgets and schedules, hiring personnel and assembling project teams, assembling resources and equipment, managing conceptual design, and managing production. Skills needed by these people include a good understanding of the capabilities of multimedia tools, good communication and negotiation skills, thorough management and human resource skills, and knowledge of copyright and other laws.

- **Multimedia Director/Architect**—The goal of the multimedia director or architect is to integrate all of the multimedia pieces developed by the other multimedia team members. Using an authoring program, this person will develop or refine a design process and efficiently create a cohesive and well-planned product. This must be accomplished by integrating technical concerns, marketing issues, and input from the client and project team. Skills required of the multimedia director or architect include excellent graphic, video, and sound skills, good communication skills, programming experience, and expertise with a multimedia authoring program.

- **Art Director**—It is the art director's responsibility to create all of the artwork for the project. Traditionally, art directors have primarily worked with visual and graphic artwork. However, with interactive media, the art director is also responsible for sound, animation, and video. Art directors need good graphic, video, and sound skills, as well as good management skills.

- **Interface Designer**—This person is responsible for the look of the multimedia interface. Interface designers create and design icons, backgrounds, and other on-screen elements. In addition, this person is responsible for what users hear, touch, and feel. This person must have good graphic, video, and sounds skills, good design skills, and the ability to see the big picture, but be able to work with the details.

- **Interactive Scriptwriter**—The interactive scriptwriter is part traditional writer (film scriptwriter, novelist, or storybook writer) and part interactive designer. Because most interactivity is non-linear, the scriptwriter must bridge the gap between traditional writing and interactivity. In other words, the interactive scriptwriter must write all of the scenarios for the different choices the user may make. Interactive scriptwriters must have excellent writing and planning skills, the ability to create storyboards and scripts for the overall project as well as scripts for each character, and a good understanding of multimedia authoring tools.

- **Editors**—These people are responsible for providing a point of view and either originating or filtering information. Editors must work closely with the scriptwriters to ensure that the text is grammatically correct and that the content flows in a logical fashion. Editors must have excellent writing and editing skills, the ability to focus on details, and knowledge of multimedia authoring tools.

- **Content Specialist**—The content specialist is responsible for providing some measure of authenticity or accuracy to the information in an interactive project. After conducting research , this person will oversee the content of the multimedia application including the scripting, characters, text, and interactivity. Content specialists should have knowledge in the content area or the ability to conduct research through the library or Internet, good writing skills, and the ability to summarize information. The person filling this role may also be referred to as the subject matter expert.

- **Instructional Specialist**—These people are experts in designing instructional projects for education or computer-based training. Their responsibilities include defining learning objectives and outcomes and establishing the delivery and flow of a project around the best educational strategies and practices. They are responsible for designing multimedia applications that appeal to a variety of learning styles and increase the learner's decision making and problem solving skills. Finally, they are responsible for designing tools that assess learning. Instructional specialists should have a background in educational theory and curriculum development as well as knowledge of the basic principles of multimedia authoring.

- **Graphic Designer**—Graphic designers are responsible for creating and designing all of the graphic images for a project. This includes buttons, bars, backgrounds, text, illustrations, 3D objects, logos, and photographs. This person works closely with the interface designer and the multimedia director/architect to create the "look" of the multimedia application. The graphic designer needs skills in 2D and 3D graphic creation and design, expertise in working with various graphic creation tools, and knowledge of multimedia authoring tools.

- **Animation Specialist**—Animators may create 2D or 3D animation. To create two-dimensional animations, animators take a sequence of static images and display them in rapid succession on the computer screen to create the illusion of motion. Animators who create three-dimensional animations command top dollar to create special effects for multimedia, film, TV, and advertising. The animation specialist must have graphic design skills, interactive multimedia development skills, and 3D modeling skills.

- **Audio Specialist**—This person is responsible for ensuring that appropriate sound is delivered in real time. They work with musical scores, sound effects, voice-overs, vocals, and transitional sounds, and are responsible for recording, editing, and selecting voices and sounds. Audio specialists should have in-depth knowledge of digital sound, skills in sound engineering, and knowledge of multimedia authoring tools.

- **Sound Engineer**—The sound engineer handles the equipment while the audio specialist edits sound files for length, tone, and effect and then converts the sound files to the appropriate format. Sound engineers must have an in-depth knowledge of the various types of equipment used in the production of high-quality voice and music.

■ **Video Specialist**—These people manage the entire process of shooting, capturing, and editing original video for use in interactive products. Video specialists need in-depth skills in digital video, skills in video production, and knowledge of multimedia authoring tools.

■ **Videographer**—The videographer shoots the video to be used with interactive technology. This person must have good artistic and photographic skills, as well as vision. Background knowledge of multimedia authoring tools is also beneficial.

■ **Computer Programmer**—These people create the underlying software that runs a multimedia program and responds to the user's actions. They help implement the technology strategy for the project by writing code lines or "scripts" that define the structure, interactions, and technical implications of certain decisions. Computer programmers are the foundation of the project because they help the multimedia team realize their collective vision. There are usually several levels of programmers. Programmers should have expertise in Lingo, Java, C++, Visual Basic and other programming languages and scripting tools. They should also have a solid understanding of multimedia authoring tools.

■ **Web Master**—This is a relatively new role in multimedia production. These people are responsible for creating and maintaining Internet Web pages. They convert multimedia application to Web pages or create Web pages with multimedia elements using HTML tags, Web editors, and other Web creation tools. They are also responsible for understanding and becoming skilled in new Web page creation tools and technology. They may write scripts using Java, JavaScript, or other programming and scripting languages. They are also responsible for making sure the Web page is technically correct and functional on the Web server. The Web master is the foundation of any project on the Internet. It is important that Web masters have skills in multimedia authoring tools, scripting and programming languages such as Lingo, Java, JavaScript, and VBScript and knowledge of multimedia Web page tools.

■ **Support Positions**—Other support positions are also important in the planning, production, and delivery of multimedia applications. **Test managers** and **alpha and beta testers** are responsible for testing the multimedia product and looking for problems before the application is delivered. **Sales** and **marketing** people identify and approach potential clients and markets that might be interested in the multimedia application. Once the product is delivered, **customer support personnel** respond to customers with questions and problems.

SUMMARY

Multimedia means using more than one media element. It implies using the computer to integrate **text, graphics, animation, sound,** and **video** to create a multisensory experience for conveying messages and ideas. Because multimedia involves multiple senses, it accommodates different learning styles and therefore enhances learning.

Interactive multimedia allows users to respond directly to and control media elements. Users of interactive multimedia become active participants in an application instead of passive recipients of information.

Linear media has a beginning and progresses through a set sequence of events until it reaches the end while **non-linear media** leaves the order of events to the discretion of the user.

Because text is still an effective way to communicate, it remains vital to multimedia applications. In addition, the use of **hypertext,** links that give users nonlinear access to information on the topics that they are most interested in exploring, is growing.

Most people are quite visual, therefore, both 2D and 3D images or **graphics** are crucial to the development of successful multimedia applications. Graphics can be created with **graphics creation software;** captured with **scanners, digital cameras,** and **digital video cameras;** and edited with **image editing software.** In addition, commercially prepared drawings and photographs are also available.

Animation refers to graphic images that change or move. Animation can convey information, add visual interest or draw attention to important information or links in a multimedia application. Like other graphics and photographs, animation can be created using animation software, or libraries of animated objects are available on CD-ROM and the Internet.

In multimedia applications, sound that has been digitized is called **audio.** Audio can be obtained by capturing sound into a personal computer using a microphone, CD-ROM, or other input device. It can also be played from a synthesizer, keyboard, or other musical instrument that is connected to the computer using a **MIDI (musical instrument digital interface) port.**

Video can be used to enhance a presentation, illustrate a proper technique, or advertise a product. **Video files** are photographic images played at speeds that make it appear as if the images are in full motion. Because video files are so large, they may need to be **compressed,** or reduced in size, for storage and transfer, and then **decompressed** for use.

At one time, multimedia was primarily used in **entertainment** and **games.** Though it is still used extensively in these two industries, the uses of multimedia have expanded beyond the world of entertainment. More and more multimedia applications are found on the **Internet** and **World Wide Web** where multimedia is being used for **advertising** and **marketing,** as well as **virtual shopping.** Multimedia is also used in **computer-based training, electronic periodicals, references, books,** and on information **kiosks.** Multimedia can also be used to create an artificial environment complete with 3D images that can be explored and manipulated. This is called **virtual reality (VR).**

Because more and more industries are discovering the value of and creative uses for multimedia, there are more and more multimedia-related jobs advertised each day. Opportunities for individuals with multimedia skills are plentiful and varied.

Multimedia applications are all around us. Our society depends on information and multimedia is an effective and user-friendly way to present it. Though working with multiple media is not new, working with multiple digital media is relatively new. In the future, multimedia will involve even more of our senses. It will provide us with greater opportunities to control our environment and it will continue to evolve into an extremely rich and powerful information environment that can be shared across networks.

KEY TERMS

Multimedia	VRML	QTVR
Non-linear multimedia	Interactive multimedia	Linear media
Animation	Text	Graphics
Hypertext	Sound	Video
Graphics creation soft-	TrueType fonts	Charts
ware	Scanners	Digital cameras
Digital video cameras	Image editing software	Clip art
Stock photography	Animation	Audio
MIDI	Compressed	Decompressed
Internet	World Wide Web	Virtual shopping
Computer-based training	Electronic periodicals	Virtual reality

Matching Questions

a. clip art	**b.** hypertext	**c.** zine
d. animation	**e.** audio	**f.** virtual reality
g. kerning	**h.** leading	**i.** push technology
j. digizine	**k.** VRML	**l.** QTVR

_____ **1.** Graphic images that change or move.

_____ **2.** Multimedia used to create an artificial environment complete with 3D images that can be explored and manipulated.

_____ **3.** Commercially prepared drawings that come packaged with many application programs.

_____ **4.** Sound that has been digitized.

_____ **5.** Text that gives you nonlinear access to information.

_____ **6.** This technology enables Web page developers to create 3D objects that users can manipulate with a pointing device such as a mouse, trackball, or joystick.

_____ **7.** This is a net-based document generally targeted to a very specific audience through e-mail.

_____ **8.** This is when the server automatically delivers information to your desktop.

_____ **9.** This is Apple Computer's technology that allows developers to create 3D interactive environments for the Web.

_____ **10.** The amount of space between characters.

_____ **11.** The amount of space between lines of text.

_____ **12.** Print magazines translated into a digital format.

Fill-In Questions

1. At the most basic level, _____ means using more than one media element.

2. _____ allows the user to respond directly to and control any or all of the media elements.

3. With _____, users start at the beginning and progress through a set sequence of events until they reach the end, while _____ leaves the order of events to the discretion of the user.

4. When media elements have been _____, it means they have been captured as a series of 0's and 1's and can now be interpreted by the computer.

5. Photographs can be digitized through a _____ or taken directly with a _____.

6. In addition to storage, _____, the amount of data a communication channel can carry, is also an obstacle to the delivery of video.

7. In order to be used effectively, video is often _____, or reduced in size, for storage and transfer, and then _____ for use.

8. The type of virtual reality that requires additional equipment is called _____ and is most often encountered in electronic games and simulations.

DISCUSSION QUESTIONS

1. How does multimedia aid learning?
2. What are three methods of obtaining digital photographs? How do these methods differ?
3. What is the primary obstacle encountered when trying to deliver video files? How is this obstacle overcome?
4. Why are good balance and design so important when creating multimedia applications?
5. What are some practical applications of virtual reality?

HANDS-ON EXERCISES

1. Using magazines, newspapers, the World Wide Web, and any other applicable resource, find several advertisements requesting the services of individuals with a background in multimedia. What skills are required? What training/education is required? What is the starting salary for the positions advertised?

2. Visit Educorp's site at http://www.educorp.com. Give the title and a brief description of two multimedia applications you would be interested in using.

3. Go shopping online at the Internet Mall at http://Internet-mall.com. Record your shopping experience. When you find an item(s) you are interested in purchasing, what payment options are available? Which payment option would you be most likely to choose? Why?

Case Study: Chapter 1

Digital Design is a multimedia production company located in Seattle, WA. It began as a desktop publishing company in the 1980s. Recognizing that the market was evolving away from print media toward real-time, 3D multimedia, Digital Design began its transition from print to primarily digital formats around 1992. In 1993, it changed its name from Desktop Design to Digital Design.

Working with clients throughout western Washington, Digital Design creates and designs multimedia interfaces for information kiosks; edits video for commercials and infomercials; designs logos, graphics, and animation; creates training materials; and designs Web pages. With the exponential growth of the Internet and World Wide Web, over half of the staff at Digital Design is now devoted to the creation and design of interactive Web pages for a diverse clientele.

Island WaterCraft (IWC) rents and sells SeaDoo personal watercraft such as wave runners and jet skis. Located in Friday Harbor on San Juan Island, Island Watercraft is interested in having Digital Design create an Interactive Web page that will help it market the sale and rental of its SeaDoo personal watercraft to the many tourists who visit the San Juan Islands during the summer.

Jamie Hunt, Production Manager for Digital Design, has been assigned to work with Island WaterCraft. As production manager, Jamie will be responsible for the overall creation, design, and delivery of a fully functional interactive multimedia Web site for IWC. She will prepare and manage the budget, resources, and schedule, as well as hire and assemble a project team to complete the Web site.

In assembling a team for the project, Jamie will need a graphic/interface designer, an animation specialist, an audio specialist, a videographer/video specialist, a scriptwriter, a content specialist, a multimedia architect, and a Web master.

Multimedia Equipment

1. Understand that a computer used for multimedia requires more powerful specifications
2. Understand the difference between the PC and Macintosh platforms in regard to multimedia
3. Explain the purpose of the Multimedia PC Marketing Council (MPC)
4. Discuss the various MPC levels
5. Describe Intel's MMX™ technology
6. Identify the manufacturers of the PowerPC microprocessor and explain how this microprocessor differs from the Intel microprocessors
7. Explain the importance of RAM in viewing and creating multimedia applications
8. Define digitizing
9. List and describe the different types of hardware used to capture images
10. List and describe the different types of storage devices commonly used when working with multimedia applications
11. Define bus
12. List and describe the different types of bus structures used to transfer multimedia data
13. List and describe the different types of hardware used to output multimedia applications

Introduction

A few years ago, purchasing a multimedia computer was quite complicated, but because of the tremendous growth of multimedia applications, most computers that you buy today are already designed to run multimedia applications. If you are interested in developing multimedia applications, however, you should consider a more powerful computer. If your computer is too slow, productivity will be lost; and in today's fast-paced technological society, you need a fast computer to keep up.

We are assuming that you have a solid background understanding of the basic computer hardware components like CPU and RAM. Therefore, in this book, we have selected to focus only on those features that are particularly relevant to multimedia computers.

The Computer

Before you purchase equipment, determine how you will use it. You are much more likely to get what you need if you examine what you will create and the software you will use to create it before you purchase the hardware.

Effectively developing and delivering multimedia applications requires a more powerful personal computer than one used to write a letter, prepare a budget, or answer e-mail. Because personal computers are becoming more and more powerful, most of those purchased today have built-in multimedia capabilities that allow you to deliver and display multimedia applications. However, if creation of high-end multimedia applications is your goal, you will definitely want to consider certain specifications that have been established specifically for multimedia.

Platforms

In discussing the creation and delivery of multimedia products, there are basically two computer platforms. The **IBM-compatible personal computer,** now

FIGURE 2.1

Some typical hardware components of a multimedia personal computer system.

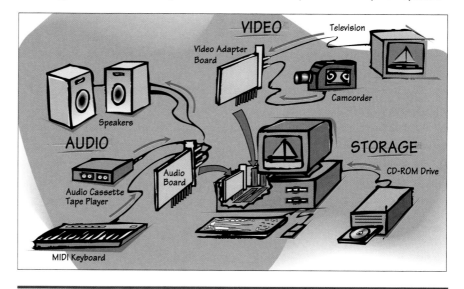

referred to as the **PC,** and the **Macintosh** platform. Most multimedia developed today is created for both platforms.

Of the two platforms, the PC or IBM-compatible is the platform most widely used and encountered in the marketplace. The PC is made by a number of computer manufacturers though the microprocessors found in PCs are most often manufactured by **Intel Corporation.** To function and develop in the PC multimedia environment, it is important to understand one or all of Microsoft's operating systems including **Windows, Window 95,** and **Windows NT.**

Though PCs are the more common platform encountered on the multimedia-user end, the Macintosh is still the multimedia king in the design and development world. Well over half of all multimedia CD-ROM titles and Web pages are developed on a Macintosh.

The processor found in the Macintosh and Macintosh compatibles is manufactured by **Motorola** if it is an original Macintosh, or by a joint venture between **Motorola, IBM,** and **Apple** if it is a **Power Macintosh.** All new Macintosh computers sold today are PowerMacs. To develop multimedia effectively for the Macintosh, you should be familiar with **System 7.5** or **System 8,** which are the two most recent operating systems found on this platform.

Today, most of the development and authoring software used to create multimedia applications is available on both platforms. Therefore, either of these two platforms can be effectively used to create, modify, design, and develop multimedia applications. Keep in mind that there are differences, some of which we have already discussed. In addition to different processors and operating systems, however, there are also differences in color depth, palette, speed, and disk format.

FIGURE 2.2

The microprocessors in most PCs is manufactured by Intel.

FIGURE 2.3

If you plan to work with or develop multimedia applications on the PC, you should understand the PC operating systems including Windows, Windows 95, and Windows NT.

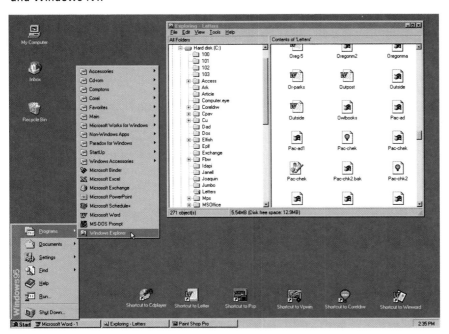

FIGURE 2.4

If you are working with or developing multimedia applications for the Macintosh, you should know System 7.5 and System 8.

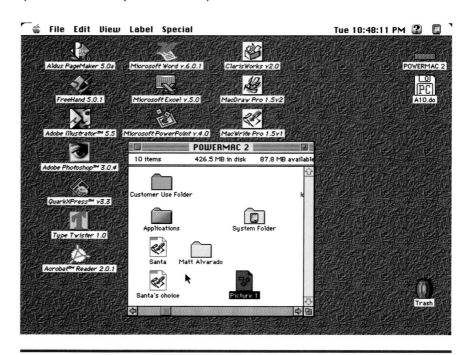

Multimedia Standards

The computer industry continues to struggle with standards. This is positive in the sense that it is the result of competition. However, it can be quite frustrating for developers and consumers of computer paraphernalia. When a new computer technology arises, several different manufacturers are likely to create hardware or software to work with this new technology. Each one possesses its own format and tries to get the market to endorse its format as the standard. In some situations, over time, one format will emerge as the standard not necessarily because it is the superior product, but simply because it is used so much more than the other formats.

In other arenas, a standard format never does emerge. As you read this book, you will soon realize that one of the reasons there is a need for books like this is because there is a lack of standardization in multimedia elements. One reason for this lack of standardization is that computer multimedia is relatively young, and another is that multimedia pulls from so many different elements. For example, in Chapter 3 we discuss the different formats for storing graphics, in Chapter 5 we discuss the different formats for storing sound files, and in Chapter 6 we discuss the different formats for storing video files.

Multimedia Personal Computer

The **Multimedia PC Marketing Council (MPC)** is a special interest group of the **Software Publishers Association (SPA).** It was created to help sustain the organized expansion of multimedia in the home and workplace. In conjunction with several major computer manufacturers including Creative Labs, Fujitsu, IBM, Intel, Gateway 2000, Dell, and Disney Interactive, MPC first established a set of minimum standards for multimedia hardware and software for the PC in 1991. Since then, they have revised the minimum multimedia standards several times. Currently there are three MPC levels, **MPC1, MPC2** and **MPC3.**

Multimedia personal computers designated with a certain MPC level are verified to have met the set of minimum standards established by the MPC. Therefore, when you purchase a multimedia computer with an MPC "stamp of approval," you are assured that your computer complies with the specifications set forth by this group.

The MPC specification was developed to serve as a "baseline" standard for the implementation of multimedia as an extension of the PC standard. It has been accepted around the world as the standard for the hardware implementation of multimedia on the PC. Keep in mind that this set of standards was established primarily for users of multimedia, not necessarily for the creators or developers of multimedia.

To determine whether a new MPC specification, MPC4, has been created since this textbook was published, visit the Software Publishers Association (SPA) site at http://www.spa.org.

As further verification that multimedia is becoming commonplace in the PC environment, Intel has added **MMX**™ technology to all of its new Pentium processor instruction sets. This new technology offers a 50 to 100 percent improvement in the clarity and speed of audio, video, and speech.

Though the CPU in the PC now includes technology designed specifically for multimedia, it is still the **PowerPC** microprocessor that is most often used in the creation of high-end multimedia products. The PowerPC microprocessor was jointly developed by IBM, Apple, and Motorola and is used in the Power Macintosh and high-end IBM server computers. It is based on **RISC (reduced instruction set computing)** technology where Intel processors are based on **CISC (complex instruction set computing).**

FIGURE 2.5

The Multimedia PC Working Group has established three levels of MPC standards for multimedia computers.

	MPC1	**MPC2**	**MPC3**
RAM	2MB	4MB (8 recommended)	8MB
Processor	16MHz 386SX	25MHz 486SX	75MHz Pentium
Hard Drive	30MB	160MB	540MB
CD-ROM Drive	150KB/sec—1X, maximum average seek time 1 second, 64KB onboard buffer recommended	300KB/sec—2X, maximum average seek time 400 milliseconds, CD-ROM XA ready, multisession capable, 64KB buffer recommended	600KB/sec—4X, average access time 250 milliseconds, CD-ROM XA ready, multisession capable, on-board read-ahead buffer required
Audio	8-bit digital sound, synthesizer, MIDI playback	16-bit digital sound, 8-note synthesizer, MIDI playback	16-bit digital sound, wavetable, MIDI playback
Video Display	640 X 480, 16 colors (256 colors recommended)	640 X 480, 65,536 colors	640 X 480, 65,536 colors
Video Playback	N/A	N/A	MPEG 1 (hardware or software) with OM-1 compliance

Purchase hardware that is expandable. Systems with additional expansion slots and bays, as well as the ability to upgrade logic boards and RAM, may add years to the usable life of your computer.

FIGURE 2.6

More RAM will make your multimedia applications run faster.

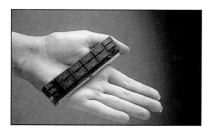

At this time, the PowerPC chips have nothing similar to MMX™ technology, however, the very nature of RISC chips makes them excellent for multimedia. In addition, IBM and Motorola have both announced that future PowerPC designs will include instructions to further optimize multimedia performance. Apple and other Macintosh-clone vendors are also planning to add dedicated multimedia chips and other hardware to their logic board design. One such implementation is the Trimedia chip by Philips.

At the time of this writing, the Power Macintosh is the fastest home computer available for multimedia development. Because processor capabilities and speeds change so quickly, it would be wise to visit Intel at http://www.intel.com and Motorola at http://www.motorola.com to discover how things have changed and to get breaking information on the latest processor technologies.

In addition to the microprocessor, many other computer components and peripherals are important in a multimedia computer system. Much of the impact of multimedia is lost if the system is not fast enough or powerful enough to deliver the product as intended. **RAM (Random Access Memory)** is extremely important because it reduces data movement to secondary storage devices and therefore improves processing speed. RAM is also important in development. Without an appropriate amount of RAM the developer will spend too much time waiting and the computer will spend too much time thrashing (moving data between RAM and the hard drive). Most home computers allow RAM expansion up to 128MB and high-end computers permit expansion up to 1GB. Because it is relatively cheap and easy to upgrade RAM in your computer system, if you are working with multimedia, you should seriously consider upgrading your system to include as much RAM as possible.

Input and Image Capture

There are a variety of images used in multimedia production including graphics, photographs, and video. Special equipment is needed to **capture** or **digitize** these images. Digitized images are stored as 0's and 1's so they can be interpreted by the computer's microprocessor.

VIDEO CAPTURE CARDS

Video capture cards are placed into an open expansion slot on the main board of the computer. Once installed, video capture cards allow you to connect a camcorder, VCR, or TV to the computer. Special software enables the images to be stored as graphic files or compressed as full-motion video clips. Though lower-quality cards can be purchased for under $50, you should expect to pay a few hundred to thousands of dollars for an average to upper-end video capture card.

Different video capture cards come with different **compression technology.** Compression technology reduces the file size for transfer and storage. **MPEG** compression is one type of compression that was developed by the Motion Pictures Experts Group. Another type of video compression is **DVI,** digital video interleave. This is Intel's proprietary compression technology. MPEG and DVI are both capable of reducing the size of the file while maintaining image quality.

At one time, playing video on the computer required additional hardware. For example, many compressed files required video output cards to reverse the compression process and allow the video files to be played. Today, both MPEG and DVI create video files that can be played without additional hardware or adapters. The only requirement to replay captured video is processor power and software decoders.

FIGURE 2.7

With a video capture card, you can capture video from a VCR or camcorder.

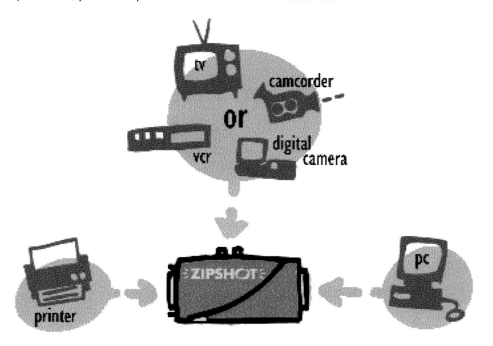

SNAPPY VIDEO SNAPSHOT

Snappy Video Snapshot offers an even easier alternative for video capture over a video capture card. Snappy connects directly to the computer via the printer (parallel) port. A video cable is then used to connect Snappy to a camcorder, VCR, or TV. After you install the software, you'll be able to capture digital images from video without installing anything inside your computer.

Snappy is also quite inexpensive, so you can get high-resolution images into a computer without spending a fortune on difficult-to-install equipment. Snappy can capture up to 16 million colors and resolutions of 1,500 × 1,125. Keep in mind that Snappy does not capture video, it merely "snaps" still images from video.

Snappy is only available on the PC. To get the details and a current price list on Snappy, visit http://www.play.com where you will read about Snappy holding the world record for highest resolution video captures ever.

VIDEO CAMERAS

With the right adapters, software, and hardware, camcorders and **digital video cameras** can be used to capture full-motion images. Although regular camcorders store video on film, digital video cameras store images as digital data. This enables the digital images to be transferred directly into the product being created. Digital video cameras range in price from under a hundred dollars for small desktop cameras like the Connectix QuickCam, to thousands of dollars for higher-end equipment.

Digital video cameras offer an inexpensive means of getting images into your computer, however, you should be aware that the resolution is often quite low and the color is sometimes questionable.

FIGURE 2.8

Snappy Video Snapshot enables you to capture frames of video without a video capture card.

DIGITAL CAMERAS

Digital cameras allow you to take pictures just as you would with a regular camera, but without film developing and processing. Unlike regular cameras, photographs are not stored on film but are instead stored in a digital format on magnetic disk or internal memory. The photographs can be immediately recognized by the computer and added to any multimedia product.

Digital cameras are generally small and lightweight. They are easy to use and include many of the same features found on a regular camera. Features like auto focus and auto flash make using a digital camera a snap. Transferring the photos to the computer is also quite simple. By connecting the camera to one of the serial ports on the computer and using the software that comes with the camera, you can easily transfer the images to any Windows or Macintosh computer. Once the image has been transferred, you can immediately pull it into your multimedia application, or you can edit the image using image-editing software such as Adobe Photoshop.

At this time, the portable digital cameras are somewhat limited in storage and image size, while the studio units are less limited because they are generally attached to a host computer. The quality produced from these cameras is quite good and improving all the time. Most offer the option of storing pictures in 16-bit or 32-bit resolution. The number of photographs that can be stored in the camera depends on the resolution selected and the amount of RAM or storage capacity of the magnetic media used.

Apple, Kodak, Casio, and many other companies manufacture digital cameras. Prices range from a few hundred dollars to as high as $55,000 for the high-end, studio-quality cameras. At least on the lower end, the cost of these cameras can be quickly recovered from savings in film development and processing alone. Undoubtedly, these digital wonders will eventually outsell traditional cameras because they are fast, quiet, convenient, inexpensive, environmentally friendly, and great for multimedia applications.

SCANNERS

Scanners digitize already developed images including photographs, drawings, or pages of text. By converting these images to a digital format, they can be interpreted and recognized by the microprocessor of the computer. **Handheld scanners** are

When purchasing image capture equipment such as scanners and digital cameras, make sure the resolution at which they capture the image is at least two times higher than the final output. Most monitors will only display a resolution of 72 dpi, so make sure the equipment will capture at least 150 dpi. Remember, you can always scale back, but you can't scale up.

FIGURE 2.9

With a digital camera, there is no need for film processing.

MVC-FD5

quite small, convenient, and inexpensive. A roller on the bottom of the device allows you to pull it over the top of an image. The image is then digitized. Handheld scanners can only digitize an image the width of the scanner. However, software is available that enables these smaller images to be patched together to create a larger image. Though this method can be effective, it does require some skill and time. Visit http://www.logitech.com for information on Logitech's ScanMan.

A better way of scanning larger images is to use a **page** or **flatbed scanner.** These scanners look like small photocopiers. Page scanners are either gray-scale scanners that work well with black-and-white photographs or color scanners that can record millions of colors. Depending on the quality and features, scanners range in price from as little as a few hundred dollars to thousands of dollars. Many different companies manufacture page or flatbed scanners. More information on flatbed scanners can be obtained from Agfa's site at http://www.agfa.com, or check out Hewlett-Packard and Epson scanners by visiting http://www.hp.com and http://www.epson.com.

Page-fed scanners also exist. These scanners have a slot through which a sheet of paper is fed. Page-fed scanners are generally set up to digitize pages of text using **Optical Character Recognition (OCR)** software. In the past, much of the text converted with OCR software had to be revised because it wasn't recognized accurately. For example, a typed letter l might be digitized as a number 1. Today, OCR software is quite sophisticated and often converts text with almost 100 percent accuracy. OmniPage leads the industry in OCR software. To find out more about this software, visit http://www.caere.com.

PHOTO CDS

Another excellent method of storing and using photographic digital images is on **Photo CD**. To view Photo CDs, you need a CD-ROM drive. Other than a roll of film, that's about all you need. Authorized service bureaus and developers can process your roll of film and supply you with digitized images on a CD-ROM. As you have additional rolls of film developed, the photos can be added to the original CD

FIGURE 2.10

Handheld scanners offer an inexpensive way to capture images.

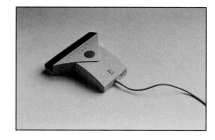

FIGURE 2.11

A page scanner looks and works much like a small photocopying machine, but stores images in the computer instead of printing them on paper.

until it reaches full capacity. The quality of these images is usually very good and they provide you with several sizes of each individual image. These compact disks can hold over a hundred images and can be read by most any computer equipped with a CD-ROM drive.

DIGITIZING TABLETS AND GRAPHICS TABLETS

A **digitizing tablet** is a touch-sensitive board that converts points, lines, and curves drawn with a stylus or digitizer device to digital data. A digitizing tablet is often used by professional architects, engineers, and mapmakers to create drawings or to trace sketches, drawings, and photographs precisely.

FIGURE 2.12

Photo CDs store digital photographs.

A **graphics tablet** is similar to a digitizing tablet, however, it contains additional characters and commands. Like the digitizing tablet, each location on the graphics tablet corresponds to a specific location on the screen.

MICROPHONES

As is true with most equipment, all microphones are not created equal. If you are planning to use a microphone for input, you will want to purchase a superior, high-quality microphone because your recordings will depend on its quality.

Next to the original sound, the microphone is the most important factor in any sound system. The microphone is designed to pick up and amplify incoming acoustic waves or harmonics precisely and correctly and convert them to electrical signals. Depending on its sensitivity, the microphone will pick up the sound of someone's voice, sound from a musical instrument, and any other sound that comes to it. Regardless of the quality of the other audio-system components, the true attributes of the original sound are forever lost if the microphone does not capture them.

Microphone sensitivity is directly related to how much feedback is around it. If there is a lot of feedback, the microphone will have to be turned down to reduce its sensitivity. If there isn't much feedback, the microphone can be turned up. In addition to the sounds around it, many other factors affect the sensitivity of a microphone. These include the shape of the room, the materials used, equalizers, and the position of the microphone.

Macintosh computers come with a built-in microphone, and more and more PCs that include Sound Blaster sound cards also include a microphone. These microphones are generally adequate for medium-quality sound recording of voiceovers and narration. These microphones are not adequate for recording music.

Microphones basically fall into two main groups, **moving coil** and **condenser.** Moving coil microphones have wires connected to the microphone diaphragm. Sound waves change the pressure of the air they travel through, which causes the

FIGURE 2.13

Digitizing tablets are excellent for tracing or drawing objects to be recognized by the computer.

FIGURE 2.14

A high-quality microphone is an important factor in any sound system.

diaphragm to vibrate and the coil to move. This creates an audio frequency. These microphones are extremely rugged and reliable.

Condenser microphones use the front electrode as the microphone's diaphragm. As it moves, a voltage comparable to the acoustic signal is produced. The electrodes used in condenser microphones allow a permanent electric charge to be stored or frozen. Therefore, low voltage internal batteries can power condenser microphones. These microphones can also be very compact.

RF condenser microphones are a unique, sophisticated class of condenser microphones that fulfill the highest demands made on sound quality and versatility. These microphones are known for their high quality, accurate sound reproduction, durability, wide frequency response, and extremely low self-noise.

To find out more about microphones, visit http://www.sennheiser.ca/english/mics.htm or go to http://www.audixusa.com/useaudix.htm to find out what type of microphone your favorite professional singer uses.

FIGURE 2.15

On a PC, a sound card is necessary if you intend to play or record sound.

SOUND CARDS

In order to play sound through external speakers attached to your computer system, or to record sound, you need a **sound card** or **audio board** on a PC. Multimedia computers that meet the MPC standard must have the ability to record and play waveform digital audio files. The most common sound card found on PC computers is the Sound Blaster manufactured by Creative Labs. On a Macintosh, the sound circuitry is built into the logic board.

Most computers that you purchase today will have a sound card already included. Because the dynamic range of sound depends on the sound card, make sure the sound card in any system you purchase is at least 16-bit. A 16-bit sound card will produce a dynamic range of 98dB (decibels).

MIDI HARDWARE

MIDI (Musical Instrument Digital Interface) is a standard that was agreed upon by the major manufacturers of musical instruments. The MIDI standard was established so musical instruments could be hooked together and could thereby communicate with one another.

To communicate, MIDI instruments have an "in" port and an "out" port that enables them to be connected to one another. Some MIDI instruments also have a "through" port that allows several MIDI instruments to be daisy chained together.

In addition to hooking one MIDI instrument to another MIDI instrument, today it is also possible to connect MIDI instruments to computers. This connection is possible through the use of an **interface** that translates messages between the computer and the MIDI instruments. If you are planning to use live instruments in creating music for your multimedia productions, be sure your computer and the musical instruments you plan to connect it to are MIDI ready. We will talk more about the MIDI standard and MIDI technology in Chapter 5.

Storage

Multimedia products require much greater storage capacity than text-based data. All multimedia authors soon learn that huge drives are essential for the enormous files used in multimedia and audiovisual creation. Floppy diskettes really aren't useful for storing multimedia products. Even small presentations will quickly consume the 1.44 MB of storage allotted to a high-density diskette.

In addition to a hefty storage capacity, a fast drive is also important. This is because large files, even if they are compressed, take a long time to load and a

FIGURE 2.16

A MIDI port allows you to connect MIDI instruments to computers that also have a MIDI connector.

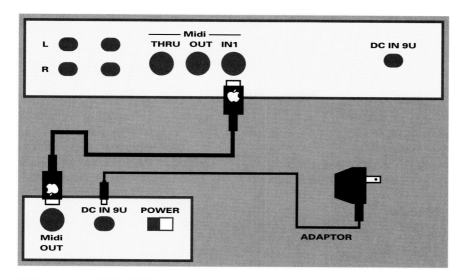

long time to save and back up. Consequently, if the drive is slow, frustration and lost productivity will undoubtedly follow. When purchasing a storage medium, consider the speed of the device—how fast it can retrieve and save large files—as well as the size of its storage capacity.

HARD DISKS

Magnetic media solutions beyond floppy diskettes are a must when working with multimedia. Internal, external, and removable hard disks contain the necessary storage capacity for working with multimedia applications. Hard disks range in both physical size and storage capacity depending on their intended use. Storage capacities also range from a few hundred megabytes to over 10 gigabytes. The MPC3 specification is only 540MB, but if you plan to work primarily with multimedia, you will definitely want a huge hard disk. Get the biggest one you can afford.

REMOVABLE HARD DISKS

Removable hard disks or cartridges are quite common when working with multimedia applications because they provide an appropriate amount of storage capacity as well as a format that is easy to transport. Removable hard disks include **Iomega's Zip** and **Jaz** drives, which hold 100MB and 1GB respectively, as well as **SyQuest's Easy Drive** and **SyJet,** which hold 135MB and 1.5GB respectively. These drives cost around $200, and the disks average about $20 each. For updated information on the products these two manufacturers sell, visit Iomega at http://www.iomega.com and SyQuest at http://www.syquest.com.

OPTICAL DISKS

Optical storage offers much higher storage capacity than magnetic storage. This makes it a much better medium for storing and distributing multimedia products that are full of graphics, audio, and video files. In addition, reading data with

FIGURE 2.17
Hard disks offer greater storage capacity and speed over floppies.

FIGURE 2.18

A removable hard disk blends the convenience of a floppy with the storage capacity of a hard disk.

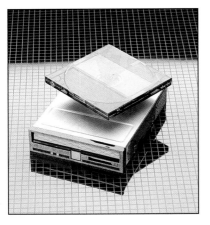

lasers is more precise. Therefore, when working with multimedia, optical storage media such as **Magneto-Optical Disks (MO)** and **CD-ROM (CD)** is more common than magnetic media. **Digital Versatile Disk (DVD),** a newer optical storage medium with even greater storage capacity than a CD, will probably take the place of these other optical media within the next few years.

The disadvantages of optical storage over magnetic storage include cost and speed. In general, optical storage devices are more expensive and slower than hard disks. However, the advantages of optical storage outweigh the disadvantages when it comes to working with multimedia applications. In addition, the disadvantages are disappearing as the technology continues to improve.

MAGNETO-OPTICAL DISKS

Not all optical storage disks are write once or read only. **Magneto-optical (MO) disks** are rewritable. MO disk drives read optical disks and also rewrite to them through the use of a laser. The laser heats the surface of the disk and permits a magnet to polarize another pattern of spots. This is promising technology for use in multimedia applications.

CDs

CD-ROM stands for compact disk read only memory. A CD-ROM can hold about 650MB of data. Because CDs provide so much storage capacity, they are ideal for storing large data files, graphics, sound, and video. Entire references such as encyclopedias complete with text and graphics, as well as audio and video to further enhance the information, can be stored on one CD-ROM. In addition, interactive components that enable the user to respond to and control the medium ensure that the user will be even more attentive and likely to retain information. For these reasons, CDs have been the medium of choice for publishing multimedia applications..

Because a CD-ROM is the most common type of optical disk, computers sold today include a CD-ROM drive as standard equipment. In fact, in order to have a multimedia personal computer based on the standards set by the MPC, you must

FIGURE 2.19

Magneto-optical (M-O) disks are rewritable.

have a CD-ROM drive. Therefore, when considering the purchase of a multimedia computer, the important consideration in regard to the CD-ROM drive is the **speed of transfer.**

CD-ROM speed is measured in kilobytes (KB) per second. This refers to the speed at which data is transferred from the CD to the computer processor or monitor. Double speed (2×) CD-ROM drives can transfer data at a rate of 300 KB per second, quadruple speed (4×) can transfer data at a rate of 600 KB per second, and so on up to 24× and higher.

In addition to transferring the data to the computer or monitor faster, a faster transfer rate will also result in higher quality graphics, audio, and video. Therefore, if you are working with multimedia, it is probably worth a few extra bucks to get a faster CD-ROM drive.

Another factor that will speed the transfer of data from a CD-ROM is the size of the **buffer.** A buffer is a temporary storage area where data from the CD can be stored until the computer is ready to process it. A computer accesses data more quickly from the buffer than from the CD.

Some CD-ROMs are classified as **CD-ROM XA.** The XA stands for extended architecture, and those CDs with this technology can hold more audio than audio CDs. Though they are fine for speech, CD-ROM XA are not as consistent and reliable as regular CDs for music.

CD-ROM Recordables are drives that allow you to record CDs. Unfortunately, these drives only allow you to write to the CD one time. Though this is an excellent way of storing data that should not be modified, it is a big disadvantage to storing data that may need to be modified at a later time. Because **WORM** (Write Once Read Many) technology definitely has its pitfalls, newer technology, the **CD-ROM Rewritable** drive, is taking its place.

CD-ROM Rewritable drives enable users to modify data on a CD-ROM just as they are able to modify the data on magnetic media such as floppy disks. By using

FIGURE 2.20

Because of their large storage capacity, CDs are often used to store multimedia applications.

a laser to change the shape and location of the pits that are read, users are now able to write over the top of data on a CD-ROM.

CD-ROM Multisession allows you to record to a CD in more than one session. With this technology, everything doesn't have to be recorded at one time. This is common with Photo CDs. If you don't fill up an entire CD, you can have additional photos added at a later time. **CD Plus,** also called **CD Extra** and **Enhanced CD,** is also considered a multisession CD-ROM drive. This format allows you to add multimedia to a regular audio CD. Users can listen to the audio CD on a regular audio player or view the other multimedia materials on a computer. Some experts are predicting that within the next few years, most new music CDs will be CD Extras.

LASER DISKS

Laser disks are also read-only. Laser disks are larger than CDs and they also have a larger storage capacity. In general, laser disks aren't as popular as CD-ROM for distributing multimedia. This is probably because of their awkward size, high cost (as much as $600 per disk), and the fact that they are analog rather than digital technology and therefore need additional hardware and software to communicate properly with the computer system.

There are two recording methods used with laser disks, **CAV (Constant Angular Velocity)** and **CLV (Constant Linear Velocity).** CAV recording creates 30 minutes/side of freeze-frame video. This recording technology is often used in education due to the importance of freezing frames that are clear and stable. CLV recording creates 60 minutes/side of video. You can also freeze frames on CLV-recorded laser disks, but these frames will flicker.

Though laser disks aren't usually used to distribute most multimedia applications, they have been used quite extensively to deliver video. Because video files are so large and require so much storage capacity, CD isn't effective and can't compete with the larger storage capacity of a laser disk. In addition, laser disks offer several advantages over videotapes. Laser disks are non-linear technology. This means that users can instantly access any track on the disk without rewinding or fast forwarding. Though laser disks can only be recorded to one time, they are far more stable and durable than videotapes. Laser disks also support more audio tracks than videotapes. Among other things, this means that video can be recorded in different languages and the viewer can choose the appropriate language. The playback of video on laser disks can also be controlled from the computer, which has made laser disks a superior medium for computer-based training and educational multimedia applications.

In the past, laser disks were used as the primary medium for the distribution of video. However, this is changing. DVD technology is taking the place of laser disk technology for distributing full-motion video.

DVDs

DVD, which stands for Digital Versatile Disk, is the newest and most promising multimedia storage and distribution technology. DVD technology offers the greatest potential to multimedia because its storage capacity is extensive.

DVDs are the same size as CDs, but they offer much more storage capacity. DVDs are either single or double sided. A double-sided DVD is actually two single DVDs glued together. By using more densely packed data pits together with more closely spaced tracks, DVDs can store tremendous amounts of data. DVD disk types and capacities include the following four:

1. DVD-5: one layer, one side—max. capacity about 4.7GB.
2. DVD-9: one layer, dual sided—max. capacity about 8.5GB.

3. DVD-10: two layers, one side—max. capacity about 9.4GB.

4. DVD-18: two layers, dual sided—max. capacity about 17GB.

At its smallest storage capacity of 4.7 gigabytes, the DVD will hold approximately seven times the capacity of a CD. At its greatest storage capacity of 17GB, each DVD can hold the equivalent of approximately 27 times more than a CD. This is equal to nine hours of digital audio, four hours of digital video, or a mix of audio and video. In addition, audio and video on the DVD will be sharper, clearer and superior compared to CDs, LDs, and VHS. There are already hundreds of movie titles available on DVD. Some people project that the DVD format will eventually take the place of VHS, S-VHS, Audio CD, LD, CD-ROM, and Audio Tape.

The tremendous storage capacity of the DVD enables movie producers and multimedia software developers an opportunity to add myriad extra features. For example, DVD discs have the capability to present soundtracks in eight different languages and 32 distinct subtitles. Multiple story lines can be created on one DVD disc that allows the user to interact by determining the story line and ending. In some cases, one DVD will hold a movie that can be viewed at different ratings—PG, PG-13, or R. Parents will have the ability to choose the rating of a movie their children view.

Most exciting is the future potential of DVD in a broad range of multimedia and computer applications. DVD discs will be used to distribute software. A single DVD disk will meet the storage requirements of almost any multimedia software, including upcoming DVD games. Because DVD consists of a suite of disk types, the format holds tremendous growth potential for data-intensive home and business applications. DVD players entered the marketplace in the fall of 1997 with prices ranging between $300 and $700.

DVD does not wear out with use. In fact, it is guaranteed to have a 100-year life. It is not affected by magnetic fields, and it is also more resistant to errors than other optical technology. Consequently, DVD equates to flexibility and interactivity and is a great new technology for the distribution of multimedia products. To find out more about DVD, visit Toshiba on the World Wide Web at http://www.toshiba.com.

Speed and storage are vital to good multimedia viewing and production. If you can afford it, purchase a fast, powerful processor, as much RAM as possible, and a huge hard drive with options for transportable storage devices such as CDs, DVDs, MOs, and removable hard disks (Zip, Jaz, and SyJet).

AV-TUNED DRIVES

AV-Tuned Drives are hard drives specifically designed to work with audio and video. AV-tuned drives are a key tool for media professionals, particularly those professionals working with audiovisual material.

FIGURE 2.21

DVDs look like CDs but they offer much greater storage capacity.

DVD SPECIFICATIONS	
Disc Diameter:	120mm (5 inches)
Disc Thickness:	1.2mm (0.6mm tick disc X2)
Memory Capacity:	4.7 gigabytes/single side
Data Transfer Rate:	Variable speed/average rate of 4.69 megabits/second
Image Compression:	MPEG-2 digital image compression
Audio:	Dolby AC-3 (5.1 ch), LPCM for NTSC
Running Time (movies):	133 min. per side

AV-tuned drives are not necessarily designed to be faster, but they are designed to provide a smoother flow of data. Gaps in a digital video or audio data stream can result in dropped video frames and flaws in sound. Therefore, multimedia applications require steady, uninterrupted data transfers that may last for minutes.

Regular hard drives periodically take breaks to **recalibrate. Thermal recalibration** occurs when the drive temporarily interrupts what it's doing to measure the size of its platters and adjust them for expansion and contraction due to changes in temperature. The recalibration process does not affect most types of data. However, it does affect audio and video data capture.

If you are in the middle of capturing a segment of video when your drive decides to recalibrate, you may lose frames. This means your video will be choppy and imperfect instead of smooth. By sensing a long, continuous data transfer, AV-tuned drives are designed to postpone recalibrations. Therefore, AV-tuned drives capture a continuous stream of data because they do not allow the drive to take breaks to recalibrate while video or audio is being captured. In addition to providing better continuity by postponing recalibration, AV-tuned drives also offer internal caches that are tuned to read ahead. This guarantees that data will be ready before it's needed. For multimedia developers, an AV-tuned drive is an excellent choice, and they are crucial if you plan to write to a CD-ROM.

FLASH RAM

Flash RAM, also called **flash memory,** is a relatively new type of storage. Flash memory is as fast as RAM, however, it retains data even when the power is turned off. Flash memory is generally found on PCI cards and is most often used in portable devices. Though flash memory is fast, it is also very expensive. Therefore, at this time, it is rather unlikely that you would be using flash RAM to store complete multimedia applications, however, you might encounter flash RAM as a storage device in digital cameras.

DIGITAL TAPE

Magnetic tape or **digital audio tape (DAT)** records digital data on a magnetic tape. Access to the data on digital tape is linear, which means you basically have to fast-forward and rewind to find the data you need. Because this process is slow and cumbersome, using digital tape in multimedia applications is useless for accessing data on a regular basis. However, digital tape is quite beneficial as a backup medium because it is cheap and will store extensive amounts of data.

RAID

RAID stands for Redundant Array of Inexpensive Disks. Essentially, RAID takes two or more hard drives and treats them as one. There are different levels of RAID, each designed to serve a slightly different function. In general, RAID technology is designed to increase speed and offer improved security. Of course, all of this technology costs money. However, because AV professionals need speed, many are willing to pay the price.

WHAT MAKES A DRIVE FAST?

Certain drive specifications affect the overall performance of a drive. Hard disk drives find information by positioning a read/write head over the track on the disk that holds the required data. The time it takes the head to move into position over the data is called the **seek time.** The time it takes for the data to be located is called **access time.**

Once the head gets to the right track, it has to wait for the data to rotate underneath it. This is called **rotational delay.** The faster the drive spins, the shorter the

rotational latency. Rotational latency is not as critical during long, sustained data transfers, such as large-still-image transfers or digital-video work, as the drive does not have to seek out data as frequently during these operations.

If the cylinders on a drive are larger and can store a larger amount of data, this also improves speed. This is because the drive can read more data from a large cylinder without having to move to a new position. In other words, it spends less time seeking. Therefore, between drives of the same capacity, those with more platters and higher recording densities (fewer cylinders) tend to be faster.

Disk optimization is also important. If the disk is **fragmented,** data is stored in noncontiguous tracks and sectors. This means that data from one file may be spread throughout the disk because there was not a large enough chunk of free space on which to store the file. To keep related data together and therefore improve seek and access time, you should defragment your drives on a regular basis. In addition, if you are performing a CD-R operation, you must "defrag" your hard drive first to prevent an interruption in data flow.

Another way to speed up the disk drive is by adding RAM and designating some or all of it to **disk cache.** Disk cache is the section of RAM that will be accessed first. This additional cache can improve speed by keeping the drive head from having to access the **FAT,** or **VFAT** in Windows 95. The FAT is the file allocation table. It serves as an index or table or contents that the operating system uses to find data on the disk. By storing this data in cache, the read/write head doesn't have to make additional stops at the FAT whenever data is requested from the drive.

Buses

A **bus** is any line that transmits data between memory and input/output devices or between memory and the CPU. **Parallel bus** structures transmit eight bits of data at one time while a **serial bus** transmits one bit of data at one time.

In the past, controller chips had a hard time processing a lot of data coming in all at once in one very fast data stream from a serial bus. They could, however, handle slower streams of data delivered from parallel ports. For this reason, parallel bus structures were the type most often found in computers.

This is changing. Silicon-chip speed has increased and allowed for faster processing of data streams. Because today's processors can handle it, serial processing, driving bits of data lined up one behind another down a single digital cable as quickly as possible, is a more effective method of transmitting data. In addition, carrying data in a parallel format requires a lot of expensive wire and connectors. It is also difficult to keep all of the parallel signals harmonious and in sync. With serial processing, there are no expensive cables, no termination issues, no short bus lengths, and no conflicting SCSI-ID numbers. With serial transmission there is merely a lot of data moving very quickly down a long, thin, cheap cable.

Bus structure can be quite important when you are working with large multimedia files. Large files that include digital artwork, audio tracks, or digital video clips require a long time to open and upload. A five-minute full-screen video can easily consume over 2 GB of storage. In addition, video editing is very finicky and requires steady, reliable, ultra-high-speed data flow. The video-editing card needs the digital-video data immediately, not when your hard drive and SCSI cable can manage to deliver it.

At the time of this writing, engineers are sharpening several new bus structures designed to speed up the rate at which data is transferred. Unfortunately, accepted standards have not yet been accepted. The following are the common bus structures as well as those that are currently being created and examined within the computer industry.

SCSI

SCSI (Small Computer System Interface) is the interface currently used by all Macs and most higher-end PCs to connect hard drives and other peripherals. SCSI is convenient and reliable, but it is also painstaking. In addition, it requires expensive cabling and is limited to a relatively small number of closely spaced connections.

There are different types of SCSI including **Fast, Wide, Fast and Wide,** as well as **Ultra.** SCSI offers a top speed transmission of 40 MB per second.

ULTRA SCSI

Ultra SCSI doubles the theoretical maximum throughput of current Fast and Fast and Wide SCSI-2 to 20 and 40 MB per second, respectively. Ultra2 promises even greater speed. However, both are still too slow for the tremendous loads being put upon them by multimedia professionals.

SSA

SSA (Serial Storage Architecture) is backed by IBM and Conner. SA offers simplified ports and cabling over SCSI. SSA maxes out at about 80 MB per second. Each scheme can connect as many as 126 devices simultaneously, each one accessible at full speed at all times. SSA allows multiple reads and writes at one time.

FC-AL

FC-AL (Fibre Channel Arbitrated Loop) is backed by Seagate, Hewlett-Packard and Quantum. It also offers simplified ports and cabling over SCSI. FC-AL is currently clocked at 100 MB per second, with 200-MB-per-second products promised for next year. 400-MB-per-second devices are just over the horizon. FC-AL can connect as many as 126 devices simultaneously, each one accessible at full speed at all times. FC-AL is a one-transfer-at-a-time technology.

FC-EL

FC-EL (fibre channel—enhanced loop), is a planned hybrid of SSA and FC-AL. Though it holds great promise in theory, it won't be a reality right away.

FIREWIRE

FireWire or **IEEE-1394** is a Sony-backed standard that was developed by Apple Computer. It appears on Sony's latest digital video cameras. The goals of FireWire are to reduce network bottlenecks and sluggish file transfers. FireWire can connect up to 63 devices always accessible at full speed. FireWire has already been adopted as the transmission standard for digital video. Therefore, it will probably be used as an audio and video interconnect with multimedia applications, but its future beyond that is uncertain.

There are a few unanswered dilemmas with high-speed serial interfaces. For example, because all users have access to all files at all times, it is possible for two users to read, modify, and overwrite the same file at the same time. Though some software protects the integrity of the file, other software does not.

Hardware manufacturers such as Apple, Truevision, Miro, and Adaptec are creating products that provide FireWire connectors for personal computers. The availability of FireWire connectors on personal computers means that users will be able to digitally transfer sound and video captured with DV cameras into their computers. The video and sound quality of these DV clips are of very high quality, in part because of the many advantages of the digital tape format and digital data transfer.

FIGURE 2.24

Firewire will probably be used as an interconnect for audio and video.

USB

Universal Serial Bus (USB) is a low-cost, low-speed interconnect designed to connect PCs to keyboards, mice, joysticks, telephones, and low-end scanners using a daisy chain configuration. Due to its low speed, its storage use will probably be limited to midrange CD-ROM drives. USB will become the standard on the PC, and although no specification for the Macintosh currently exists, the possibility is being explored and it will probably become a Macintosh standard as well.

Image Output

Most multimedia productions are viewed and heard directly from the computer. Therefore, when we discuss image output in multimedia, we are primarily concerned with how the image will appear projected on the computer monitor or from a projection device. We are also concerned about the quality of the sound coming from the speakers. We are not usually interested in how the production will print, therefore, printers will not be discussed in this textbook.

MONITORS

The image displayed on the computer monitor depends on the quality of the monitor and software, as well as the capability of the video adapter card. For multimedia applications, it is critical that all of these elements work together to create high quality graphic images. However, because all display systems are not the same, you will have very little control over how your images appear on other people's systems. Consequently, it is a good idea to test your projects on different display systems to see how your digital images appear.

When purchasing a computer monitor to be used with multimedia applications, you will want to consider purchasing a larger screen. Screen sizes are measured along the diagonal and range in size from eight to more than 50 inches. You will probably want at least a 17-inch monitor. Though this larger monitor will cost you a bit more, it will prove well worth it if you intend to spend any time at all either designing or otherwise working with multimedia applications. In fact, after you have spent some time working with multimedia applications, you may even want to consider purchasing two monitors if you are using a Macintosh or PC setup that will support two monitors.

In addition to size, clarity and **resolution** are also key elements to quality image output. The number of **pixels,** picture elements, or lighted dots the monitor can display is sometimes called the resolution. More accurately, this measurement is the **screen size.** The resolution is the number of **pixels** per inch. Keep in mind that people often say resolution when they really mean screen size. Whether we measure the entire screen or just an inch, the greater the number of pixels, the higher the resolution. The resolution will be listed first by the number of horizontal dots displayed on the screen followed by the number of vertical dots displayed. For example, a monitor with a screen size or resolution of 1360 x 1024 would have 1,360 dots across and 1,024 down. The minimum resolution for a multimedia computer is 640 pixels across by 480 pixels down. Monitors that display different resolutions are called **multisync monitors.** These monitors can handle various scanning frequencies. If a monitor cannot multisync, it will display poor quality images at higher resolutions.

When viewing two monitors with the same resolution, one monitor may still appear to be superior over another. This is probably a result of the **dot pitch.** The dot pitch is the distance between pixels and should definitely be considered when purchasing a computer monitor. Dot pitch is built in by the manufacturer and cannot be changed at a later time. Although you will want to buy a screen with a large

FIGURE 2.25a

A comparison of three common resolutions for displaying video.
Low-resolution (640 × 480 pixels) with only 16 colors at once.

FIGURE 2.25b

Medium resolution (800 × 600 pixels) with 256 colors.

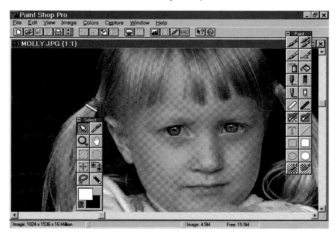

FIGURE 2.25c

High resolution (1024 × 768 pixels) with 65,536 colors.

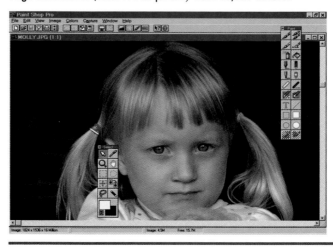

number of pixels, when you are analyzing dot pitch, the smaller the number the better. Remember, dot pitch is the distance between pixels. The less space you have between pixels, the sharper the image. Look for a dot pitch of .26mm or lower.

The number of colors that the monitor can display is also important. The number of colors is dependent on the amount of memory installed on the video adapter board as well as the monitor itself. The number of colors a monitor can display varies as listed below:

1. 4-bit system will display 16 different colors
2. 8-bit system will display 256 different colors
3. 16-bit system will display 65,636 different colors
4. 24-bit system will display more than 16 million different colors.

Most monitors can display at least 256 colors (8-bit), which is probably adequate for multimedia presentations, particularly if the presentation is delivered via the Web, but it may not be adequate for video. Eight-bit images are the most compatible across multiple platforms and they also take up very little disk space. Computer monitors capable of displaying thousands of colors (16-bit) are quickly becoming the multimedia standard. Images on these displays not only look better, they also display much faster.

Though nothing quite compares to a 24-bit display, these monitors are expensive and the file sizes are huge. However, if everything is set up correctly, you certainly won't feel limited by the number of displayable colors because the maximum is more than 16 million and is nearly comparable to photographic images or 35mm slides.

Keep in mind that if you are designing multimedia applications, the more colors you choose the greater the amount of storage space required by the image. This factor has important implications when designing images for the Internet where you want images to download as quickly as possible. Therefore, we will discuss this issue in greater depth in Chapter 8.

Though color is important, one of the biggest problems with computer monitors is their lack of consistent colors. This problem is heightened by the endless combination of cards and monitors that make it nearly impossible to predict what the final image will actually look like when it is displayed.

PCs are particularly problematic because there is no standard for color management under Windows. Macs display approximately 72 ppi, and a cable that connects the monitor to the computer tells the system the size of the monitor. Consequently, the Macintosh is far more predictable, but it still isn't perfect.

Finally, when choosing a monitor make sure the display is **non-interlacing.** With a non-interlacing monitor, lines on the monitor will be lit in consecutive order. If the monitor is **interlacing,** every other line will be lit from top to bottom. A second pass will be made to light those lines that were missed during the first pass. This interlacing process often causes flickering on the screen. Though most monitors claim to be non-interlacing, they may switch to interlacing at higher resolutions.

FLAT PANEL DISPLAYS

Flat panel displays are already common on portable computers, but they are becoming more and more common as larger units where they are often found mounted on walls and other surfaces. Within the next few years it may be quite common to hang your monitor on the wall almost like a painting. **Flat panel displays** do not use the cathode ray tube (CRT) technology found on most desktop monitors. Instead, they use **liquid crystal display (LCD)** or **gas plasma technology** to produce the image on the screen. Gas plasma screens offer a higher display quality than LCD screens, however, they are also more expensive. For this reason,

Purchase monitors that support multiple resolutions and millions of colors so that you can test a range of viewing possibilities. Monitors that permit color calibration will reflect a truer, more accurate image.

And remember, do not purchase a monitor with a dot pitch higher than .26 mm.

you are probably more likely to encounter or purchase an LCD screen. If you do consider purchasing an LCD display, you will want to pay the extra money to get an active matrix screen. **Active matrix screens** use individual transistors for each crystal cell while **passive matrix screens** use only one for each row and column. For this reason, active matrix screens will create a sharper, brighter image. Active matrix screens are also necessary if you want to display motion video.

PROJECTORS

If your multimedia presentation will be displayed to a room full of people, you will want to purchase a projection system that will project the image that displays on the computer monitor to a larger screen. There are several different projection systems that make this possible. In choosing a system, be sure to match

FIGURE 2.26

Flat panel displays are already common on portable computers.

FIGURE 2.27

Though large screen flat panel displays are still very expensive, they are becoming more and more common.

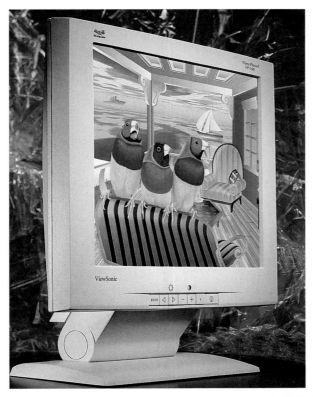

the projector resolution with the resolution of the multimedia application. For example, if the projector projects at 640 × 480, you will want to make sure that your multimedia application is written for a resolution of 640 × 480. If it is written at 800 × 600, it may not project on a 640 × 480 projector. If it does project, viewers may only see two-thirds of the application screen.

On the lower end are **LCD projection panels.** LCD projection panels use liquid crystal display (LCD) technology. These projectors are connected to the computer and then placed over a light source such as an overhead projector. The advantages of LCD projection panels include their portability and relatively low cost compared to most other projection equipment. The disadvantages include the need for a light source and the lower quality of the image displayed compared to other projection systems. Because they do not have their own light source, images projected from an LCD panel often need to be viewed in a dark room.

Unlike LCD projection panels, **LCD projectors** are self-contained. This means they have a built-in light source and do not require a separate overhead projector. These projectors offer a much higher quality image that is easier to see in a lighted room. Like the panel, LCD projectors are portable. In fact, all-in-one projectors that deliver graphics, video, and sound are great for presenters who travel. Though they sometimes lack the consistent delivery quality offered by individual components, they are convenient. The biggest drawback to this superior technology is the higher cost.

More expensive, stationary projectors are also available. These units have individual red, green, and blue lights that must be focused and set a certain distance from the screen. This is why these projectors are generally installed in auditoriums and large meeting rooms.

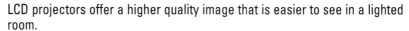

FIGURE 2.28

LCD projectors offer a higher quality image that is easier to see in a lighted room.

A fourth projection option is the large screen television. Some computers can be connected directly to large screen TVs, others require converter boxes that convert the image from the screen to an image that can be viewed on a large screen TV. The room size and setup, as well as the potential size of the audience should guide you in selecting the most appropriate projection system. Visit Epson's site at http://www.epson.com or InFocus's site at http://www.infocus.com for additional information and current pricing on different types of projection systems.

SPEAKERS

To listen to the sound produced by your computer, you will need a pair of audio speakers. Most computer speakers are powered, which means the amplifier is built into the speakers. If they are not powered, you will need to purchase an amplifier.

Many computer manufacturers as well as stereo system manufacturers make computer speakers. You'll find that Apple, Radio Shack, Bose, Yamaha, Sony, and others manufacture computer speakers that range in price from under $20 to hundreds of dollars. They also range in quality. Keep in mind that sound has a major influence over the mood and effect created in a multimedia application, so buy speakers that effectively enhance the mood.

CD BURNERS

If you intend to produce your own multimedia CD-ROMs, you'll need a **CD burner.** Check out the specifications of any CD burner that you intend to purchase. Yamaha and other manufacturers make CD burners that allow you to burn CD-ROMs, audio CDs, and hybrid CDs in less than half an hour provided you have the right software. Visit http://www.yamaha.com for more information.

FIGURE 2.29

Because sound is a very important element in a multimedia application, you should buy high-quality speakers.

Emerging Technologies

New technologies are always on the horizon. Take a look at the major manufacturer's Web sites to find out the latest or visit http://www.chalk.com for a user-friendly description of many new computer technologies.

SUMMARY

Because of the tremendous growth of multimedia applications, most computers that you buy today are designed to run multimedia applications, and most multimedia developed today is created for both the PC and Macintosh platforms. Though PCs are the more common platform encountered on the multimedia-user end, the Macintosh is still the more common platform encountered in the multimedia design and development world.

The **Multimedia PC Marketing Council (MPC)** created a set of minimum standards for multimedia hardware and software for the PC in 1991. Currently there are three MPC levels.

As verification that multimedia is becoming commonplace in the PC environment, Intel has added **MMX™** technology to all of its new Pentium processor instruction sets. This new technology offers a 50 to 100 percent improvement in the clarity and speed of audio, video, and speech. The **PowerPC** is a RISC chip, which is excellent technology for use in multimedia. In addition to the microprocessor, a sufficient amount of **RAM (Random Access Memory)** is extremely important because it improves speed.

Special equipment is needed to **capture** or **digitize** images. **Video capture cards** allow you to connect a camcorder, VCR, or TV to the computer to capture images. Different video capture cards come with different **compression technology** to reduce the file size for transfer and storage.

Snappy Video Snapshot connects directly to the computer and a video cable is then used to connect Snappy to a camcorder, VCR or TV. With Snappy, you can capture digital images without installing anything inside your computer.

Camcorders or **digital video cameras** can be used to capture full-motion images. Although regular camcorders store video on film, digital video cameras store images as digital data. Similarly, **digital cameras** allow you to take pictures that are stored in a digital format on magnetic disk or internal memory.

Scanners digitize already developed images including photographs, drawings, or pages of text. There are different types of scanners including **handheld scanners, page** or **flat-bed scanners,** and **page-fed** scanners. Another excellent method of storing and using photographic digital images is on **Photo CD.** **Digitizing** and **graphics tablets** convert points, lines, and curves drawn with a stylus or digitizer device to digital data.

Next to the original sound, the microphone is the most important factor in any sound system. Microphones fall into two main groups, **moving coil** and **condenser.**

In order to play or record sound on a PC, you need a sound card while the sound circuitry is built into the logic board on a Macintosh. **MIDI (Musical Instrument Digital Interface)** is a standard that was agreed upon by the major manufacturers of musical instruments. With MIDI, it is possible to connect musical instruments to computers.

If you plan to work with multimedia, you need huge storage capacities. Internal, external, and removable hard disks contain the necessary storage capacity for working with multimedia applications. Removable hard disks including **Iomega's Zip** and **Jaz** drives and **SyQuest's Easy Drive** and provide an appropriate amount of storage as well as a format that is easy to transport.

Optical storage including **Magneto-optical (MO) disks** and **CD-ROM (CD)** is more common than magnetic media when working with multimedia. **Digital Versatile Disk (DVD),** a newer optical storage medium with even greater storage capacity than a CD, will probably take the place of these other storage media within the next few years.

AV-tuned drives are specifically designed to work with audio and video by providing a smoother flow of data. **Flash RAM** is a relatively new type of storage often used in portable devices such as digital cameras. **Magnetic tape** or **digital audio tape (DAT)** records digital data on a magnetic tape and is quite beneficial as a backup medium. **RAID** (Redundant Array of Inexpensive Disks) is designed to increase speed and offer improved security. **Seek time, access time,** and **rotational delay** are used to measure drive speed. The size of the cylinders, disk optimization, and **disk cache** are important in improving disk drive speed.

A **bus** is any line that transmits data between memory and input/output devices or between memory and the CPU. **Parallel bus** structures transmit eight bits of data at one time while a **serial bus** transmits one bit of data at one time. There are many different types of bus structures. **SCSI** is the interface currently used by all Macs and most higher-end PCs to connect hard drives and other peripherals. **FireWire** or **IEEE-1394** is a Sony-backed standard that appears on digital video cameras and will probably be used as an audio and video interconnect with multimedia applications. Newer bus structures—including **SSA, FC-AL,** and **FC-EL**—are also being explored.

The image displayed on the computer monitor depends on the quality of the monitor and software, as well as the capability of the video adapter card. Size, clarity, and **resolution** are key elements in determining the quality of the image output. The minimum resolution recommended for a multimedia computer is 640 pixels across by 480 pixels down with a dot pitch of .26mm or lower. The number of colors that the monitor can display is also important. Most monitors can display at least 256 colors (8-bit), which is probably adequate for multimedia presentations.

Flat panel displays are common on portable computers, and large units mounted on walls are becoming more common. If you purchase an LCD display, pay the extra money to get an active matrix screen, which will produce a sharper, brighter image.

You can project your multimedia presentation using **LCD projection panels** or **projectors** and listen to the sound with a pair of high-quality, audio speakers.

KEY TERMS

MPC	MMX™	PowerPC
RISC	RAM	Capture
Digitize	Compression	MPEG
DVI	Snappy	Digital video camera
Digital camera	Scanner	Photo CD
Graphics tablet	Moving coil	Condenser
MIDI	Zip	Jaz
Easy Drive	SyJet	CD-ROM
Laser disk	DVD	MO disk
WORM	AV-tuned drives	Flash RAM
DAT tape	RAID	Bus
Seek time	Access time	Rotational delay
Disk cache	SCSI	FireWire
Resolution	Pixels	Screen size
Dot pitch	Flat panel displays	Active matrix
Passive matrix	Multisync monitors	LCD projection

Matching Questions

a. digitized   **b.** video capture card   **c.** compression

d. pixels   **e.** dot pitch   **f.** scanner

g. sound card   **h.** recalibration   **i.** bus

j. seek time   **k.** access time   **l.** rotational delay

_____ **1.** The time it takes for the data to be located.

_____ **2.** This technology reduces file size for transfer and storage of data.

_____ **3.** This occurs when the drive temporarily interrupts what it's doing to measure the size of its platters and adjust them for expansion and contraction due to changes in temperature.

_____ **4.** This refers to picture elements or lighted dots displayed on the monitor.

_____ **5.** The time it takes for the data to rotate underneath the head.

_____ **6.** Cards or boards placed into an open expansion slot on the main board of the computer that allow you to connect a camcorder, VCR, or TV to the computer.

_____ **7.** The distance between pixels.

_____ **8.** Equipment used to digitize images such as photographs, drawings, or pages of text.

_____ **9.** This is any line that transmits data between memory and input/output devices or between memory and the CPU.

_____ **10.** Data stored as 0's and 1's so it can be interpreted by the computer's microprocessor.

_____ **11.** The time it takes the head to move into position over the data.

_____ **12.** These cards are necessary on a PC if you want to play sound through external speakers or record sound.

Fill-In Questions

1. The _____ is a special interest group of the _____. It was created to help sustain the organized expansion of multimedia in the home and workplace.

2. With the right adapters, software, and hardware, camcorders or _____ _____ _____ can be used to capture full-motion images.

3. _____ is a standard that was agreed upon by the major manufacturers of musical instruments.

4. Removable hard disks including _____ _____ and _____ drives, can hold 100MB and 1GB respectively, as well as _____ _____ _____ and _____, which hold 135MB and 1.5GB respectively.

5. _____, a newer optical storage medium with even greater storage capacity than a CD, will undoubtedly take the place of both of these media within the next few years.

6. _____ are rewritable CDs.

7. _____ stands for Redundant Array of Inexpensive Disks.

8. _____ _____ structures transmit eight bits of data at one time while a _____ _____ transmits one bit of data at one time.

9. If the disk is _____, data is stored in noncontiguous tracks and sectors.

Discussion Questions

1. What are some of the differences between the PC platform and the Macintosh platform? Why are these platform differences important to consider when you are creating and designing multimedia applications?

2. What is the purpose of the Multimedia PC Marketing Council (MPC)? What are five of the standards listed as part of MPC3?

3. Why is optical storage technology generally preferred over magnetic storage technology when working with multimedia applications?

4. Why are AV-Tuned Drives an excellent choice for multimedia developers working with audio and video?

5. Why are serial bus structures becoming more common on today's computers?

Hands-On Exercises

1. Using current computer magazines, catalogs, and the World Wide Web, research three different video capture cards. Compare specifications and prices.

2. Using current computer magazines, catalogs, and the World Wide Web, research three different digital cameras. Compare the specifications and prices.

3. Prepare a research report on a new and emerging multimedia technology. In preparing your paper, use and cite three distinct sources of information. (Hint: The Web will probably be your best research source because the information found there will probably include the most recent and relevant information available.)

Case Study: Chapter 2

After meeting with the owner and president of IWC, Mr. Luke Scott, Jamie believes she has a good feel for the image IWC would like to portray on its Web page—fast and fun. After all, speed and fun are what personal watercraft are all about. In order to portray this fast and fun image, Digital Design will incorporate lots of graphics, animation, sound, and video into the site. To accomplish this, the company needs equipment.

The graphics and animation for this Web site will be created on a Micron Pentium Pro II with MMX technology running at 250 MHz with 128 MB of RAM. This computer has a 4 GB Fast and Wide SCSI hard drive and an internal Iomega Jaz drive for easy backup and transfer.

Still images will be scanned from the manufacturer's marketing brochures using an Agfa StudioStar scanner with a 30-bit, 600×1200 image-capture resolution. Additional images will be taken with an Olympus D-320L digital camera.

Sounds recorded from video equipment will be used for the personal watercraft revving engines. A synthesizer will be connected via a MIDI port to a PowerMac 8600 with a 200 MHz 604e processor and built-in AV capabilities to create the sound of rushing water. The built-in microphone will be used to record the narration. Wave music files will be selected to serve as background music, so no recording will be necessary, though the music may need to be modified with sound processing software and saved in a cross-platform file format.

Sony Digital camcorders will be used to record full-motion video that will then be captured using a Radius MotoDV™ video capture card. This capture card uses FireWire to transfer the video in and out to the 21" radius monitor that's perched on top of a Power Computing 250 MHz PowerTower Pro. With FireWire and 128MB of RAM this capture process won't take long.

The pieces will be pulled together using Macromedia Director and Adobe Pagemill running on another Power Computing 250 MHz PowerTower Pro. After they have been assembled, they will be delivered via the Internet and tested on a variety of different computers and platforms including a 386SX PC with a 14" EGA monitor on the low end and a PowerMac G3 with a 21" monitor on the high end.

CHAPTER THREE

Graphics

1. Explain why graphic images are vital to multimedia applications
2. List the different ways graphics can be used in multimedia applications
3. Describe the different technologies that can be used to capture digital images
4. List several sources of still images
5. List the four items that should be logged in reference to graphic images
6. Discuss the responsibilities of a graphics designer
7. Define common terms used in computer graphics
8. Describe some of the common tools found on a tool palette
9. Explain the difference between paint programs and draw programs
10. Explain the difference between bitmapped graphics and vector-based graphics
11. Describe several features of common graphics programs
12. Explain jaggies and how they occur
13. Explain the process of creating 3D graphics
14. Discuss the different types of images that can be used in a multimedia application
15. Discuss the two different types of resolution related to graphic images
16. Explain several disadvantages of high resolution graphics
17. Discuss copyright law as it applies to graphic images

Introduction

Still images are vital to multimedia applications. We are a very visual society. With the advent of technology, we have become even more visual. This is because our society is fast-paced and in many circumstances, a picture really is worth a thousand words. One table, chart, graphic, or photograph can illustrate what might take many pages of narrative text to communicate. In the end, the image may still do a better job of creating a lasting impression. In societies such as ours where communicating information quickly is crucial, the importance of graphic elements in multimedia applications cannot be overstated.

Graphics can be used in multimedia applications as backgrounds, buttons, icons, navigational items, colors, maps, and charts; illustrations to explain concepts, information, and moods; and logos to communicate corporate image.

In addition to being able to use graphics in many different ways within a multimedia application, developers also have a variety of sources from which they can obtain the graphics they use in their designs. Some of the new technologies discussed in Chapter 2 including scanners, video capture cards, and digital cameras, allow developers to create these different types of digital images for multimedia projects.

In addition, once images are in a digital format, image-editing software such as Adobe Photoshop can be used to edit and manipulate them even further. Using image-editing software, multimedia developers can combine text and images to create almost any work of art they can imagine.

FIGURE 3.1

The data portrayed in this simple pie chart would consume pages of text if explained in words alone.

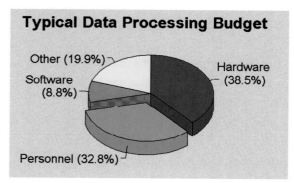

FIGURE 3.2

Graphics can be used as backgrounds, buttons, and icons.

Because still images are so vital to a multimedia project, care and time in searching for or creating just the right image is important. When searching for just the right image for your multimedia application, you should first create a list and description of the images you need for your project. Once you know what you want, you can choose to create the images yourself, obtain the images from a commercial image provider, or hire a graphic designer to create them for you.

Regardless of which source you use to obtain your images, you should keep track of the vital information and correspondence surrounding each image you have selected. It is good practice to log the following information:

- description of the image
- source of the image
- rights negotiated from the source including special conditions
- amount paid for each image.

The Graphic Designer

It's not always practical or even wise to find or create your own image. This is where the professional graphic designer steps in. Chances are, if you are working as part of a multimedia production team, a graphic designer will be part of that team. It is the graphic designer who is responsible for creating images for all different types of multimedia applications. It is also the responsibility of the graphic designer to be very selective and ensure that the multimedia project contains the highest quality images. If you are not working as part of a multimedia team, you should still consider hiring a graphic designer if you feel you can't find or create the image you need, or if you don't have time to do it.

Many professional graphic designers and photographers do freelance work and use the computer and technology as tools to express their creativity. You can usually hire them by the hour, by the day, or by the project. When hiring professionals, don't hesitate to ask for recommendations and samples of their work. If

FIGURE 3.3

Use a Multimedia Image Log to track vital information about the images used in your multimedia application.

MULTIMEDIA IMAGE LOG			
Description	Source	Right Negotiated	Amount Paid

FIGURE 3.4

Graphic designers use the latest tools and technology to create computer art forms.

they are professionals, they should be more than willing to show you what they have done. It is also wise to inquire about additional expenses such as travel and determine up front who will be paying these expenses.

Because the technology used by the graphic designer changes daily, this person must always be learning about the improvements and possibilities in graphics technology. In this chapter, we focus on some of the technologies a graphic designer can use to create the many images used in multimedia applications.

Digitized Images

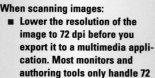

When scanning images:
- Lower the resolution of the image to 72 dpi before you export it to a multimedia application. Most monitors and authoring tools only handle 72 dpi images.
- Always work from the original image.
- Do not increase image resolution after it has been lowered. Some of the original color will have been deleted, so the image won't be as sharp.

In order to be used in a multimedia application, images must be in a digital format. **Digitizing** is the process of converting images into a format that the computer can recognize and manipulate. In other words, the image is converted into a series of binary data or 1's and 0's. There are many different sources of preexisting digitized images, or you can digitize images that are currently photographs, slides, or line art.

In this chapter we will discuss software programs called draw and paint programs that allow you to create digital images. Whenever you create graphic images with draw or paint programs, the image is digitized. Pre-existing graphic images in the form of clip art are also stored in a digital format. In Chapter 2, we discussed the different types of hardware used to digitize images. Scanners allow you to digitize photographs, line art, and drawings. Video capture cards allow you to connect video cameras, VCRs, videodisc players, television, or other live video source directly to your computer to capture frames of video. Or, on a PC, you can also use Snappy to get high-resolution images into a computer without purchasing and installing a video capture card.

FIGURE 3.5

There are many different ways of obtaining digital images. Graphics software can be used to create them, they can be scanned, or they can be captured from video.

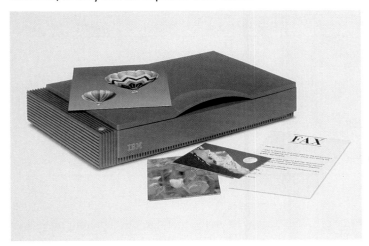

If you don't have a scanner, a video capture card, or a Snappy Video Snapshot, you can still use digitized multimedia images in your multimedia application if you have 35mm slides or photographs. Many film-processing companies will now place your photos on diskette or Photo CD for a minimal charge. Once these photos or frames are digitized, they are stored as bitmap images that can be manipulated just like any other bitmap image.

Types of Images

There are many different types of images used in multimedia production. A solid foundation in the terminology associated with these different images will help you work as part of a multimedia team. When working with multimedia, you'll need to understand the following terms:

Line Art

Images that contain only black and white pixels are called line art. This term is also used to describe drawings that contain flat colors without any tonal variation.

Grayscale

A grayscale image is a continuous tone image consisting of black, white, and gray data only. This is an image comprised of a range of grays, typically up to 256 levels of gray.

Color

Color images are dependent upon the equipment and will range from 4-bit color (16 colors) to 24-bit color (16 million colors). Actually, images can now have up to 36-bit color. Though the difference between 24-bit and 36-bit color depth can't

FIGURE 3.6

Color images can range from 16 colors to 16 million colors and more.

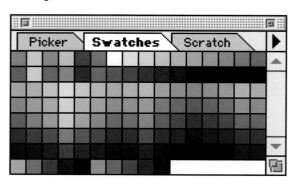

be discerned by our eyes and displayed on the monitor, the captured image will be higher quality. This means there will be less distortion, particularly when scanning, and the image will be truer. Increased color depth results in an increased file size. Although 36-bit color depth will produce a higher quality image, it will also make the file size much bigger. Therefore, there is a trade-off between color depth and file size.

Color on a computer monitor is referred to as **RGB,** which stands for red, green, and blue. These are the primary additive colors used in computer monitors and image recorders.

2D or 3D

By adding depth to **two-dimensional (2D),** flat images, they become **three dimensional (3D)** images. Actually, computer 3D graphics merely represent a three-dimensional scene in two dimensions because at this time, the medium on which the scene is viewed is a flat computer screen. Three-dimensional images are much more lifelike than 2D images, however, they are more difficult to create and they require greater computer resources.

Though both types of images have an application in multimedia, the two-dimensional desktop we are currently comfortable with may eventually be replaced by real-time 3D graphics. Because the real world is three dimensional, the 2D interface is often stifling, particularly for applications such as educational software, architectural design software, games, and training simulators. As evidence of this, three-dimensional environments are becoming more common on the Internet. **VRML** (Virtual Reality Modeling Language) is the programming language used to create these 3D environments on the World Wide Web. These Web-based 3D environments are often called **Live3D.**

Hypergraphics

In multimedia applications, graphic images can also serve as **hypermedia** or **hypergraphics.** These are clickable graphics that allow you to link to other locations within the same multimedia application, or even outside of it. They may also serve to trigger different events within a multimedia application.

When a graphic is also a trigger, the mouse pointer will generally change shape when it's placed on a hotspot. Each graphic can contain one trigger, or the

FIGURE 3.7
3D images are more lifelike than 2D images, but they also require greater computer resources.

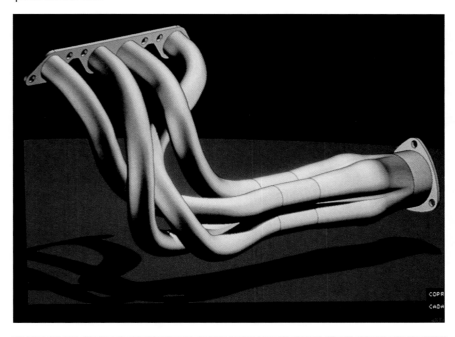

same graphic may contain several triggers. Graphics that contain more than one trigger are called **image maps**. Like hypertext, hypergraphics are quite useful in expanding the capabilities of an application.

Image Quality

Just as image color is dependent on the equipment, so is image quality. Image quality is dependent upon the medium by which the multimedia application will be disseminated. For example, due to bandwidth considerations that will be discussed in Chapter 8, images created for CD will be of much higher quality than images created for the Web. Let's take a look at what we mean when we talk about the quality of an image.

When it comes to multimedia, resolution can be a pretty confusing term. This is because it is used with several different multimedia elements, and it means something slightly different each time it is used. In other words, there are many different types of resolution. In Chapter 2, we discussed resolution as it relates to computer monitors. We said that device resolution or output resolution measures the number of dots per inch (dpi) that the output device—monitor, LCD panel, projector—can produce, and that screen resolution refers to the number of dots per inch on the screen. In Chapter 5, we will define resolution as it relates to sound. In this chapter, we are more concerned with resolution as it relates to the image itself.

FIGURE 3.8

3D environments are becoming more and more popular on the Web.

There are two types of resolution related to graphic images that you need to be familiar with. **Bit resolution** or **color resolution** measures the number of bits of stored information per pixel or how many tones or colors every pixel in a bitmap can have. You may also see this referred to as **bit depth** or **pixel depth,** with the most common ranges being 8-, 16-, and 24-bit. An image with a greater bit resolution will be more colorful and of higher photographic quality. **Image resolution** refers to the amount of information stored for each image. Image resolution is typically measured in pixels per inch (ppi).

When deciding upon an appropriate resolution for your image, keep in mind that a higher resolution will display a superior image, but it will also result in a larger file size. This means the file will require more storage space and it will take longer to display. In other words, there is a trade-off for higher resolution images. For example, when creating images for Web pages, we must be willing to give up some quality in order to ensure that the graphic file sizes are small enough to download quickly.

Image Compression

As it is, graphics take up a lot of space. A five-page text document will average about 50K to 100K while even a small graphic file can easily be ten times larger

FIGURE 3.9

Hypergraphics use images to link visitors to related information.

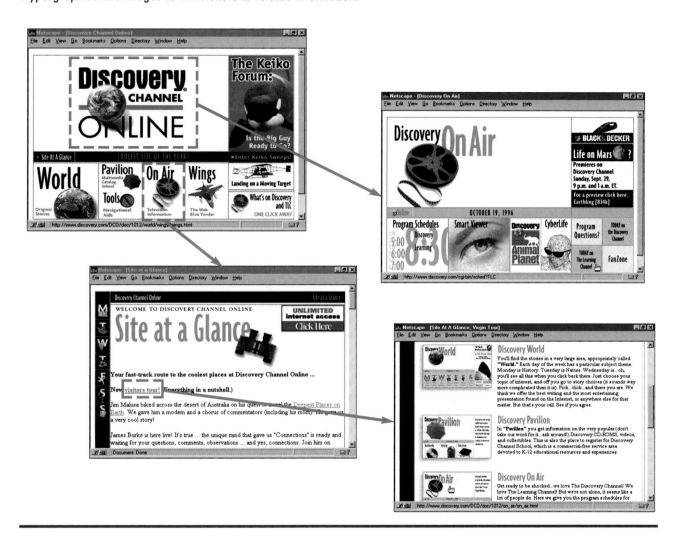

at 500K to 1000K. Because graphic files take up a lot more storage space than text, it is quite easy to run out of disk space or to spend a significant amount of time waiting for graphic files to transfer or download. For these reasons, you may find it necessary to compress your image files. **Compression** is simply an algorithm that is used to create smaller file sizes. There are two types of compression: **lossy** and **lossless.**

With lossless compression, none of the data is actually lost during compression. Instead, mathematical algorithms eliminate redundant data. If there isn't a lot of redundant data, the file size may not be significantly reduced. In fact, in some instances file size will actually be increased. Many graphic formats and compression utilities like **PKZIP, WinZip,** and **StuffIt** use lossless compression.

In lossy compression some of the data is actually lost. The idea behind lossy compression is that some of the data isn't important to an image and therefore that data is expendable. The advantage to using lossy compression is that it offers greater image compression than lossless compression. For this reason, it is very popular with multimedia professionals, particularly when images are delivered over the Internet.

FIGURE 3.10
The quality of an image is dependent upon both the bit depth and the image resolution.

FIGURE 3.11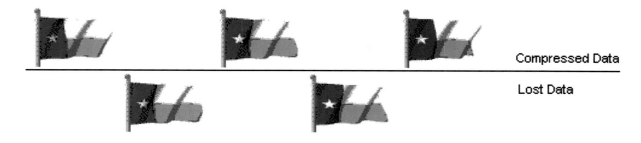

Lossy compression is often used with video while lossless compression is used with text.

Compressed Data

Lost Data

Graphics Software

There are many programs available that allow you to create or modify two-dimensional graphic images. These programs are called **graphics editors** and include drawing programs, painting programs, and image editing programs. Programs that allow you to create or modify three-dimensional graphic images are called 3D modeling programs. Typically, to create on-screen graphics in one of these programs, you use a **tool palette.** The tool palette contains electronic drawing tools such as pencils, paintbrushes, and erasers. Once you have created or modified images using the available drawing tools, you can resize them, move them, rotate them, or change their shape. Once completed, the images can be incorporated into an on-screen multimedia presentation or application.

There are many advantages to creating your own images. When you create them, you own them. Therefore, you don't have to worry about copyright, permission, and possible royalties. You can edit and manipulate the images any way you desire. If you have a clear vision of the images you want, you may find it easier to create them yourself rather than explain them to someone else who may

FIGURE 3.12

These tool palettes contain electronic drawing tools that allow you to create and modify graphic images.

have a hard time sharing your vision. With today's tools, you can either create the images using image editing, painting, drawing, and modeling software or you can draw them, paint them, and edit them using traditional methods and then digitize them with a scanner.

Graphics editors can be classified as one of two types. **Bitmap graphics editors** or **paint programs** allow you to create bitmap graphics. **Vector graphics editors** or **draw programs** allow you to create vector graphics. Let's look at the fundamental differences between these two types of graphics and graphics editors.

Paint Programs and Bitmapped Graphics

When you use a paint program the image you create is considered a bitmapped image. Bitmapped images are stored in memory as **pixels.** Pixels are picture elements. To illustrate, imagine that each piece of a graphic image is broken down into small squares. Each small square represents one pixel. This pixel records the screen location and color value on a **bit map** in memory. A bit map is a grid similar to graph paper from which each small square will be directly mapped back onto the computer screen as a pixel.

Bitmapped graphics editors or paint programs are the only programs that allow you to edit images at the pixel level. This means they are the only type of program that can be used to accomplish effects like touching up photographs. In addition, paint programs are typically easier to learn and use than draw programs. Though bitmap-based paint programs are easier to use than vector-based draw programs, the resulting bitmapped images are not as flexible as vector graphics.

Because bitmapped images are pixel-based, when you enlarge these images the squares simply get bigger. In other words, because bitmapped images have a specific resolution or number of pixels per inch, if the image is enlarged without

FIGURE 3.13

If we zoom in on a bitmapped image, we can edit it pixel by pixel.

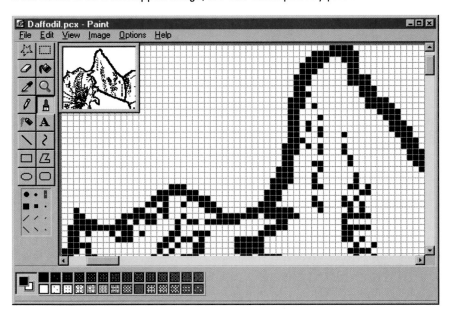

FIGURE 3.14
Some of the icons in a typical toolbox.

Scissors (known as a *Lasso* in some programs) select an object on the screen to be moved, copied, or erased. For example, to move the ice cream cone in Figure 3.18, select the Scissors tool, draw a line around the ice cream cone by dragging the mouse, click the mouse, and then drag the cone to a new location.

Select (known as *Pick* in some programs) also is used to move, copy, or erase objects. The difference is that Select marks off a rectangular area, while Scissors can mark off irregularly shaped areas. Pick could not be used to move the ice cream cone, for example, because it would move part of the red line, too.

Airbrush (also known as *Spray Paint*) spatters dots on the screen wherever you move the tool. To spray a denser pattern of dots, move the Airbrush tool more slowly.

Text lets you type words on the screen. Then you can use a pull-down menu to adjust the font and size of what you have written.

Eraser erases whatever it is dragged across. You can make the eraser tiny (for detailed work) or large (for quick erasing) by clicking on the width adjustment scale in the screen's lower, left-hand corner.

Fill blankets any enclosed region of the screen with a solid color or pattern. The Fill tool is a speedy way to color in backgrounds or shapes. To select a different fill color, click on one of the colors in the palette at the bottom of the screen.

Brush lets you draw curves and shapes freehand, somewhat like an artist's brush. You can change the brush width from thin to thick by clicking on the width adjustment scale in the screen's lower, left-hand corner.

Line (also called *Rubber Band*) draws straight lines when you drag the mouse between two points. If you hold down the Shift key while you drag, the lines will be perfectly vertical or horizontal.

Rectangle draws a box when you drag the mouse diagonally across the screen. The Rounded Rectangle tool makes boxes with rounded corners, while the Filled Rectangle tool makes solid boxes. To make a perfect square, hold down the Shift key while you drag the mouse.

---

adding extra pixels, the size of each pixel is increased. Consequently, the pixels are larger, but there are fewer pixels per inch. Obviously, this decreases the resolution. Enlarging an image too much may result in **staircasing** or **jaggies.** Jaggies are the stairstep-shaped edges that result when you enlarge a bitmapped image too much.

FIGURE 3.15

This bitmapped image has been enlarged too much. The smooth edges have been replaced by jaggies.

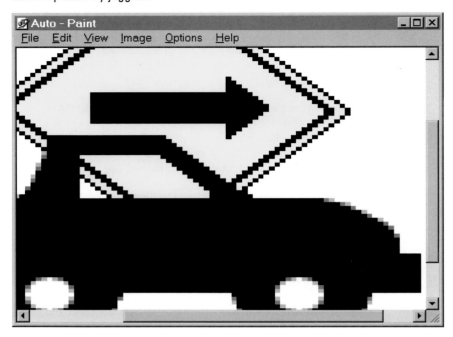

When you reduce the size of a bitmapped image, the opposite occurs. Pixels become smaller, therefore, there are more of them per inch. Although this increased resolution is aesthetically pleasing, it may create an unnecessarily large file size. The large file size may pose problems depending on how you plan to deliver your multimedia application. For example, if you are planning to include the image on a Web page, you must take extra care to ensure that the file size of your graphic images are small and will download quickly.

Some of the more common paint programs include Claris Works and Microsoft Paint. Let's take some time now to look at several common features found in most paint programs by checking out Microsoft Paint.

GEOMETRIC FIGURES

With paint programs, there are many tools available that allow you to create geometric figures or combine geometric figures to create forms. For example, from the Microsoft Paint tool palette you can choose the line tool, the rectangle tool, the oval tool, and the freeform tool to create images like this ice cream cone.

EDIT

All paint programs offer some method of editing mistakes; the eraser tool is one of the more common tools for removing mistakes. If you place a line where you later decide you don't want one, or if you draw the line too long, you can use the eraser tool to get rid of it. In addition, the Undo command from the Edit pull down menu will allow you to undo what you have done.

FIGURE 3.16

Microsoft Paint is a paint program that comes as an accessory with Windows 95. You can use it to create and edit bitmapped images.

FIGURE 3.17

From the tool palette, you can select lines and other geometric figures that allow you to create images like this ice cream cone.

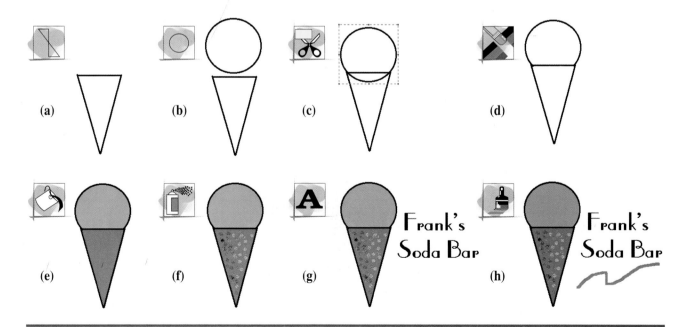

ADD COLOR AND PATTERNS

After you have created the image, you can add color to it by using the Fill tool, the Brush tool, and the Airbrush tool. With the Fill tool you can cover entire areas with solid color or special patterns of color. Adjust the brush width on the Brush tool and apply color only where you want it, or spray patterns of dots on the screen with the Airbrush tool. Combined, these three tools allow you to apply color to objects and backgrounds.

CUT AND PASTE

Using the Select (often called Pick) tool and the Scissors (often called Lasso) tool you can select any part of an object or objects. This selected area can then be deleted. It can also be copied or moved using the Edit pull down menu and the cut, copy, and paste commands.

ROTATE AND STRETCH

Change the horizontal or vertical position of an image using the Rotate command. In some programs, you can only flip the image horizontally or vertically. However, more sophisticated paint programs allow you to specify the direction and number of degrees to rotate an image. The Stretch command allows you to distort part or all of an image to fit into a new set of borders.

Draw Programs and Vector Graphics

Drawing programs excel as art production and illustration tools for creating original artwork. When you use a draw program, the resulting graphic is **vector based**. Unlike bitmapped graphics, vector graphics are created and recreated from mathematical models. These models actually create the image as a series of

FIGURE 3.18

Paint programs allow you to rotate, flip, or stretch images.

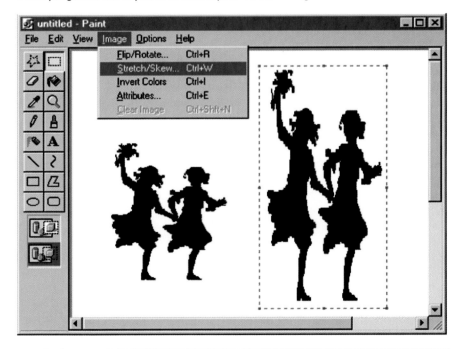

mathematical formulas that connect vectors or simple geometric shapes like lines and arcs that ultimately become circles and boxes.

Vector-based graphics can be resized or contorted without losing the quality of the image. Vector-based graphics are smoother and more precise than bitmapped graphics. They also require a lot less memory. Because vector graphics are more versatile and more precise than bitmapped images, professionals in art and drafting often use them. In addition to draw programs, most 3D graphics programs and Computer Aided Drafting (CAD) programs also produce vector graphics.

Some of the more common draw programs used today include **CorelDRAW, Adobe Illustrator, MacDraw, Claris Works,** and **Macromedia FreeHand.** By looking at some of the features found in Adobe Illustrator, you should get a feel for drawing programs and how they differ from paint programs.

FULLY EDITABLE SHAPES

Adobe Illustrator contains more than 27 different tools that can be used to create a variety of shapes. There are tools that allow you to create almost any type of polygon imaginable, from a 30-point star to a 15-sided polygon. Though you could also create this shape in a paint program, it would require a lot more time and patience. In addition, when shapes are created with a draw program, they are fully editable. This means that they can be reshaped at any point.

BÉZIER CURVES

The curve tool in a draw program works differently than it does in a paint program. This is because all curves in Adobe Illustrator and most drawing programs are **Bézier curves.** These are curves named after Pierre Bézier that are defined mathematically by four control points. The control points are the two directional **nodes** at the end of each line, and the **handles** tangent to each curve. These

FIGURE 3.19

This draw program, MacDraw II, is being used to plan the conversion of a small bedroom into a bathroom. Nonprinting grid lines and automatically dimensioned arrows aid in aligning objects and measuring distances.

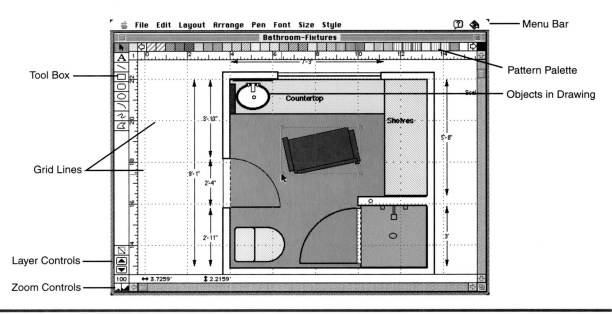

FIGURE 3.20

Vector objects can be picked up, moved, deleted, stretched, or shrunk. In this screen, a chair has been stretched into a couch. First, the chair was selected by clicking the mouse on it, thereby exposing its "handles" (the red spots around its edge). Then, dragging one of the handles caused the chair to stretch.

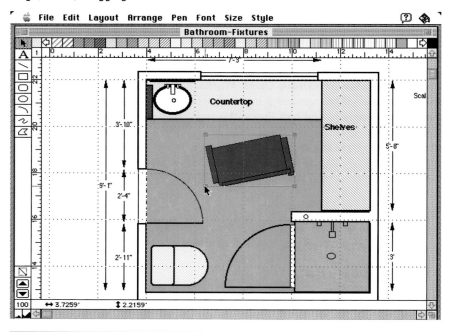

FIGURE 3.21

This image can be changed at any point.

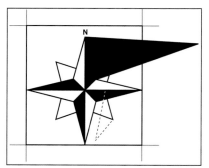

control points allow you to fine-tune a curve into almost any shape imaginable. You can create a **smooth node** by keeping the protruding handles on opposite sides of the node or create a **cusped node** by moving the handles anywhere else.

When we use a draw program, freehand drawings are converted into Bézier curves. Using Bézier curves creates a professional look. Notice how much smoother the red stripe underneath the text in our ice cream cone appears when it is converted to a Bézier curve. In Illustrator, Bézier curves are created using the famous Pen tool. This is the industry's most powerful tool for creating precise paths.

FIGURE 3.22

Changing the shape of a Bézier curve by moving its handles.

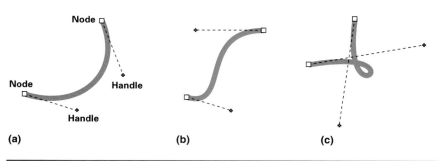

(a)   (b)   (c)

FIGURE 3.23

(a) Two Bézier curves will connect smoothly when connected by a smooth node.
(b) A cusped node makes it possible to "crimp" the joint.

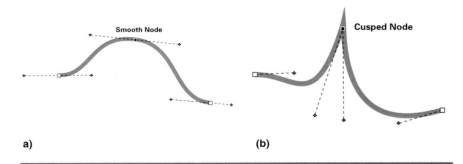

a)   (b)

GRADIENT FILL

In Adobe Illustrator, a **gradient fill** is a graduated blend between colors. This blending can be either linear or it may radiate from a specific point. This blending may occur between a single starting and ending color, or it may consist of multiple intermediate blends between a number of colors. In some programs, a gradient fill may be referred to as a **fountain.**

The gradient fill is another draw feature that makes an object look more professional. Notice how applying a gradient fill to both the ice cream and the cone

FIGURE 3.24

The Pen tool in Adobe Illustrator is the most powerful tool for creating precise paths.

FIGURE 3.25

The illustration from Figure 3.18, redrawn with a draw program. Although it is harder to learn to use a draw program than a paint program, the results can look more professional.

FIGURE 3.26
A gradient fill was added to give this ice cream cone a three-dimensional appearance.

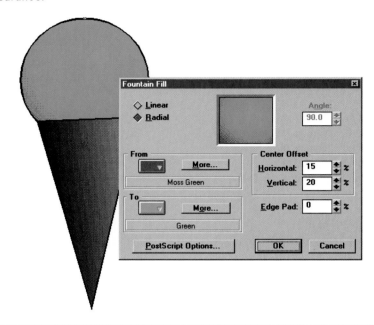

gives our illustration a 3D effect. By simply blending color our illustrations in drawing programs look more professional than those created in paint programs where the gradient-fill feature isn't always an option.

BLENDING

Blending allows you to create a series of intermediate colors and shapes between two selected objects. Illustrator and other drawing programs do an excellent job of blending one object into another. This process is often called **morphing** and is not an available tool in most paint programs.

GROUPING OBJECTS

When you use a drawing program to create a graphic image, each part of the image is considered a separate piece. For example, if you were to draw a bicycle in a drawing program, the wheels, the handlebars, the seat, and the frame would be separate drawings. Stated differently, we could say the bicycle is **ungrouped**

If you wanted to resize, reshape, or rotate the bicycle, you would have to modify each piece of the bicycle separately. This would be an inefficient and time-consuming way of working with an object. Therefore, drawing programs allow you to **group** the pieces together. After individual pieces are grouped together, the pieces become one object. The drawing program and other programs recognize all of the pieces of the object as one unit. For example, by selecting all of the pieces of the bicycle and using the group command, the pieces become one object that can then be manipulated as one unit instead of many individual pieces.

RASTERIZE

Each time items on a screen change, the entire screen must be redrawn. This is called the **refresh rate.** Because performance is critical in multimedia applica-

FIGURE 3.27

This figure is ungrouped. Each of the pieces is independent and must be edited individually.

FIGURE 3.28

Drawing programs allow you to group pieces together making it easier to edit the entire object.

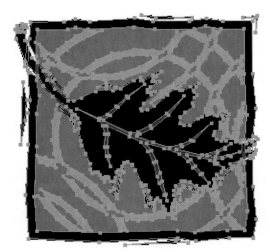

tions, a fast refresh rate is also critical. In multimedia applications, bitmapped graphics are often considered superior to vector-based images because the refresh rate of a screen containing bitmapped images is faster than the refresh rate of a screen containing vector images. With vector-based images, the computer must recalculate all of the vectors each time the screen is redrawn. As you might imagine, this can take time depending on the complexity of the image. For this reason, working with bitmapped images may allow you to work more productively. Many draw programs, including Adobe Illustrator, allow images to be exported to a multimedia application in a bitmapped format. **Rasterizing** is the process of converting a vector-based image to pixels or a bitmapped file format.

FIGURE 3.29

This image is being rasterized or converted from a vector-based graphic to a bitmapped graphic.

3D Modeling Programs

As mentioned above, three-dimensional objects help create a virtual world by adding depth to 2D objects. **Modeling** and **rendering programs** are used to create and manipulate 3D images.

In creating 3D objects, **geometric forms** or **wire frame models** serve as basic building blocks. For example, cubes and cylinders are combined to form models.

FIGURE 3.30

The objects in these figures serve as wire frame models for developing 3D images.

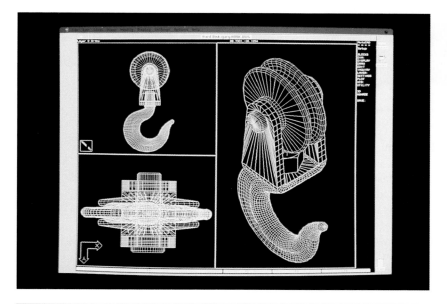

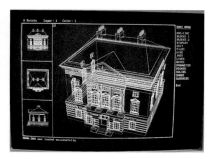

Different surfaces or **textures** are then applied or **mapped** to the models to give them shadows and provide special effects. This wire-frame model concept comes from clay modeling where artists first create a wire frame model to which they apply clay.

After the model has been created and a surface has been applied, the next step in most programs is to select a perspective (top, front, or side) and lighting from which the object is to be viewed.

Once a scene has been modeled in three dimensions and a perspective has been established it must then be converted to an image that will be visible on your computer screen. This conversion process is called **rendering.** Rendering adds the three-dimensional quality to the object based on its surface and shape properties, as well as the selected perspective. Though 3D objects created in modeling programs are quite impressive, rendering requires a great deal of processing power. Depending on the complexity, it may take hours or even days to render a 3D drawing.

There are many software programs available on Macintosh, Windows, and UNIX platforms that allow you to build 3D objects, add colors and textures to these objects, arrange the objects in a scene, light the scene, and finally render it. Some of the common modeling programs used today are **Ray Dream Designer Studio, Electric Image, Form-Z, Specular Infini-D, Macromedia Extreme 3D, RenderMan,** and **AutoDesk 3D Studio.** On high-end Unix workstations, you are likely to find a sophisticated program called **SoftImage** being used to create 3D images. To give you a better understanding of several common features found in a 3D modeling program, let's take a look at some of the features found in Ray Dream Designer Studios, a leader in 3D illustration.

MODELING

In the Ray Dream Designer Studio program, a document is called a **scene.** In order to create an object, a scene must be open. Creating an object to place in the scene is called **modeling.** There are three different ways to model an object. You can use **primitive objects,** which are 3D geometric figures such as cones, spheres, and cylinders. You can design your own **free form objects** with the drawing tools. Or, you can create **text objects,** which are blocks of 3D type.

ARRANGING AND DEFORMING OBJECTS

The 3D workspace in Ray Dream Designer is called the **universe.** In this workspace is a tool bar from which every basic arrangement operation (alignment, orientation, positioning, sizing) can be performed. Arranging objects is the process of positioning and orienting them. As you can imagine, arranging objects is very important when you are trying to create a realistic three-dimensional scene. An object's spatial relationship to other objects is particularly important. This means resizing objects as they change position may also be necessary. Setting lighting and cameras is important in establishing a perspective and is another part of arranging objects.

Deformers serve as a powerful class of manipulation tools that enable you to twist and modify objects and groups of objects. There are deformers to stretch, shatter, bend, twist, and scale an object.

SHADING

The process of assigning surface properties such as color, texture, and finish to an object is called **shading.** These surface properties are called **shaders.** Shaders determine whether an object appears rough or smooth, shiny or dull, transparent or opaque. In Ray Dream Designer, trying different shading features is quite simple because of the drag and drop interface. After several surface attributes have

FIGURE 3.31
You can design your own free form objects using the drawing tools in Ray Dream Designer.

FIGURE 3.32

Arranging objects is very important when you are trying to create an accurate 3D effect.

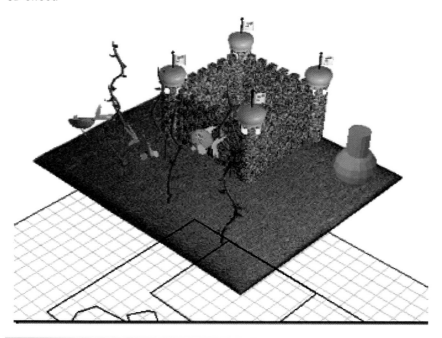

been defined, objects can simulate complex materials such as hammered gold, polished wood, or rough granite.

The **texture map** feature allows you to use a 2D image in your shader. If done well, texture maps can give your objects unparalleled realism. For example, you can use a scanned photograph or illustration as a texture map. This is helpful because many complex real-world surfaces are difficult or nearly impossible to design even with today's sophisticated tools.

To apply shaders to a limited area on the surface of an object, you can use **3D Paint tools** that allow you to create paint shapes directly on the surface of an object. The 3D Paint tools are not limited to painting with color; you can load your brush with gold, marble, or concrete and apply color, bump, reflection, transparency, and other shading attributes. Once these shapes have been painted, they can also be moved, resized, or layered.

SETTING LIGHTS AND CAMERAS

Lighting conditions are important in creating high quality 3D objects. The exact same scene rendered under different light can create an entirely different result. Two types of light are supported in Ray Dream Designer. **Ambient light** is uniform throughout the scene while several types of **specific light** sources are also available. You can create several types of specific lights with the standards set to **distant, bulb,** and **spot.** Color and other characteristics can also be set for both ambient light and specific light.

The position and orientation of a camera is called a **viewpoint.** Cameras provide viewpoints for the perspective and for rendering. As you work and build the scene, several cameras can be placed at different locations. By switching between the cameras you can see alternate perspectives of your scene. However, when you are ready to render the scene, you can choose only one camera.

FIGURE 3.33

Surface attributes can be applied to the entire object or to parts of an object.

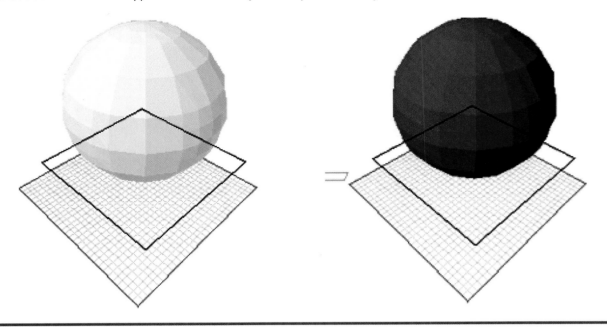

In creating a viewpoint, you can choose the type of camera used, and just as a regular camera has different lenses and settings, the cameras in Ray Dream Designer can also be set to properties such as **wide, telephoto,** and **zoom.**

RENDERING

Rendering is the process of capturing a view of a 3D scene and saving it as a 2D image. When a scene is rendered, all of the forms, colors, and textures of all objects, as well as the lights and surfaces are considered.

FIGURE 3.34

In this figure, a 2D image or texture map is being applied to give the image a real-world surface.

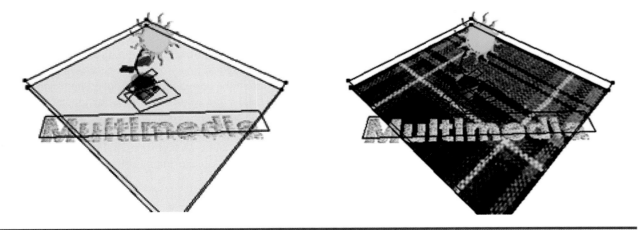

FIGURE 3.35

The vector-based model for this image was drawn with a 3-D modeling program. The computer then rendered a realistic picture of the model by tracing the course of theoretical rays of light.

If you wanted to see a 2D object created from a drawing program from another side, you would have to redraw it. With 3D scenes, you can see different views of it by changing the lighting and the camera angles and re-rendering the scene based upon the new settings. The original scene is a separate file and is stored on disk in a different format than the rendered scenes. Rendering produces a 2D, photorealistic, bitmapped image of a scene. Therefore, in order to open an image in another program such as an image-editing program, it must be rendered first. In Ray Dream Designer, rendered scenes can be saved as PICT, EPS, BMP, TIFF, Adobe PhotoNative, and other popular image formats.

Image-Editing Programs

Image editing software allows you to manipulate digitized images using a variety of features that combine painting, editing, and other image composition tools. There are several good image-editing programs to choose from, including **Macromedia XRES, Fractal Design Painter, KPT Live Picture, Deneba Canvas, Corel Photo-Paint, Adobe PhotoDeluxe,** and **Adobe Photoshop.**

Though there are several good image-editing programs to choose from, by far the most used image-editing program in the design world is Adobe Photoshop. This is because it is comprehensive, versatile, and accurate. It is used by graphic designers, photographers, and illustrators, and can do just about anything with almost any kind of graphic file format. Although image editing programs offer many more features than we can possibly cover here, let's take a look at some of the more predominant features available in Photoshop and most image-editing software programs.

CROPPING

Because image-editing software is used extensively to manipulate photographs, one of the first tasks you may encounter is the need to remove or **crop** areas of a

FIGURE 3.36

Image-editing programs allow you to enhance and modify photographs.

photograph you don't wish to include in a multimedia application. The crop tool in the tool palette makes it easy for the designer to select a section of an image and remove the rest.

BRIGHTNESS, CONTRAST, AND COLOR CORRECTION

Slider controls allow you to adjust the brightness and contrast of an image. As you use the slider, you can preview the change in a preview box and establish just the effect you are trying to achieve. Because it is rare that an image you scan will appear on your screen with the same color values as the original, you can also adjust the hue, saturation, and luminosity of a color using color sliders; or you can completely change the colors in an image. In general, you will want to keep your images to an 8-bit color depth to ensure that your viewers will be able to display

FIGURE 3.37
The crop tool can be used to remove unwanted areas of a photograph.

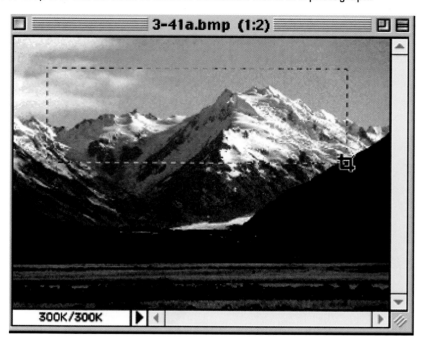

it on their computers. Though most newer computers have enough memory to display at least 16- and 24-bit color depth, if you want to guarantee that your application will be available to the masses, keep your images at 8-bit color depth and the resolution to 72 dpi (dots per inch). Aiming your finished images for the lowest installed base ensures a wider audience.

FILTERS

Filters are special effects applied to an image or part of an image. Filters can be used to blur or sharpen an image, create a mosaic effect, or distort the image with noise. Filters are available with the program or additional filters can be purchased from third-party vendors. To apply a filter in Adobe Photoshop, you can use the Lasso, Magic Wand, or Marquee to select the area and then apply the filter to that area alone or you can apply the filter to the entire image. A dialog box allows you to preview the result of the filter before you apply it.

LAYERING

Another wonderful feature of some image-editing programs is their ability to add layers. **Layers** are different levels in a document. For example, in every Photoshop

FIGURE 3.38

FIGURE 3.38
Image-editing software can be used to enhance this poorly scanned illustration.

document there are at least two layers, a background layer and a foreground layer. When pixels appear on a layer, the layer is opaque; otherwise, it is transparent and the background or previous layer is allowed to show through. On each layer, you can draw, paste images, or reposition artwork without affecting the pixels on any other layer. To create really interesting effects, you can continue to add layers until your computer runs out of memory.

FILE FORMAT CONVERSION

Though there are programs designed specifically to convert graphic files from one format to another, image-editing programs are also quite good at doing this. For example, if a file is in a TIFF format, and you need to use it on a Web page that only supports GIF or JPEG files, you can open the TIFF file in an image-editing program and save it as a GIF file. (The differences between these formats are discussed later in this chapter.) In other words, if you need a file in a particular format, Photoshop will probably allow you to save it in that format.

Image Enhancement Plug-Ins

Many third-party developers create **plug-ins** or add-on features that enhance the capabilities of paint, draw, 3D modeling, and image-editing programs. For example, there are programs that expand the number of filters available in Adobe Photoshop. Some of the more common image enhancement plug-ins available for graphics software are **Kai's Power Tools, PhotoTools,** and **WildRiverSSK.**

File Formats

Graphic images may be stored in a wide variety of file formats. In choosing a format, you should consider how and where the image will be used. This is because

FIGURE 3.39
Using an image editor to edit the previous mountain photograph.

(a) The Deskew command straightens the photo, and the Eyedropper tool helps repair the sky.

(b) Other commands improve the contrast, increase the sharpness, and crop the edges.

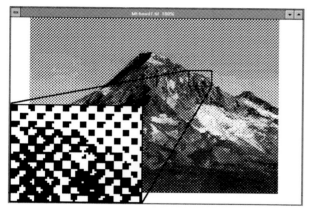

(c) The dot pattern in this computer-generated halftone shows up clearly in the enlarged inset.

(d) The image in (b) was quickly converted into this nightscape with a few additional commands.

the application must support the file format you select. Some formats are proprietary while others have become universally supported by the graphics industry. Though proprietary formats may function perfectly in their own environment, their lack of compatibility with other systems can create problems.

In the Macintosh environment, the PICT format, a vector-based file format, is the image format supported by almost all Macintosh applications. Recently, the Windows environment has standardized on the BMP file format. Prior to this, there were multiple file formats under DOS that made it difficult to transfer graphic files from one application to another. The most common file formats are described below.

TIFF (TAGGED IMAGE FILE FORMAT)

The TIFF file format is probably the most widely used bitmapped file format. Image-editing applications, scanning software, illustration programs, page-layout programs, and even word processing programs support TIFF files. The TIFF format

FIGURE 3.40

Layers can give an image interesting effects.

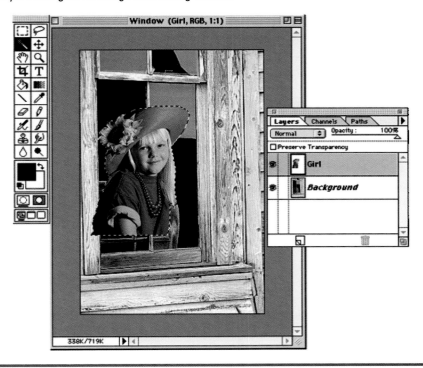

FIGURE 3.41

In Photoshop, you can choose from a variety of graphic file formats.

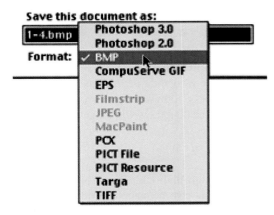

works for all types of images and supports bit depths from 1 to 32 bits. In addition, TIFF is cross platform. Versions are available for the Mac, PC, and UNIX systems. The TIFF file format is often used when the output is printed.

EPS (ENCAPSULATED POSTSCRIPT)

The EPS format is a vector-based graphic. Like the TIFF format, EPS is popular for saving image files because it can be imported into nearly any kind of application. The biggest disadvantage to the EPS file format is that it requires more storage space than any other format.

BMP (SHORT FOR BITMAP)

The BMP format has been adopted as the standard bitmapped format on the Windows platform. It is a very basic format supported by most Windows applications. It is also the most efficient format to use with Windows.

DIB (DEVICE-INDEPENDENT BITMAP)

This format is also a Windows format. It is used to transfer bitmaps from one device or process to another. This is an older file format that is not used much today.

GIF (GRAPHICS INTERCHANGE FORMAT)

CompuServe created this format. Consequently, you may see it listed as CompuServe GIF. It is one of two standard formats used on the Web without plug-ins. It is the method of storing bitmaps on the Web. The GIF format only supports up to 256 colors.

PCX

This is an earlier, low-end PC standard format. It was a popular format used in DOS applications. Some older PC programs are still using it and because of its early adoption, it is still supported by most Windows applications. It is also used with Paintbrush.

PICT/PICT2 (SHORT FOR PICTURE)

These are formats for the Macintosh. They are generally used only for screen display. Some Mac programs can only import images saved as either PICT or EPS. Unlike the EPS format, PICT does not provide information for separations, which means graphics saved with this file format will be smaller than EPS files. PICT2 added additional levels of color to the PICT format.

JPEG (JOINT PHOTOGRAPHIC EXPERTS GROUP)

This format creates a very compact file. Because of its small file size, it is easy to transmit across networks. Consequently, it is one of only two graphic file formats supported by the World Wide Web without plug-ins. Do keep in mind that in order to make the file so small, lossy compression is used when a file is saved or converted to this format. This means pixels will be removed from the image. JPEG files are bitmapped images.

TARGA

This is also an earlier, though high-end, PC standard. It is more popular with video editing and therefore may be encountered in multimedia applications. However, it is not very common in working with graphics simply because most people prefer using TIFF or EPS files. It is a bitmapped file format.

PHOTOSHOP NATIVE

The Photoshop Native file format is a proprietary format used with Adobe Photoshop. Because this program is so popular in editing images, quite a few other image-editing programs now support this proprietary format. Photoshop Native files are bitmapped files.

MACPAINT

This is the format used by the Macintosh MacPaint program.

PIC

This is the graphics format used by the PC Paint program.

PCD (PHOTO CD)

This is Kodak's Photo CD graphics file format. It is a bitmapped format that contains different image sizes for each photograph.

PLOT FILE

This is a vector-based format used with some Computer Aided Drafting (CAD) and drawing programs.

AUTOCAD

AutoCAD is also a vector-based graphics format used with CAD and drawing programs.

WINDOWS METAFILE (WMF)

This is a metafile, bitmapped, and/or vector-based file created by Microsoft.

WORD PERFECT GRAPHICS (WPG)

These are bitmapped files for Word Perfect graphics.

This is only a small sample of all of the different graphic file formats available. There are also many proprietary formats. If you plan to transfer files from application to application, consider using the most common file format supported by all of your applications. If you get stuck because an application does not support a graphics file format, graphic conversion software is available to help you change the file format so that you can import and export graphic images from almost any application to another.

FIGURE 3.42

These are the most common computer graphics formats:

FILE FORMAT	FILE EXTENSION	TYPE OF FILE
Tagged Image File Format	.TIF, .TIFF	Bitmapped
Encapsulated PostScript	.EPS, .EPSF	Vector
Windows Bitmap	.BMP	Bitmapped
Device-Independent Bitmap	.DIB	Bitmapped
Graphics Interchange Format	.GIF	Bitmapped
MacPaint		Bitmapped
Photo CD	.PCD	Bitmapped
PC Paint	.PIC	Bitmapped
PCX	.PCX	Bitmapped
Picture	.PICT, .PICT2	Bitmapped
Joint Photographic Experts Group	.JPG, .JPEG	Bitmapped
Targa	.TGA	Bitmapped
Photoshop Native		Bitmapped
Plot File		Vector
AutoCAD		Vector
Windows Metafile	.WMF	Bitmapped, Vector
WordPerfect Graphics	.WPG	Bitmapped

Sources of Still Images

When obtaining digital files:
- Make sure the file is in a format that is compatible with your system software and your application software.
- Make sure the resolution is appropriate for the multimedia application you are creating.

There are many sources of still images. In fact, there are **commercial image providers** or **stock photography houses** whose entire business is to find and sell the rights to images. CDs often contain thousands of images including photographs, clip art, and animated graphics. Many image collections are also available online via the World Wide Web. Today, it is easier than ever to get access to images from around the world just by logging onto the Internet and taking a few minutes to download the image.

Keep in mind, that in most situations, commercial image providers are only selling the rights to use the image, they are not selling the image itself. In other words, they may sell you the right to use the image in one multimedia application, but the image does not become your property. If you want to use it again in a different multimedia application, you may very well have to pay another royalty. The agreements vary depending on the image, the original artist, and the commercial image provider. Take caution and read the licensing agreement carefully before you include an image from a CD or the Web in a multimedia application. Just because you purchased the CD or were given access to the image on the Web, that doesn't necessarily mean you own it.

Clip Art

In addition to creating your own graphics, you can also purchase pre-existing digitized images called **clip art.** Clip art is a collection of drawings generally organized by category. Extensive clip-art libraries are available with some software packages, on CD-ROM, or for download from the Internet. Generally, clip art files are available in EPS, PIC, PICT, and BMP formats. To get a taste of what's out there, check out http://www.ist.net/clipart/, http://imageclub.com, or search

FIGURE 3.43

This CD is full of photographs divided into categories.

on "clip art" using any search engine. Don't be surprised if the number of hits totals well over a million!

Clip art is also an excellent alternative if you aren't an artist, don't have time to create your own image, or don't have the money to hire a graphic designer. Some graphic images available as part of a clip art library are **public domain.** When images are public domain, it means you can use these images at your discretion for no charge (other than what you may pay up front to purchase the clip-art library). Others, however, have restrictions and charge royalties. Royalties are more commonly charged if you plan to use the graphic for commercial purposes. The royalty may be charged each time you use the image or it may be a one-time fee. Be sure to read the licensing agreement carefully before you include someone else's clip art in your multimedia application.

Photographs

Photographs can be used in multimedia applications to reference real people, places, and events. If you have a background in photography or just enjoy taking pictures, you can digitize and use your own photographs or slides in your multimedia application. Today, most cameras, including digital cameras, make it easy to take quality photographs.

When taking pictures for multimedia applications, take a lot and take them from many different angles. This way, you can create sequences in the multimedia project. If you are using film, this can get quite expensive, but with a digital camera, cost per photograph is not a consideration.

When snapping pictures:
- Photograph people from many different angles and in many different poses.
- Shoot people in indirect light.
- Shoot in the morning or evening when the light is filtered through the clouds. Midday light creates too many contrasts.
- Use a variety of angles and perspectives to record details and panoramas.
- Try shooting objects both indoors and outdoors. Shoot from a variety of angles and play with the light and color to get the effect you wish to create.

FIGURE 3.44
Clip art libraries are available on CD-ROM or the Internet.

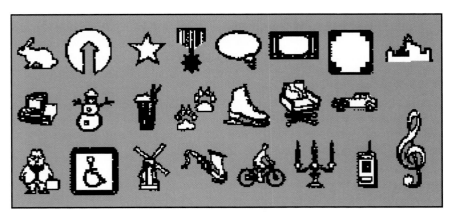

If you choose not to take your own pictures, there are many other alternatives. You can purchase photographs from commercial image providers or stock photographers in either analog or digital format. You can also hire a photographer to take pictures for you. Or, like clip art, many professional-quality photographs are also available with commercial software packages, on CD-ROM, or from the Web.

Once you have selected the photo or photos you intend to include in your multimedia application, you can modify them using image editing software such as Adobe Photoshop or Corel Photopaint. As discussed earlier in this chapter, these programs allow you to modify images by cropping, combining, removing, sharpening, and applying special filters and effects.

Digital Video

As we discussed in Chapter 2, you can use a video capture card to connect a camcorder, VCR, or TV to the computer. Special software enables you to freeze and save still images from video footage. You can then edit these frames using image-editing software just as you would edit a photograph.

Charts

Charts or **graphs** are used to present numerical data. Charts provide a much more effective means of communicating data than text alone. People are much more likely to grasp trends or the relationship between the parts to the whole by looking at a line graph or pie chart than by reading text alone.

Electronic spreadsheets contain the best tools for preparing 2D and 3D charts. As a result, many multimedia authoring packages and presentation programs now include integrated spreadsheet and chart-making tools. In fact, some of these programs even allow you to animate charts. For example, in an animated chart, different pieces of the chart may fly into the screen as you click the mouse.

If these tools are not available in the authoring software you are using to create your multimedia product, you can generally develop the chart with an electronic spreadsheet such as Lotus 1-2-3, Quattro Pro, or Microsoft Excel. Once it is developed, you can either export it to your application or take a screen shot of the chart. If you take a screen shot, the image on your screen is saved as a graphic file. Usually it will be saved as a PICT or BMP file. Once the file is saved it can be edited or imported directly into the multimedia-authoring program being used. Of course, another option would be to copy and paste the chart into an authoring program where it could be further modified.

Maps

Maps are obviously used to illustrate locations. They are becoming more and more prevalent in multimedia applications, particularly multimedia applications running over the World Wide Web. More and more companies are including maps on their Web pages so that people know where to find them. Maps are also quite common on information kiosks in places such as airports and tourist information centers.

If you just need a general map, there may be clip art to meet your needs. If you need a more detailed map and you have the map in an analog format, you can scan the map. Provided the original map, your scanner, and your scanning software are of high enough quality, this should work fine. A third and more exacting option is to use **mapping software.** By selecting the geographic area, scale, and proposed perspective you can use mapping software to create a custom map illustrating precisely what you want viewers to see.

FIGURE 3.45

Spreadsheet programs offer several standard chart types; Quattro's options include 12 varieties of 3-D charts.

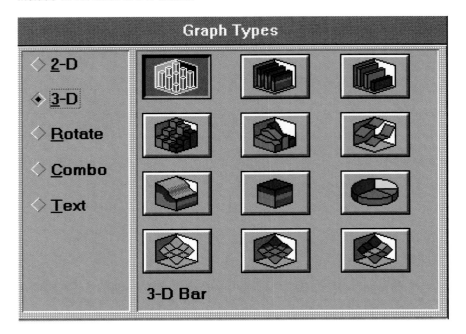

Line charts show linear trends, such as stock market prices. Three-dimensional line charts are called *ribbon charts*.

Area charts dramatize quantitative trends, such as sales or water-use volumes.

Vertical bar charts (also called *column charts*) are best for displaying quantitative trends where there are only a few data points.

Horizontal bar charts should be reserved for displaying horizontal concepts such as distance or time.

Pie charts portray statistics that add up to 100 percent, such as budget analyses.

Scatter graphs (or *xy graphs*) depict points of data with two variables, such as weight versus height.

Combination graphs overlay two chart types in order to show relationships between pairs of trends.

FIGURE 3.46

A spreadsheet program can quickly convert highlighted data into a chart. Microsoft Excel includes a ChartWizard tool bar button that leads the user through the steps of selecting the data to be graphed, choosing the chart type, and providing labels.

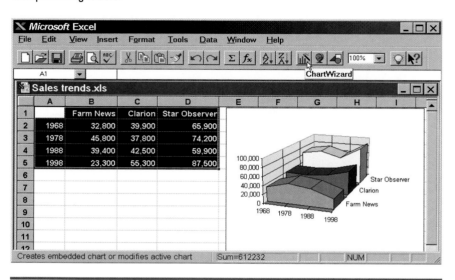

Images created with mapping software are usually vector-based graphics or EPS files. This is because most mapping programs are draw programs. Consequently, if you need to edit these files after they are created, you will probably need to edit them using a drawing program like Adobe Illustrator or Macromedia Freehand.

Copyright

Don't try to get away with merely altering an image. Adobe has pioneered a new embedded signature that enables a graphic designer to embed a signature into an image. This embedded signature won't show up when the image is displayed or printed, but it will serve as proof of artistic ownership if needed.

Keep in mind that most images are **copyright protected.** If an image is copyright protected, you must obtain permission from the artist in order to copy or use the image, or even part of the image. If you fail to obtain permission to use someone else's work, you are violating copyright law, and you could be liable for damages including statutory damages, legal fees, and compensation to the artist.

Remember that maps are subject to copyright law just like any other original work. When reproducing and digitizing maps, be sure to follow copyright law as outlined.

If in doubt, assume an image is copyright protected. The 1976 Federal Copyright Act stipulates that copyrighted images are property of the creator from the time they are created to 50 years beyond his or her life. If the creator is a corporation or business, the image is property of the creator up to 75 years after publication or 100 years following creation, whichever is shorter.

After the copyright period has expired, the image becomes public domain. **Public domain** images can be manipulated and used without permission from the artist and without having to pay the artist any royalties for using them.

When images or other copyright protected works are used strictly for instruction and research in an educational setting, copyright permission may not be necessary. This exclusion is referred to as a **fair use policy.** There are many factors

FIGURE 3.47

Maps like this Atlas are also available online.

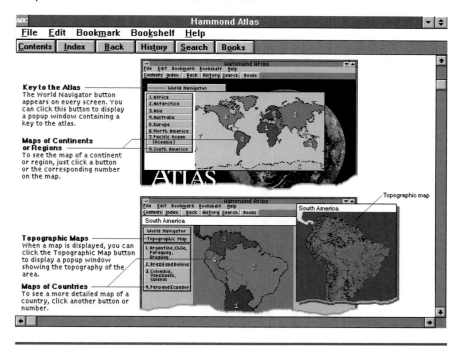

that determine when this exception applies and when it does not. If you are uncertain as to whether or not an image is copyright protected, don't take chances; assume that it is copyright protected and seek the advice of a legal expert.

In summary, the only time you can alter or manipulate images is if:

- you receive permission from the original artist
- you create the image yourself
- the image is clearly public domain
- the image is being used strictly for instructional purposes in an educational setting.

SUMMARY

Still images are vital to multimedia applications. Graphics can be used in multimedia applications for a variety of purposes.

Graphics for multimedia applications can be created with graphics creation software, captured with scanners and digital cameras, and edited with image-editing software. Images can also be obtained or purchased from clip art libraries and stock photography houses.

If you don't have time to find or create your own images, you can also hire a **graphic designer.** If you are working as part of a multimedia team, a graphic designer will probably be part of the team. **Digitizing** converts images into a format that the computer can recognize and manipulate. In your multimedia application, you can use pre-existing digital images or you can digitize photographs, slides, or line art using a scanner. Many film-processing companies will also digitize your photos and save them to disk or CD for you.

Graphic images also serve as **hypermedia** or **hypergraphics** and three-dimensional environments are becoming more common on the Internet. **VRML** (Virtual Reality Modeling Language) is the programming language used to create these 3D Web pages.

Image quality is determined by the **bit depth,** which measures the number of bits of stored information per pixel and the **image resolution,** which is the amount of information stored for each image.

Graphics take up a lot of storage space, often making it necessary to compress image files. There are two types of compression, **lossy** and **lossless.** Some common compression utilities include **PKZIP, WinZip,** and **StuffIt.**

There are many programs used to create or modify two-dimensional graphic images. These programs are called **graphics editors** and include drawing programs, painting programs, and image editing programs. Programs that allow you to create or modify three-dimensional graphic images are called 3D modeling programs.

Graphics editors can be classified as **bitmap graphics editors** or **paint programs** that allow you to create bitmap graphics, and vector graphics editors or **draw programs** that allow you to create vector graphics. Bitmapped images consist of **pixels.** Unlike bitmapped graphics, vector graphics are created and recreated from mathematical models or formulas that connect geometric shapes like lines and arcs. **Modeling** and **rendering programs** are used to create and manipulate 3D images.

Image-editing software allows you to manipulate images using a variety of features that combine painting, editing, and other image composition tools.

Graphic images may be stored in a wide variety of file formats. In choosing a format, consider how and where the image will be used. Some of the more common formats include: TIFF, EPS, BMP, DIB, GIF, PCX, PICT/PICT2, JPEG, TARGA, Photoshop Native, MacPaint, PIC, PCD, WMF, and WPG.

If you need a still image for a multimedia application, there are many sources to choose from. **Commercial image providers** and **stock photography houses** sell the rights to images. Images can also be found on CDs and the Internet. Still images can be captured from **digital video. Charts** and **graphs** can be created from electronic spreadsheets. **Mapping software** can be used to create maps. Maps can also be scanned or found as clip art.

Most images are **copyright protected.** This means that you must obtain permission from the artist in order to copy or use the image or part of the image. By failing to do so, you are violating the law. If you obtain permission or purchase the rights to use an image, be sure to read the **licensing agreement** carefully. Don't take chances! If in doubt, assume that an image is copyright protected.

KEY TERMS

Graphic Designer	Pixels	Copyright protected
Hypergraphics	Crop	Digitizing
Bit depth	Stock photography	VRML
PKZip	houses	Image resolution
Graphics editors	Charts	WinZip

Paint programs	Licensing agreement	Draw programs
Modeling programs	Digital video	Rendering programs
Filters	Hypermedia	Layers
Commercial image providers	lossless	Mapping software
Graphs	lossy	
	StuffIt	

Matching Questions

a. digitizing	**b.** RGB	**c.** VRML
d. hypergraphics	**e.** image maps	**f.** bit depth
g. image resolution	**h.** rasterizing	**i.** shading
j. rendering	**k.** plug-ins	**l.** filters

_____**1.** Measures the number of bits of stored information per pixel or how many tones or colors every pixel in a bitmap can have.

_____**2.** The process of assigning surface properties such as color, texture, and finish to an object.

_____**3.** The process of converting images into a format that the computer can recognize and manipulate. Converting the image into a series of binary data or 1's and 0's.

_____**4.** The amount of information stored for each image.

_____**5.** The primary additive colors used in computer monitors and image recorders.

_____**6.** Graphics that contain more than one trigger.

_____**7.** The process of capturing a view of a 3D scene and saving it as a 2D image.

_____**8.** The programming language used to create 3D environments on the World Wide Web.

_____**9.** The process of converting a vector-based image to pixels or a bitmapped file format.

_____**10.** Clickable graphics that allow you to link to other locations within the same multimedia application, or even outside of it.

_____**11.** Add-on features that enhance the capabilities of programs.

_____**12.** Special effects applied to an image or part of an image.

Fill-In Questions

1. By adding depth to _____, flat images, they become _____ images.

2. _____ is simply an algorithm that is used to create smaller file sizes. There are two types of compression: _____ and _____.

3. Typically, to create on-screen graphics in one of these programs, you use a _____ _____.

4. When you use a draw program, the resulting graphic is _____ _____.

5. Each time items on a screen change, the entire screen must be redrawn. This is called the _____ _____.

6. The position and orientation of a camera is called a _____.

7. There are many sources of still images. In fact, there are _____ _____ _____ or _____ _____ _____ whose entire business is to find and sell the rights to images.

8. _____ _____ images can be manipulated and used without permission from the artist and without having to pay the artist any royalties for using them.

DISCUSSION QUESTIONS

1. What are three different technologies used to capture digital images? How are these three technologies different?

2. What is the difference between paint programs and draw programs? How are bitmapped graphics different from vector-based graphics?

3. How do staircasing or jaggies occur? What can be done to prevent this?

4. What is the difference between lossy and lossless compression? Why would you be more likely to use lossy compression with video than with text?

5. How do layers help you create special effects in image-editing programs?

6. How can a 3D image be created on a flat screen?

7. When can you alter or manipulate images without violating copyright law?

HANDS-ON EXERCISES

1. Using the search engine of your choice, search the Internet for two Web sites that distribute clip art or stock photography. One of the sites should distribute public domain images royalty free, the other should have a licensing agreement. What are the addresses of both sites? Print or save the details of the licensing agreement.

2. Find a Web page with well-designed graphics. What is the address? What do you find particularly appealing about the graphics? What makes these graphics work? Would you change anything about the graphics? If so, what would you change?

3. Find a Web page with poorly designed graphics. What is the address? What do you find particularly distressing about the graphics? What's wrong with these graphics? What would you change about the graphics? What else could be done to improve the design of this page?

Case Study: Chapter 3

Marc Giráldes will be the Graphic/Interface Designer for this project. Marc is a skilled professional with a special knack for designing fast and fun graphics using both analog tools (traditional pencils, paints, etc.) as well as the latest computer technologies. Marc was hand-picked for this project because he is a talented designer with a contemporary, sporty style and love of water sports that make him a perfect match for this project.

In creating the interface for the Web site, Marc intends to use the waters surrounding the San Juan Islands as a metaphor. For example, docks, buoys, personal flotation devices (PFDs) and even marine wildlife will be incorporated into the interface. He will incorporate lots of bright, vibrant colors such as fluorescent orange and green to establish the contemporary, fast and fun feel of the site.

Marc will use traditional tools as well as Adobe Illustrator to create navigation buttons, backgrounds, and icons of jet skis, waverunners, and other personal watercraft and marine paraphernalia. These cartoon-like illustrations will give the site a laid-back, fun feeling.

Adobe Photoshop will be used to enhance digital photographs of the different types of personal watercraft available for sale or rent. These photographs will provide the serious user with a real-life look at the equipment.

Animation

1. Define animation
2. List several applications of animation
3. Describe the different types of animation
4. Understand the animation process
5. Describe the roles and responsibilities of the animation specialist
6. Explain the different methods used to create animation
7. List and describe the different animation tools used to author animated objects
8. List and describe the different programming languages used to create animated objects
9. List and describe some of the key features found in Macromedia Director

Introduction to Animation

Technically, animation is the illusion of movement. It has been around for many years. Though early animation included flip books and pop-ups, fifty years ago, Walt Disney was creating animated objects and characters like Mickey Mouse that were making us laugh and sometimes cry. Others have joined Disney, and today on the big screen, animation is still making us laugh, cry, and jump out of our movie seats in anticipation and fear. If you've seen *Jurassic Park, Toy Story,* or *The Lost World,* you are probably well aware of how sophisticated animation has become.

In order to realize animation of today's caliber, the process used to create animated objects has had to change. Today, creating animation involves high-end computer technology, and, like other computer-related technologies, it is changing as you read this paragraph.

Though animation is predominantly found in the entertainment industry, it isn't restricted to video games, television, or movies. Many industries now use animation for computer-based training, kiosks, and Web pages. Many of the items that include animation today didn't exist fifty years ago. For that matter, they didn't exist five years ago. For example, five years ago the Web was merely a text-based infant. Today, animated objects and video are fairly common on the Web and will become more prominent players as technology continues to evolve.

Another reason animation is finding its way into other areas is that the technology has become more sophisticated, user-friendly, and powerful. Though video games have been around for quite some time now, they certainly didn't contain the sophisticated animation they contain today.

Animation is an integral part of multimedia. When used appropriately, it can add a great deal to the overall quality and content of a multimedia application. However, if done improperly, it can be a real distraction. As always compatibility and balance are key.

FIGURE 4.1

Growth in the Internet has spurred the growth of animation on the Web.

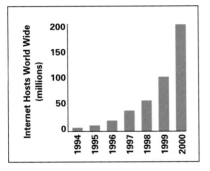

What Is Animation?

Animation is a moving graphic image. The virtual world created by animated objects has physical properties including height, width, depth, and time. The computer is used to create movement on the screen, or to trick our eyes into believing that a series of still images is actually in motion.

Use your thumb and forefinger to flip quickly through the pages of this chapter, and watch the images in the lower corners appear to move. Your computer creates a similar effect by rapidly showing slightly different images.

Uses of Animation

Animation can be used to achieve a variety of different effects. Animation grabs attention! As I was writing this book, my husband and I attended an air show. The moment any flying machine moved, regardless of its size, shape, complexity, or color, all eyes and all attention would focus on it.

Because animation is an attention-getter, it is commonly found on Web pages as animated banners used in advertising or to focus the user's attention. In games, animated characters entertain us as they interact with other animated objects. Even in computer-based training programs, animation can be found illustrating techniques from how to effectively swing a golf club to how to repair complex aerospace equipment.

Computer-Based Training Programs

Animation is often used in computer-based training programs. Animated illustrations demonstrate the correct way to assemble parts, adjust controls, or even perform surgery. Though computer-based training programs are generally used more in technical training, they can also be very effective in teaching human relations and communication skills. Animated computer-based training programs can be particularly effective for teaching cross-cultural communication skills. For example, employees involved in international business who lack knowledge of cultural differences can receive training from an animated cultural guru on traits such as appropriate body language and customs. These programs are useful not only for new employees but also as updates or reminders for employees who have been with the company for some time.

Education

Computer-based training programs are not limited to business and industry. Comparable programs are also available in education. Programs geared toward entertaining students as they learn are often referred to as **edutainment.** There are multimedia programs prepared for specific age ranges and disciplines. To get a feel for some of the programs that are available, check out Educorp's site at http://www.educorp.com. This is creativity at its finest. You'll find everything from spelling and foreign language programs for grade school children to pro-

FIGURE 4.2

Animation is very effective in computer-based training.

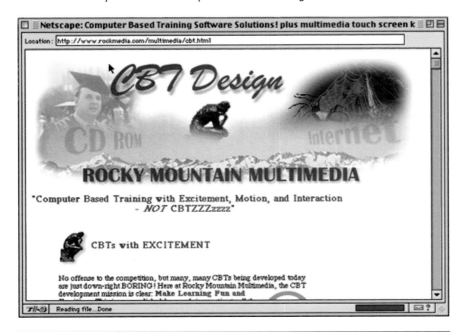

grams that prepare high school students for college entrance exams such as the SAT or ACT. You'll even find programs for college students who are preparing for a career. For example, animated counselors can teach future counselors effective and ineffective ways of working with clients by using animated demonstrations.

Animated training materials also serve as an effective way to teach other applied and hands-on skills. For example, musicians can learn to play instruments such as guitar, drums, keyboards, and violin. Athletes can learn the proper methods and techniques in football, inline skating, tai chi chuan, and yoga. Some programs even offer certification upon completion of a test. For example, Adventures in Scuba Diving and Mastering Advanced Scuba Diving offer certificates of academic proficiency that are accepted by the NAUI.

Games

It probably goes without saying that nearly all games (that remain on the market and sell) involve animation. They involve animated characters that encounter animated objects in animated worlds. All of this animation requires powerful computer processing capabilities on both the development and user end. Donkey Kong, Mario, Doom, and Myst are just a few of the games to check out. Educorp (http://www.educorp.com) also has a complete list of games. For all of you Monty Python fans, I recently heard on Dave Chalk's computer show (http://www.chalk.com) that there is now an animated Monty Python game complete with animated characters and clips from the movie.

FIGURE 4.3

Animation can be used in education to teach students skills and concepts.

Pulsed Flame Photometric Detector

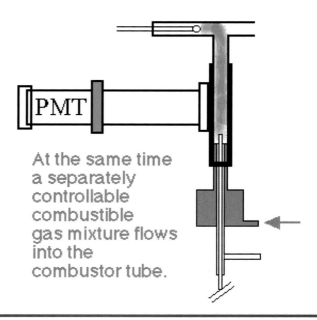

FIGURE 4.4

Animation is not new to computer games, but it has grown to be more and more sophisticated.

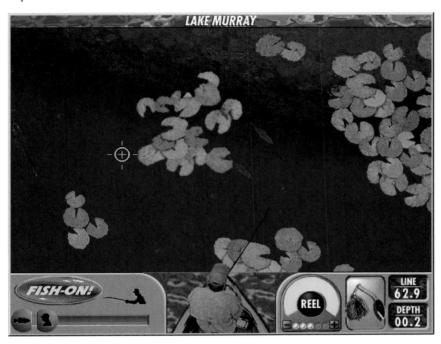

The Web

Web pages running tiny animations abound on the Internet today. Animated buttons, banners, text, and characters are used for advertising and information. At some art sites, these animated art forms themselves are the reason viewers choose to visit. We will discuss animation on the Web in greater depth in Chapter 8.

Types of Animation

Two-dimensional (2D) images are flat. Changing the position or location of the image and then recording this change causes 2D images to be animated. By replaying the sequence of changes, the object appears to move or change; in other words, it's animated.

By adding depth to 2D images, they become **three-dimensional (3D).** In other words, adding textures and shading to 2D images creates 3D objects. This creates the illusion of depth and enables an object to appear three-dimensional even though it is on a flat surface. Animation sets the 3D object in motion. When animating 3D objects, relative space must also be considered. Therefore, animating 3D objects is more complicated and expensive than animating 2D objects. As computers become even more powerful and the price of 3D modeling programs continues to drop, 3D animation will become common.

FIGURE 4.5

Animation is prevalent on the Web.

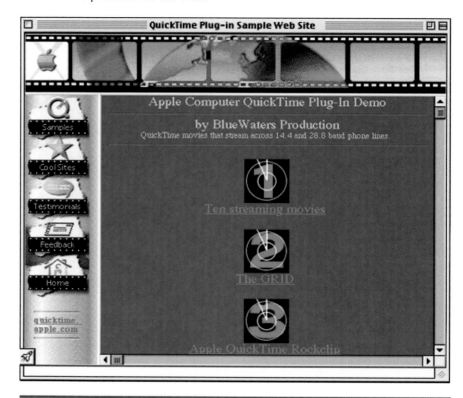

As mentioned in Chapter 3, some popular 3D Modeling programs include **Ray Dream Designer Studio, Electric Image, Form-Z, Specular Infini-D, Macromedia Extreme 3D, RenderMan,** and **AutoDesk 3D Studio.** On high-end UNIX workstations, you are likely to find a sophisticated program called **SoftImage.**

These different programs allow you to create different types of animated objects that can be distributed and used on different platforms. Though there are many animation formats just as there are many graphics formats, let's take a look at three of the most common.

Animated GIFs

Animated GIFs are a special kind of GIF file known as GIF89a. Animated GIFs enable you to create animated 2D and 3D images for Web pages. To create animated GIFs, multiple images are stored as separate blocks within one single GIF file. Consequently, animated GIFs are also called multi-block GIFs. When the animated GIF is viewed on the Web, the multiple images are **streamed,** or played one at a time. This creates the illusion of motion. Animated GIFs are very efficient because the viewer does not have to wait for the entire GIF to be downloaded before it begins running on the Web page. Animated GIFs require no plug-ins and most major browsers including Netscape, Internet Explorer, and Mosaic support them. You can include animated GIFs in Web pages without being concerned about compatibility or user accessibility.

FIGURE 4.6

3D images have the illusion of depth.

Just as clip art can be purchased or downloaded from the Internet, animated graphics can also be purchased on CD-ROM or downloaded from the Internet. Though more and more pre-made animated graphics are available, you may find that you need to create your own animated image to create an intended effect most accurately. If you do decide to create your own animated graphic, you will need several pieces of software to do it.

You will need graphics software to create the image or images. You will also need animation software to animate the image or images you created. Popular GIF animation authoring tools include **GIF Construction Set for Windows/Windows 95** and **GIFBuilder for the Mac.** We will discuss these

FIGURE 4.7

Sophisticated animation requires substantial processing power.

FIGURE 4.8

QuickTime makes it possible to create, integrate, and publish animation.

tools in greater depth in Chapter 8. You can also turn to the end of this book for the addresses to Web sites for each of these programs as well as some additional references on animated GIFs.

QuickTime Animations

QuickTime is Apple Computer's technology. It is an industry-standard software architecture that has been instrumental in the birth of animation for the computer. QuickTime makes it possible to create, integrate, and publish animation. QuickTime also recognizes still image formats such as Adobe Photoshop files, QuickDraw pictures, Bitmap (BMP) files, and on the Internet, GIF and JPEG images.

QuickTime animation is not platform-specific. You will find QuickTime files running on Macintosh computers and PCs running Windows, Windows 95, and Windows NT. Though QuickTime allows you to store your media files in other formats, the QuickTime Movie file format is among the most convenient and powerful formats for storing animation. For more information on QuickTime, visit http://www.quicktime.apple.com.

AVI

Another common animated file format is **AVI.** This is Microsoft's movie file format. Though the quality of AVI files is adequate, AVI files don't offer the sophisticated management features and cross-platform compatibility found in QuickTime files. Therefore, if you want your animation to reach the widest audience possible, save your animation as a QuickTime file. Conversion programs do exist that allow you to convert QuickTime files to AVI files and vice versa.

Planning:
- **Plan your multimedia application by following scripts, storyboards, and flowcharts.**
- **The trick to good animation is knowing what, when, and how much to animate.**

If animation is not well planned and is poorly executed, it will be the death of a multimedia application.

The Animation Specialist

This person is responsible for creating all of the animation for a project. An animator should have graphic design skills, experience and expertise with 3D modeling programs, and skill in using interactive multimedia development tools. Let's take a look at some of the different tools the animation specialist might use to create animation within a multimedia project.

In creating the animation for a project, the animation specialist will be working as part of a team. Written documents including a storyboard, a flowchart, and a program script (see Chapter 9) as well as individual scene scripts, will outline all of the pieces and ideas of the multimedia application for the client and the other team members. These documents provide a detailed description of the program. The program script and scene scripts assist the animation specialist in designing animations that are consistent with the goals and framework of the program.

In addition to designing appropriate animation for the project, the animation specialist will also need to know what will actually work based on the hardware and software used to distribute and view the final product. In other words, the animation specialist must have technical skills as well as design savvy. As a specialist, the animator will need to understand how to develop for high-end systems, as well as those that might be found in the average user's home or office.

Methods of Creating Animation

In multimedia applications, digital animation is usually created using the **flip-book** approach where a sequence of slightly different visual images is compressed and then played back to convey a sense of motion. In other words, it is a series of still images shown in quick succession, which trick our minds into seeing motion. These images might be a collection of paintings, photographs, or drawings that enable the animation specialist to create simple or extremely detailed animation.

FIGURE 4.9

You can see from this illustration how visual images appear to be in motion.

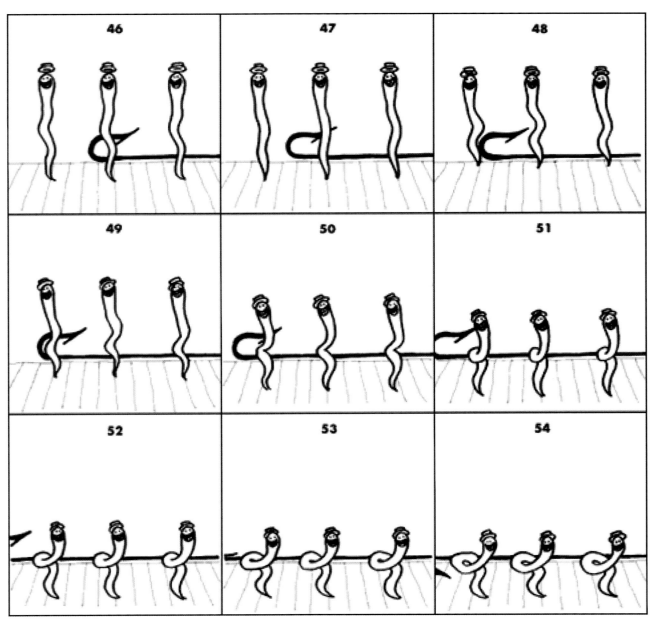

There are two rates used in animation. The **sampling rate** is the actual number of different images that occur per second. The **playback rate** is the number of images displayed per second when the animation is being viewed. The sampling rate and playback rate can be, and often are, different. Obviously, a higher sampling rate will yield a higher quality product.

To create an effective illusion of motion at full-motion video standards, the playback rate must be between 24 and 30 frames per second. When the illusion of motion fails and the animation appears as a rapid sequence of still images, the image is said to **flicker.** The speed at which animation plays is determined by the complexity of the animation as well as the specifications (processor speed and RAM) of the computer running the animation. The sampling rate and playback rate work together to create high quality animation.

Regardless of whether you are creating 2D or 3D animation, one of the following basic methods of creating animation for multimedia applications will probably be used.

Cell-Based Animation (Tweening)

Cell-based animation is also called **frame animation.** Using this creation method, **key frames** that describe a key event in the time line of animation are created on cells or frames. **Tweening,** the process of filling in the frames between the key frames, is then used to make the animation appear fluid. The artists who create the frames between the key frames are often referred to as **tweeners.** This is how cartoons have been created in the past.

Morphing is a special technique that uses frames to create the illusion of one object changing into another. By displaying a series of frames that create a smooth transition, it appears that one shape actually becomes another. Morphing is quite common on television and in the movies. It is particularly popular in horror movies and thrillers. Commercials also employee morphing to market their products to consumers.

In order for animation to be effective, it must create the illusion of natural movement. This requires frames running at least 15 per second, and to really appear professional, 24 to 30 frames or cells per second is more common. Obviously, requiring people to manually draw each cell or frame is an incredibly labor-intensive and time-consuming process. Computers really shine when it comes to this type of monotonous, redundant activity.

Theoretically, cell-based animation on the computer uses basically the same technique employed by tweeners. However, with the help of the computer,

FIGURE 4.10

Tweening can be used to create animation.

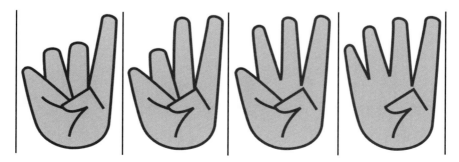

FIGURE 4.11
Morphing uses frames to make it appear as if one object actually evolves into another.

drawings can be reused and altered. This means key frames can be created and modified in a much more realistic time frame, and transitional frames can be created automatically. Though tweening and morphing are quite time consuming when done manually, creating cell-based animation is actually quite simple when using the computer and special software.

GIF Builder and **Macromedia Director** are two popular animation programs that have incorporated cell-based animation into their design.

Path-Based Animation

Path-based animation is also called **vector animation.** This type of animation creates animated objects by following an object's transition over a line or vector. More specifically, it tracks the beginning, direction, and length that an object travels. The path the line takes can be straight, curved, or jagged. With path-based animation, the artist creates only one drawing and a path. The computer program manipulates this object by drawing the frames as the object travels over the path.

Some software permits multiple means of creating animation. Macromedia Director is an example of software that allows the designer to use either cell-based or path-based animation. Other programs that permit path-based animation include **Autodesk, Hypercard, Macromedia Authorware,** and **Toolbook.**

Combination of Cell- and Path-Based Animation

Most programs, including Macromedia Director, allow you to combine cell-based and path-based animation. Typically, the animated object is created using cell-based techniques. It is then moved along a path using path-based animation.

FIGURE 4.12
With path-based animation, objects travel along a path.

Computational Animation

Computational animation allows an object to be moved across a screen by varying its x and y coordinates. By changing the x coordinate, you change the object's horizontal position. When you change the y coordinate, you change the object's vertical position. This method of animating objects is similar to path-based animation, however, instead of specifying a path for the object to travel, you vary its position on the screen based on axes.

Program- or Script-Based Animation

Using programming languages to create animation is also quite common and is often referred to as **script-based animation.** Through the use of a sometimes-elaborate set of program commands, frames can be substituted for other frames thus creating a sequence of movement or animation. Script-based animations are often more flexible than the others. In addition, script-based animation programs can be easily modified for new images. The programming language included in Macromedia Director that allows you to create script-based animation is called Lingo and is one of many programming languages used to create animated objects.

LINGO

Lingo is the scripting language found in Macromedia's Director program. It is an object-oriented scripting language that allows developers to write code that will extend Director's built-in capabilities.

To learn Lingo, you must first understand the basics of Director and how Lingo works within it. Director is based on a theater metaphor. Within this theater is a stage on which cast members (actors, backgrounds, props, etc.) interact. Though animation features are built into Director, you can also use Lingo to write a script that will animate cast members.

ANIMATED OBJECTS

Within a multimedia application, there is a multitude of opportunities to add animation. Objects and characters of all types have the potential to be animated. The animation can be quite simple. For example, an animated children's story designed to teach children about the importance of recycling might have fairly

FIGURE 4.13

Lingo is Macromedia Director's object-oriented scripting language.

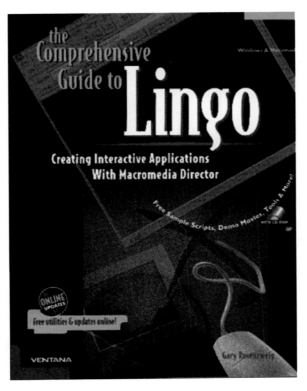

simplistic animation such as a talking recycle bin. On the other hand, full-length animated feature films such as *Toy Story* or *The Lost World* contain extremely complex animation, as do many of the video games whose characters are fully developed, lifelike human creatures. Many times the human creatures in the game represent the players who create them. More animation is needed as these characters navigate through an animated, 3D virtual world.

Because multimedia has the potential to be interactive, the animation specialist must design animated characters and objects that change as a result of a change in mood or tone within the application. In other words, as the user makes choices, the outcomes are different. Obviously, the animated characters and objects must correctly reflect this outcome. For example, in a computer-based training program a character might be designed to jump for joy if the user chooses the correct answer. However, should the user respond incorrectly, the character should reflect this mood perhaps by hanging its head and looking dejected. Thus, a multimedia application must be designed to encounter a range of motion depending upon a range of possible outcomes.

Animation Tools

Different types of software are used to create animation. To begin with, you need to create a still image or a series of still images. In Chapter 3 we discussed the

FIGURE 4.14

Animated characters in 3D games can be extremely complex.

Know the tools. There are many ways to create animation; if you have a range of possibilities to work from, you will be more productive and creative.

hardware and software needed to capture or create still images. Once you have the still images, you may need to edit them with image-editing software. The final step is to animate the still images. The animation process can be achieved through the use of programming languages, animation software, or a combination of the two. After quickly reviewing some of the software used to create and edit still images, let's take a more in-depth look at the tools used for animation.

Graphics Creation or Capturing Software

Unless the image you wish to animate already exists, the first tool you need to create animation is software to capture or create the graphic image. For a review of the software used to capture and create graphics, refer to Chapter 3. You can use almost any commercial graphics package, which would include virtually every **drawing, painting,** and **modeling** application. In fact, some of these applications actually come with an **animation engine** that will compile your graphic once it has been created.

Some of the programs used to capture and create still images and ultimately animated images include: **Adobe Photoshop, Adobe Illustrator, Adobe Dimensions, Adobe TextureMaker, Microsoft Paint, Corel Photo-Paint,**

Fractal Design Painter, Ray Dream Designer Studio, Macromedia Extreme 3D, and **Kai's Power Tools.**

Image-Editing Software

After you have captured or created your image, you may need to edit the image with an **image-editing program.** This program may be the same software used to capture or create the image, or it might be something different. Among other things, a good image-editing utility should offer you the ability to resize the object, apply different design aspects to various parts of the image, and modify the object using paint or drawing tools.

The most well-known image-editing program is **Adobe Photoshop.** In addition to the features mentioned in the previous paragraph, Photoshop comes with special effects, filters, and the ability to manipulate the color depth and resolution of each image individually. To create an animated image, each graphic image is slightly modified and then later played back together. Using this technique, the graphic appears to change or move.

Each image-editing utility has its own special features and hardware requirements, so be sure to check out the details before you purchase. A few other common image-editing programs include **GraphicConverter, Fractal Design Painter,** and **Macromedia XRES.**

Animation Programs

After your graphics have been captured, created, and edited to your satisfaction, you will need to animate the graphics. Programs specifically designed to create animation are also available. These programs range from simple presentation programs such as **Microsoft PowerPoint** and **Adobe Persuasion** to complex programs, such as **Macromedia Director,** which uses both path- and cell-based animation.

Most animation programs include a **compiling engine** that allows you to arrange still images into animated objects. Most of these animation packages will also include a **codec** (compressor/decompressor) as part of the compiler. The codecs enable you to choose the amount of compression as well as the type of

FIGURE 4.15

By slightly changing each graphic and then playing them back together, it appears as if the object is animated.

FIGURE 4.16
Simple animation is easy to create in presentation programs like Microsoft PowerPoint.

Point

ANIMA

PowerPoint

ANIMATION

PowerPoint

ANIMATION

compression used. The better packages also allow you to render or compile the images at a later time. Compilers are included in the following animation programs: **Adobe Premiere, Macromedia Director, Macromedia Authorware, Multimedia Toolbook, MotionWorks CameraMan, Dave's Targa Animator, GifBuilder,** and **Avid VideoShop.**

Macromedia Director is the industry leader for creating interactive multimedia animation. With Director, you can create simple or extremely sophisticated animation sequences. There are also many techniques you can use in Director to create unique animation. To give you a feel for how animation programs work, let's take a look at some of the key animation features available in Macromedia Director.

THE STAGE

Most animation programs establish some type of metaphor surrounding the program. Director uses a theater stage as its metaphor. Animated objects are added to the stage and become the actors who are cast and scripted to play particular parts. In other words, the **stage** is where the action takes place.

The Stage in Director is not a window. It is really just a container where the animated objects interact. This distinction is important because many of the techniques you are comfortable using in a window do not apply on the stage. For example, you cannot paste objects onto the stage from the clipboard.

You can change the size, location, and color of the stage. The size of the stage is particularly important when you are creating multimedia applications with Macromedia Director. In Chapter 2, we said that every computer monitor has a different resolution. For this reason, if you want your animated movie to get maximum exposure, it is important that you pick a stage size that is easily displayed on many types of computer monitors. At this time, a stage size of 640 x 480 will probably enable most people to view the animation you create for standard applications. For

FIGURE 4.17
Macromedia uses the metaphor of a theater. This is the stage on which the cast members interact.

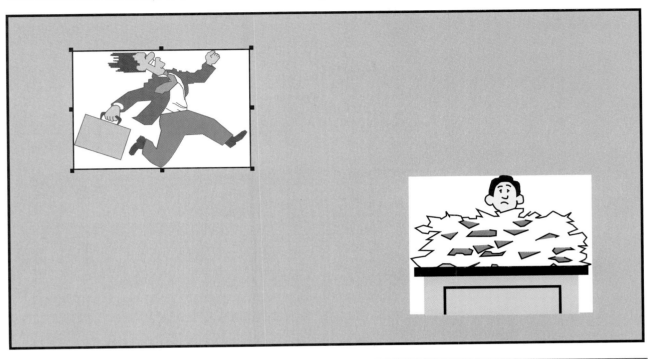

the Internet, the stage size will vary depending upon bandwidth. In general, the stage size for Web-based multimedia applications will be smaller than for other distribution methods.

THE CAST

The first window you will probably encounter when you begin working with Macromedia Director is the **Cast window.** In this window, you will place all of the items that would be considered part of the cast. **Cast members** are the basic elements of any Director movie. In other words, all of the actors, scripts, directions, backgrounds, and props need to be placed in the Cast window. Within a single cast, you can have up to 32,000 cast members.

The number of cast members available is probably more than you could ever imagine or need. If, however, you want more than 32,000 cast members, you can have multiple casts that would be similar to multiple scenes from a play. Casts can be **internal** or **external.** Internal casts are stored with the movie file while external casts are stored separately. By using external casts, libraries of commonly used cast elements can be shared. Multiple casts also make it possible to better manage large numbers of cast members because the cast members can be divided into separate casts. In addition, using external casts can greatly reduce the size of an animated movie.

Cast members can be created in Director or they can be imported from other applications. You can use most any graphics design program to create your cast member and then import that cast member into your animated movie. Macromedia Director supports a number of file formats and sources. You can import graphics, text, sound, animation sequences, and digital video from these sources. From within Director, you can add graphics, text, and scripts.

When using authoring software such as Macromedia Director, work with duplicate cast members. This way, if you make a mistake, you will always have the original to work from.

FIGURE 4.18

External casts make it possible to create libraries for sharing cast members between applications.

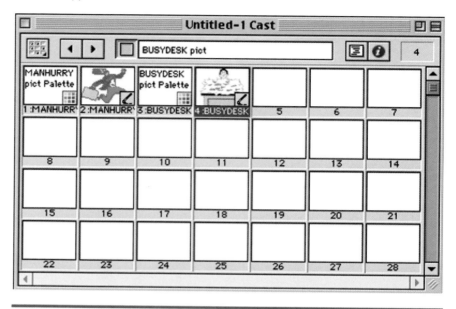

You can also use the **Paint window** and **Tool palette** in Director to create your own cast member. The Paint window and Tool palette in Director are very similar to those found in other paint programs. You will find the pencil, eraser, paint bucket, paintbrush, airbrush, rectangle, oval, polygon, and line tools. You will also have the ability to rotate, skew, and distort the image just as you can in other paint programs.

Director also offers a Text window and Text tools for creating and editing text. Using these features, you can change the font, point size, line spacing, alignment, and style of text without worrying about jaggies or staircasing that would result

Use TrueType fonts or bitmapped graphics to help ensure that the fonts you choose will appear correctly when played.

FIGURE 4.19

Macromedia supports all of these file formats and sources.

Type	Description	Create in Director?	Import?
Bitmaps	Images or text	Yes	Yes
Buttons	Interactive controls	Yes	No
Film Loops	Animation Sequences	Yes	No
Movies	(digital video and other animation files)	No	Yes
Palettes	Color controls	Yes	Yes
Pictures (PICT files)	Vector or bitmap Mac images	No	Yes
Scripts	Lingo commands	Yes	No
Shapes	Vector images	Yes	No
Sound Level Properties	Control for sounds played within a movie	Yes	No
Sounds	Sound files	No	Yes
Text	Bitmapped or editable	Yes	Yes
Transitions	Effects between sprites	Yes	No

FIGURE 4.20

The Paint Window and Tool Palette found in Macromedia Director make it easy to create cast members.

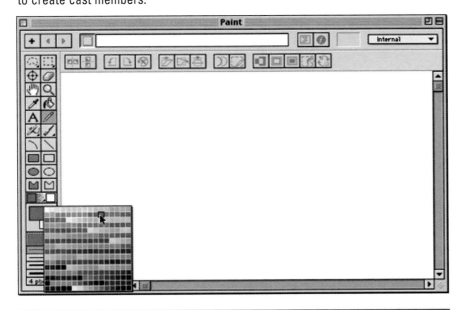

if the text were a bitmapped image. These features make it easy to create the buttons that are often found in interactive animated movies.

There are different types of cast members, and all cast members have properties that vary depending on type. Typical properties include the cast member name, number, file size, color depth, and storage location. When you are ready to add a cast member to the animated movie, you drag it to the score. Once a cast member has been placed in the score, it is called a **sprite.**

THE SCORE

The **score** ties all of the animation elements together. In addition to all the cast members, the score also contains animation controls. The score consists of columns and rows that divide it into a grid of cells. Each column represents a frame in an animated movie. Each row represents a channel.

Channels represent different activities that will take place in the animated movie. You can think of channels as layers stacked back to front. For example, there are channels designated to control transitions, those that control the tempo, and others than control the script. The following channels are used in Macromedia Director:

- **Tempo Channel**—Allows you to change the tempo and insert wait states. With this channel you can pause for a set amount of time, until a mouse or key action occurs, or while another movie or sound finishes playing. It is this channel that determines the speed at which the movie will run. Film animation runs at 24 frames per second while video runs at 30 frames per second.

- **Color Palette Channel**—You can select colors from special color palettes such as metallic or pastels, or you can create your own custom color. Changes to the color palette of the movie appear in the Color Palette Channel at the point where the change takes effect. To create an animated effect, you can use color cycling. This is a quick method of applying

FIGURE 4.21

The score contains all of the cast members. It also controls the animation.

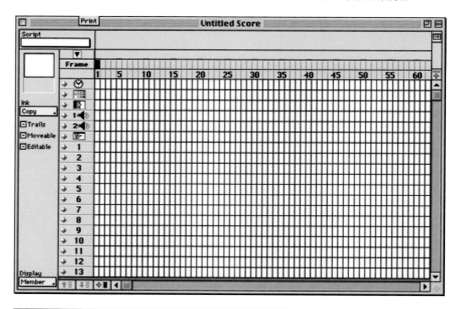

animation that requires very little memory. By cycling through several colors or blends of colors, an object appears to glow, or point, or even move.

- **Transition Channel**—Effects that occur as the movie moves from frame to frame are set in the Transition Channel. Common effects include fade, cover, wipe, strip, dissolve, reveal, and a multitude of others. Third-party transitions can also be purchased and used with Director. Consider using transitions to speed up and simplify some animation effects.

- **Sound Channels**—These channels contain the sound effects, voice-overs, and music for a movie. Director makes it possible to play music and voices at the same time by giving you more than one channel. All Macintosh computers and most PC compatibles support multichannel sound.

- **Script Channels**—The programming language included in Director is called **Lingo.** Lingo allows multimedia developers to extend Director's built-in capabilities to customize animated objects more fully. Lingo scripts can be quite simple or extremely complex. The script channels contain the Lingo programming scripts for the different cast members.

- **Sprite Channels**—The sprite channel displays all of the image cast members on the stage. Sprites can be bitmaps, buttons, text, or shapes.

ANIMATION

Animation is achieved by changing an object's position in a given cell to a new position in the next cell. By slightly changing the position of the cast member from frame to frame, it appears to move. Director offers several different methods of creating animation. Each of the techniques listed below can be used alone or combined to create even more impressive results. Keep in mind that it takes time to create smooth animation sequences.

- **In-Between**—In Macromedia Director, **tweening** is the process of adding incremental sprites between a starting and ending sprite. The **In-Between**

FIGURE 4.22

By using the in-between animation technique, the computer will fill in the frames between the beginning and ending frame.

Linear method allows you to tween between locations in a straight line. The **In-Between Special** method allows you to tween between sprites that have been resized, squeezed, stretched or otherwise modified.

- **Step Recording**—Step recording is one of the easiest methods of creating animation in Director. You animate a sprite by recording the position of the sprite in one frame. You then step forward a frame and record the position of the sprite in the next frame. In other words, animation is accomplished by recording one step at a time until you have completed an entire animation sequence. If you want, you can animate several sprites at the same time. When you do this, all of the sprites will move in the same direction.

- **Real-time Recording**—Real-time recording allows you to record movement. For example, if you wish to show movement of one sprite while the others remain stationary, you will use real-time recording. To animate a sprite, you use the mouse to establish the path. To make the movement appear smooth, you will probably need to record the movement at a slower speed, such as five frames per second (fps). Once you have the movement recorded to your satisfaction, you can adjust the speed or the number of frames per second.

- **Cast to Time**—Cast to time allows transition from one cast member to the next. As the cast member changes from frame to frame, the illusion of animation is created. To accomplish cast to time animation, a cast member is usually created and then slightly modified and saved as a new cast member. This process is continued until an entire animation sequence of still images has been created. These cast members are then dropped onto the stage where they are arranged in adjacent cells. Provided the cast members are aligned correctly, an illusion of movement is created as the movie moves from one frame or cast member to the next.

- **Space to Time**—To create smoother transitions between sprites, you can use the space to time animation technique. Space to time is also helpful if you need to have the animated object change and move. This technique allows you to position the same cast member in subsequent channels of the same frame. You can then move these sprites from multiple channels of the same frame to a single channel on subsequent frames.

- **Paste Special Relative**—Paste special relative automatically positions a sequence of selected frames on the stage where the last sequence ended. In other words, repeating a smaller sequence creates a longer animation sequence.

FIGURE 4.23

When using the trail effect, the previous image remains.

ANIMATION EFFECTS

Special features in Director allow you to create interesting animation effects:

- **Onion Skinning**—Onion skinning allows you to create new images by tracing over an existing image. It is a particularly useful technique when you are creating **parallel animation** where part of an image remains static while another portion of the image changes. For example, you may want the head of the image to remain static while the facial features change.

- **Trail Effect**—With the trail effect, the previous image is not completely erased when the image in the next frame appears on the screen. In other words, a trail of the image is left. This is particularly effective when images would be left behind. For example, you might use the trail effect to animate footprints in the snow.

- **Film Loops**—A film loop is a cast member that consists of a series of animated frames set up to play over and over again. In addition to creating a looping cast member, film loops also improves the performance of a movie by creating a shorter, cleaner score.

SUMMARY

Animation is a moving graphic image. Though animation has been around for many years, the processes that we use to create animation have evolved. Today, creating animation involves sophisticated computer technology.

At one time, animation was primarily found in the world of entertainment. Today, animated objects can be found in **computer-based training, education, games,** and on the **World Wide Web.**

There are many different types of animated objects. Flat, **two-dimensional (2D) images** can be animated, or to create a more lifelike effect, **three-dimensional (3D) images** that have depth can be animated. **Animated GIFs** are a special kind of GIF file format used to store animated 2D and 3D images for Web pages.

Planning is vital to the production of successful multimedia applications. With the help of other team members, the **animation specialist** should rely on **storyboards, scripts,** and **flowcharts** in creating animated objects that meet the goals of the project.

There are different methods that can be used to create animation in multimedia applications. Most of these methods are based on the **"flipbook" approach** where a sequence of slightly different visual images is compressed and then played back to convey a sense of motion. To effectively create the illusion of motion, the playback rate must be between 24 and 30 frames per second.

Cell-based animation is also called **frame animation.** Using this method, **key frames** define the beginning and end of an event. **Tweening** is used to fill in the frames between the key frames. **Path-based animation** creates animated objects by tracking the path that an object travels while **computational animation** allows an object to be moved by varying its x and y coordinates. Finally, **script-based animation** uses programming languages such as **Lingo** to create or enable animation.

Many different types of animation tools assist the animation specialist in creating animated objects that are appropriate to the multimedia application. A series of still images can be captured using special software together with scanners, digital cameras, and video capture cards, or images can be created with **graphic creation software.** Once created, **image-editing software** allows the animation specialist to modify images and apply special effects. Finally, the series of still images can be animated using **animation software.**

Leading the animation software industry is **Macromedia Director.** Like most animation programs, Director contains a **compiling engine** that arranges still images into animated objects. Director is based on a theater metaphor that explains some of the other key features found in Director including **the stage, the cast, the score, animation,** and **animation effects.**

KEY TERMS

Animation	Animated GIFs	QuickTime
AVI	Animation specialist	Storyboards
Scripts	Flowcharts	Flipbook approach
Sampling rate	Playback rate	Cell-based animation
Frame animation	Key frames	Tweening
Path-based animation	Computational animation	Script-based animation
Lingo		Compiling engine
Stage	Macromedia Director	Score
Animation effects	Cast	

Matching Questions

a. animation   **b.** edutainment   **c.** 2D images

d. 3D images   **e.** tweening   **f.** morphing

g. stage   **h.** cast members   **i.** score

_____ **1.** The process of filling in the frames between the key frames to make the animation appear fluid.

_____ **2.** A moving graphic image.

_____ **3.** In Macromedia Director, this is where the action takes place.

_____ **4.** Flat images that only have height and width.

_____ **5.** A special technique that uses frames to create the illusion of one object changing into another.

_____ **6.** Programs geared toward entertaining students as they learn.

_____ **7.** These are the basic elements of any Director movie.

_____ **8.** Images that have height, width, and depth.

_____ **9.** This ties all of the animation elements together and also contains all of the animation controls.

Fill-In Questions

1. When the animated GIF is viewed on the Web, the multiple images are_____, or played one at a time.

2. In multimedia applications, digital animation is usually created using the _____ _____ where a sequence of slightly different visual images is compressed and then played back to convey a sense of motion.

3. The _____ _____ is the actual number of different images that occur per second. The _____ _____ is the number of images per second displayed in the viewing process.

4. _____ _____ is also called frame animation. Using this creation method, _____ _____, which describe a key event in the time line of animation, are created on cells or frames.

5. Path-based animation is also called _____ _____. It creates animated objects by following an object's transition over a line or vector.

6. Using programming languages to create animation is also quite common and is often referred to as _____ _____.

7. Most animation programs include a _____ _____ that allows you to compile still images into animated objects. Most of these animation packages will also include a _____ (compressor/decompressor) as part of the compiler.

8. _____ represent different activities that will take place in the animated movie.

DISCUSSION QUESTIONS

1. Why are scripts and storyboards important to the animation specialist?

2. What are some of the different methods used to create animation? How would you describe each of these methods?

3. What are some of the key components found in Macromedia Director? What is the purpose of each of these components?

4. What is the difference between a cast member and a sprite in an animated Director movie? How are they similar?

HANDS-ON EXERCISES

1. Using the Internet, find two Web pages that use animation. Describe the animation used on these pages. What type of animation is it (Animated GIF, QuickTime, AVI, other)? How might it have been created?

2. Using the two Web pages from Question #1 or two different pages, answer the following questions: a) Is the animation effective? If so, what makes it effective? b) Is the animation geared toward the audience? c) Is the animation appropriate for the application? d) Is the Web a proper means of distributing this animation?

3. Describe a multimedia application that you would like to create. In planning the animation for this application, describe a) your audience, b) the purpose of the application, c) the preferred method of distribution for the application, and d) any special considerations. Draw a sequence of still images that could be combined to create an appropriate animation for this application.

Case Study: Chapter 4

Wendy Perry has been selected as the animation specialist for the project. Wendy will be working closely with Marc to ensure that the animation is consistent and compatible with the interface Marc designs for the project.

Using a series of the illustrations Marc has created of jet skis, waverunners, and other personal watercraft, Wendy will use the GIF Construction Set to animate these still images. She will then create animated GIFs of the hypermedia watercraft, which will be used as hypermedia links.

To appeal to the audience, Wendy knows that she needs to create fast animation that is full of surprises and consistent with the application. At the same time, she doesn't want the animation to be annoying or detract from the interface or the content of the site.

Wendy has decided to create animated navigation buttons and icons that don't move until the user clicks on the object. Once activated, these clickable animated watercraft will jump a wave, complete a 360-degree turn, or speed off into the sunset. Hypermedia will transport the user to a new spot within the site or off to a related site.

CHAPTER FIVE

Sound

1. Understand the importance of sound in a multimedia application
2. Define some of the basic terminology associated with sound including waveform, amplitude, frequency, decibel, Hertz, and Kilohertz
3. List several applications of sound
4. Describe the different categories of sound
5. Describe the different types of sound
6. Define rate and resolution as they relate to sound quality
7. Explain where sound should be included in the planning process
8. Describe several methods of recording analog or digital sound
9. Describe the roles and responsibilities of the Audio Specialist
10. Explain the difference between destructive and non-destructive sound processing
11. Describe how sound is incorporated into a multimedia application
12. List the key considerations for delivering high-quality sound
13. List and describe several of the more common sound file formats
14. List and describe some of the key features found in Macromedia SoundEdit 16
15. List and describe some of the key features found in Macromedia Deck II
16. List and describe some of the key features found in Macromedia Director that pertain to sound

Introduction to Sound

We acquire a great deal of knowledge through our ears. Unfortunately, other than in the entertainment industry, many multimedia developers don't take advantage of this sense by incorporating sound into their multimedia products. Sound enhances a multimedia application by supplementing presentations, images, animation, and video. In the past, only those who could afford expensive sound-recording equipment and facilities could produce high-quality, digital sound. Today, computers and synthesizers make it possible for the average person to produce comparable sound and music.

Basic Principles of Sound

A sound is a **waveform.** The **amplitude** is the distance between the valley and the peak of a waveform. The amplitude of a waveform determines its volume, which is measured in **decibels.** A decibel is the smallest variation in amplitude that can be detected by the human ear.

The **frequency** is the number of peaks that occur in one second. Frequency is measured in **Hertz (Hz)** or **Kilohertz (kHz),** which represent thousands of cycles per second. The frequency of a waveform determines its pitch.

Categories of Sound

In multimedia applications, sounds are either **content sounds** or **ambient sounds.** Content sounds furnish information. Narration and dialog are content sounds. Music and other sounds can also be considered content sounds if they are part of the topic itself. For example, the sound of a motor would be content sound if it were used to distinguish between different engine problems.

FIGURE 5.1

Sounds are waveforms.

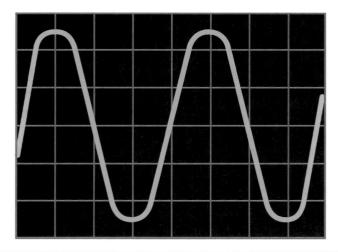

FIGURE 5.2

Narration in a multimedia presentation is considered content sound.

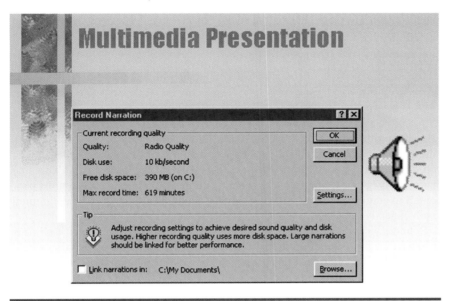

Ambient sounds include background sounds and special effects. Ambient sounds reinforce messages and set the mood. Music is a universal language that most people enjoy and appreciate. Classical music might be used in the background to set the mood for a multimedia application on literature and the arts while new age rhythms would be better for a multimedia application on the healing power of crystals.

Special sound effects can reinforce or enliven a message. Different types of laughter could be incorporated into a multimedia application that included comic relief such as knock-knock jokes. As bullets enter the presentation screen in Microsoft PowerPoint, special sounds draw attention to and reinforce the bulleted item.

FIGURE 5.3

Background music sets the mood of a multimedia application.

In multimedia applications, audio can either be synched with the occurrence of other objects in the production, or it can serve as a trigger to the user. As a trigger, it becomes a form of hypermedia called **hyperaudio.** In this format, users are given control. They can click on the sound object when they are ready to listen to the clip.

Uses of Sound

Like every other multimedia element, if you decide to incorporate sound into a multimedia application, you should have a reason for doing so. In other words, you shouldn't use sound just because you can. Along the same lines, don't assume that more is better. Using too much sound is rarely a problem because most people fail to add it where it could truly enhance an application, but do keep in mind that balance is important.

Sound adds another dimension to a multimedia application. If used well, it is an extremely powerful element that can stimulate emotional responses that would never be activated from text and graphics alone. Sound should be used selectively and appropriately whenever and wherever it will help convey the intended message or complement the purpose of the multimedia application. Sound can be used to get attention, to entertain, to give directions, to personalize an interface, or to convey an educational or persuasive message.

Computer-Based Training Programs

Sound can be used to enhance computer-based training programs. Appropriate narration can be used to augment the demonstration of correct techniques or procedures. Instructions are more likely to be followed if audio accompanies the written instructions. Sound can also be effectively used to provide feedback. For example, in a simulated experience, a buzzer noise may signal that the wrong choice has been selected.

Education

In education, sound is used to accommodate auditory learners. In educational psychology it has also been proven that students are better able to recall information when sound has been used as a cue. Though sound can be useful in almost any educational application, it is more important in some applications than in others. For example, sound is imperative in teaching the correct pronunciation of words in multimedia applications designed to teach foreign language. As in computer-based training, sounds can provide feedback such as a buzzer when an incorrect answer is given. Sound can also be used to illustrate. For example, a multimedia application geared toward assisting medical students in diagnosing disease could include the sounds of different types of breathing patterns that signify different ailments. For more examples of how sound is used in multimedia education titles, check out Educorp's site at http://www.educorp.com.

To be effective, sound must keep learners involved. Giving learners control of the sound is an effective way of keeping them involved and motivated. If learners don't have control over the sound, the sound may be lost as it blends in with the rest of the noises in the environment. Once lost, the sound becomes a useless multimedia element.

FIGURE 5.4

Instructions in computer-based training applications are more likely to be followed if audio narration accompanies the written instrtuctions.

Advertising and Marketing

Sound is much more effective in selling products and services than is text or text with graphics. Direct mail advertising is considered effective if there is a 2–3 percent return. Letters alone don't sell. Salespeople know that they have a much better chance of selling you something if you can hear them. If your goal is to sell a product or service, you will be much more successful if you add sound to your multimedia application.

FIGURE 5.5

In this program, sound is used to demonstrate the correct pronunciation of words in a foreign language.

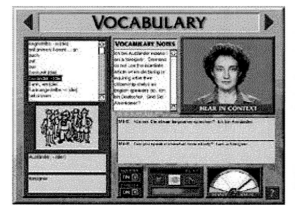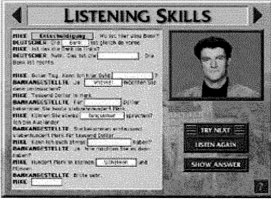

FIGURE 5.6

Nearly all multimedia games have background music that sets the mood.

Entertainment and Games

Developers of multimedia games know the value of sound. It is the entertainment and game industry that has spurred the growth of computers with multimedia capabilities. Arcade games come complete with the sounds of tilting pinball machines and bumper pool. Card and casino games use sounds to simulate the spinning of a roulette wheel, the shuffling of cards, and spewing coins from a slot machine. The sound of tornadoes, earthquakes, floods, firing guns, engines, and screeching tires can be heard throughout action games. Developers are always creating funny little animated creatures that make noises we've never heard before, and nearly all multimedia games have background music that sets the mood to light and cheery or dark and dreary.

The Web

Sound is no longer a novelty on the Web. More and more Web pages are incorporating background music, narration, and sound effects into their Web pages. On the Web, recorded testimonials from customers are used to market and sell products and services. Interviews with political candidates are designed to sway

FIGURE 5.7

Background music and special sound effects are abundant in multimedia games.

votes. Options to have tips and text narrated are available. Beeps, squeaks, claps, and whistles are all quite common sound effects found throughout Web pages.

Audio on the Web can either be **downloaded** or **streamed.** Downloadable sound files are stored on your computer before they are played. Streaming is a more advanced process that allows the sound to be played as it is downloading. These two processes will be discussed in greater depth in Chapter 8.

Other applications of sound on the Web include **one-way audio,** which offers on-demand radio listening around the world. These radio programs broadcast music, talk shows, and live interviews. Online services offer **Internet audio e-mail** or **voice mail** that enables you to listen to e-mail instead of reading it. Internet phone applications are also available. These technologies enable **Internet audioconferencing** or **Internet telephony** that allows two-way, full-duplex audio conversations over the Web. With Internet telephony you can talk to friends or family without the cost of a long-distance phone call.

The Audio Specialist

Because sound is so important to a multimedia project, yet working with sound can be a rather intricate process, you may find it worthwhile to secure the services and skills of an audio specialist. If you are working as part of a multimedia team on a larger project, an audio specialist has probably already been assigned to work with your team.

Audio specialists are responsible for recording and processing the audio files used in the multimedia application. Working with the multimedia director or

FIGURE 5.8
Sound is becoming more and more common on the Web.

architect, they will ensure that the audio is correctly incorporated into the multimedia application. Finally, audio specialists should properly prepare the application for delivery. If appropriate, they should be directly responsible for setting up the equipment in the location where the multimedia application will be delivered and the sound will be heard.

The services of the audio specialist are even more valuable to the project as the audio in the multimedia application gets more complicated. For example, when multiple sounds from multiple sources have been incorporated into a multimedia application to be delivered through different types of equipment located in a large auditorium, it's time to get an audio specialist.

Sound Quality

The quality of the sound included in your multimedia application will affect its credibility and effectiveness. Recording and playback environments and equipment have a huge impact on the quality of sound. Two other factors that determine the quality of a sound are rate and resolution. The rate and resolution are sometimes referred to as sampling speed and depth.

Rate

The **rate** is the number of waveform samples per second. The sampling rate is usually measured in kilohertz with 22 KHz and 44 KHz being the most common sampling rates. A higher sampling rate produces a higher quality sound.

FIGURE 5.9

Rate and resolution affect the quality of a sound.

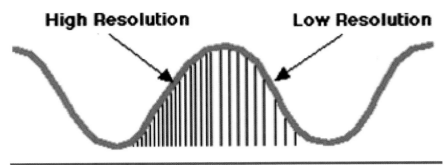

The disadvantage of using a higher sampling rate is that sound files with higher sampling rates require greater storage capacity.

Resolution

Resolution is the number of binary bits processed for each sound wave. Like all digital data, sound that has been recorded by a multimedia computer is represented in bits. Bits represent the vibrations in the sound wave. As the number of bits used to sample the sound increases, the range and the quality of the sound also improves. When more bits are processed, the recording is smoother and purer, thus the sound is more realistic. Because 16-bit recordings contain much more information than 8-bit recordings, they are higher quality. In addition, 16-bit recordings offer a dynamic range of 98dB (decibels). This makes them superior to 8-bit recordings, which only offer 50dB. According to MPC standards, MPC1 requires 8-bit sound although MPC2 and MPC3 require a higher quality 16-bit sound. Once again, there is a trade-off in recording sound with a higher resolution. A sound file with a higher resolution requires much greater storage capacity.

Mono versus Stereo Sound

Mono sounds are flat and unrealistic compared to **stereo sounds,** which are much more dynamic and lifelike. However, stereo sound files require twice the storage capacity of mono sound files. Therefore, if storage and transfer are concerns, mono sound files may be the more appropriate choice.

Types of Audio

There are two types of sound: analog and digital. **Analog sound** is a continuous stream of sound waves. To be understood by the computer, these sound waves must be converted to numbers. The process of converting analog sounds into numbers is called **digitizing** or **sound sampling.** Analog sounds that have been converted to numbers are **digital sounds.** When we are working with digital sound, we call it audio. Therefore, sound that has been converted from analog to digital is often called **digital audio.**

FIGURE 5.10

Sound sampling converts analog sounds to digital sounds consisting of 1's and 0's.

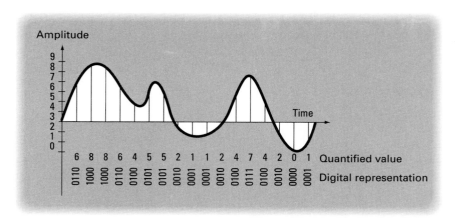

When we are working with audio (sound that has been digitized) in multimedia applications, it may be waveform audio, MIDI, compact disc audio, or 3D.

Waveform

All sounds have a **waveform.** The waveform includes the frequency, the amplitude, and the harmonic content of the sound. Just as an image has to be digitized in order for the computer to recognize it, a sound must also be converted to 1's and 0's. Waveform Audio digitizers are used to record sounds and convert them to a digital format. To accomplish this, audio digitizers sample the waveform thousands of times per second and then store the file in a wave format.

On a PC, files stored with a wave format generally have a .wav extension. Just as you can purchase clip art, you can also purchase prerecorded waveform audio sounds on CD or you can download them from the Internet. To further illustrate the importance of wave files in multimedia, the MPC3 standard now requires a **wavetable** on multimedia computers. A wavetable is a list of numbers that represent the waveshape of each sound.

FIGURE 5.11

The waveform includes the frequency, amplitude, and harmonic content of the sound.

MIDI

MIDI stands for Musical Instrument Digital Interface, and MIDI files have a .mid or .midi extension. MIDI is a format used to represent electronic music produced by a MIDI device (such as a synthesizer, sequencer, electronic keyboard, or drum machine). This format provides instructions on how to replay music, it does not actually record the waveform. In other words, there are MIDI codes for making notes loud or soft, turning them off or on, and changing their tone. MIDI is not music; it is instructions. For this reason, MIDI clips offer smaller file sizes than the other audio file formats. Though MIDI clips are small in size, they can be very high quality and can be accessed down to 1/128 second, which makes them extremely efficient. This is one of the reasons MIDI has been included as part of the MPC3 standard.

To play music files that have been generated by digitally controlled musical equipment such as synthesizers and keyboards (MIDI files), your computer must have a MIDI synthesizer driver for the sound card. If a MIDI synthesizer is not available, you will need external equipment such as an electronic keyboard connected to your computer to play the MIDI file. The MIDI synthesizer driver probably won't sound as good as external equipment, but it is significantly less expensive. If you have QuickTime installed on your computer, you won't need to worry about any of this because QuickTime contains everything you need to make these files play.

Because a synthesizer is what reproduces the sound from the instructions in the MIDI file, sounds that cannot be reproduced by a synthesizer cannot be stored in the MIDI format. For example, human voices and animal sounds are difficult to reproduce with a synthesizer. Also, all MIDI devices and computers do not create the same sound from a MIDI file. Therefore, MIDI files should be tested on a variety of different computer systems.

In general, MIDI files are superior to WAV and AIFF files when storage space or computer processing speed are concerns, though the quality of MIDI output hinges on the hardware playing it. However, to be sure the sound file will always be played back accurately, and also to create sounds that cannot be created from a synthesizer, WAV files are the better choice.

If you'd like to check out some MIDI files, visit these sites: http://www.prs.net/midi.html#index, http://www.doctoraudio.com/links.html, http://www.eeb.ele.tue.nl/midi/index.html.

CD Audio

Music that has been recorded to compact disc is already in a digital format that can be included as background music or melody in any multimedia application. Most of the sound on CDs has been sampled at almost 45,000 samples per second. In addition, CDs can hold up to 75 minutes of 16-bit sound, which can be accessed faster than 1/75 second per sample. This means that you can get very high quality sound from a CD.

CD Extra, also called **CD Plus** or **Enhanced CD,** is a dual-purpose CD. In addition to being played just like a regular music CD, it also contains computer programming that will illustrate graphics and provide interactivity like any other multimedia CD inserted into the CD-ROM drive of any computer.

3D Sound

Live sounds and music resonate and surround us. **Surround sound** or **3D sound** attempts to create this same encompassing experience by inserting delays into the sound recording. These delays attempt to simulate the time it would take for sound waves to reach our ears if we were listening to a live sound or performance. In order for this to happen, multiple speakers are necessary, and a pair of front and rear speakers is preferable.

Similarly, virtual reality attempts to create an illusion of reality by using technology to trick our senses. To trick our sense of hearing, realistic sound effects and audio are needed. Therefore, to create virtual worlds, 3D sound must be incorporated. As virtual reality becomes more and more sophisticated, the use of 3D sound in virtual worlds will become more and more common.

Sources of Digital Sound

There are many sources from which you can obtain digital sound for your multimedia applications. Although some of these sources of sound are copyright protected, others are not. If in doubt, assume that the sound you wish to use in your multimedia application is copyright protected and obtain permission through a release before you use it.

Create your own sound

MIDI instruments make it possible and affordable for even novice musicians to input digital music directly into the computer. If your musical talent is more highly developed, you can even compose your own piece. Keyboards manufactured by companies such as Yamaha and Kawai enable you to create thousands of special sound effects just by pressing a few buttons and depressing a few keys.

FIGURE 5.12

With the right equipment, you can create your own sound.

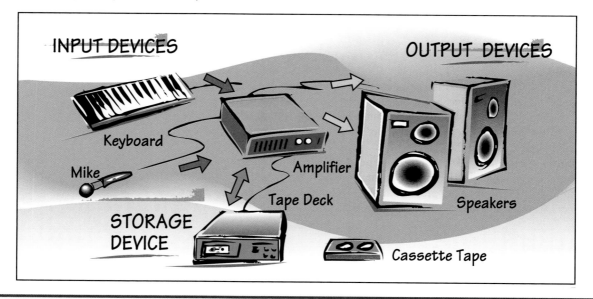

Clip Audio

Just as clip art gives you access to a variety of graphic art files, **clip audio** gives you access to prerecorded digital audio clips of music and sound effects. Clip audio can be purchased on CD-ROM or you can download it over the Internet. Visit the Music Previews Network at http://www.mpmusic.com/ for samples. As always, be sure to read carefully the licensing agreements that come with clip audio. These agreements contain information about royalties and copyright.

Audio CDs

Most authoring programs, such as Macromedia Director, allow you to modify and control the different music tracks from an audio CD. The music from any track on the CD can then be used as background music within the multimedia application.

Voice Recordings

Narrations, voice-overs, and interviews can be recorded directly into the computer. In developing your multimedia application, don't forget to analyze your audience. Hire professional talent including actors and narrators who appeal to your audience and lend credibility to your application. Two or more voices will add variety to your application. Once again, however, balance is important. If you have too many voices, your audience will get lost and will consequently lose interest. Finally, remember to get signed releases before you use someone's recorded voice in your multimedia application.

Planning Sound

It is very important to plan what, when, where, and how sound will be incorporated into a multimedia application. First you must consider what content should be delivered via sound as well as the types of ambient sounds that will be used to set the mood or create a special effect. In Chapter 9, we will discuss the documents used to plan multimedia applications. These documents include the **storyboard,** which provides the details for each screen of the application (including

FIGURE 5.13

Sound should be included in the planning documents of a multimedia application.

Scriptwriting 101

THE SOUND OF COFFEE

INTERIOR KITCHEN

CLOSEUP: Tap water filling carafe
    SOUND EFFECT: Running water filling container

CLOSEUP: Measuring cup empties coffee into filter
    SOUND EFFECT: Dry coffee filling filter

MEDIUM SHOT: Water-filled carafe moves toward filter; hits edge of sink; falls; breaks
    SOUND EFFECT: Glass container hits object, (pause) shatters; water splashes

    Coffee Cook: AAAaaarrrrrrgggghhh!

multimedia elements). The **scripts** include details about the text and narration for a multimedia application. Because there is a difference between the way words are heard and the way they are read, scripts should be written for listening rather than for reading. This involves using short, simple phrases and questions with familiar words and adequate pauses. **Flowcharts** illustrate potential choices made by users of interactive multimedia applications.

To plan the proper inclusion of sound in a multimedia application, sound files should be considered in the storyboarding phase. Storyboards should designate where appropriate sound will begin and end in the multimedia application. Scripts should include details about narration and voice dialogs including what is said and how it is said. Finally, if the multimedia application is interactive, flowcharts should distinguish between which sounds are played based upon choices made by the user. Proper planning is critical to the effective incorporation of sound into a multimedia application.

Recording Sound

For simple recording projects such as narration, a microphone and computer can serve as the recording unit. **Microphones** translate analog signals into electrical impulses. Through the use of an **analog-to-digital converter (ADC),** these impulses are converted to numbers that can be stored, understood, and manipulated by a microprocessor. If music is included, a more complex system is needed.

One way to get music or other sound into the computer is to use **digital audiotape (DAT) devices.** DAT devices convert analog sound into digital sound. These high-quality digital sounds are then stored on **digital audiotape (DAT)** that is then used to get digital sounds into the computer. Audio CDs that are made from DAT tape can also be used to get digital sounds into the computer. Other options for getting digital sound into the computer include recording digital sounds directly from a synthesizer or using appropriate software to generate a digital sound file.

The most common sampling rates are 22 KHz and 44 KHz. Most software and computer systems will support both mono and stereo recording and playback with an option for either an 8-bit or 16-bit sampling size. When you choose the settings at which to record sound for a multimedia application, you must consider your own system capabilities including storage and memory capacity, as well as the capabilities of the equipment on which your multimedia application might be delivered.

When recording sound, be sure to consider the recording environment. Record in a soundproof room, or at minimum be sure to eliminate any unnecessary noise before you begin.

Processing Sound

Once the digitized sound is in the computer, it will probably need to be modified. Unwanted noise, pauses, and other mistakes may need to be removed or files may need to be trimmed. Fade-ins, fade-outs, background music, and special effects may need to be added. Pieces of sound files may need to be copied and moved, or several sound files may need to be mixed and spliced together. All of this processing must be carefully completed to create sound that is coordinated with the rest of the multimedia application.

Some digital sound processing methods change the original sound. These methods are considered **destructive** because they permanently alter original

FIGURE 5.14
Sound files can be modified just like other documents.

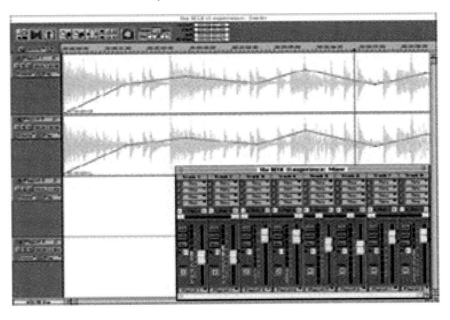

sounds. **Non-destructive** sound processing methods maintain the original file. A copy of the original file can be manipulated by playing it louder or softer, combining it with other sounds on other tracks, or modifying it in other ways. Using non-destructive processing, the original file remains untouched in case it is needed at a later time.

Incorporating Sound into the Multimedia Application

Effectively incorporating sound into a multimedia application is very important. In fact, the success of a multimedia application depends not only on sampling the appropriate sound and effectively processing it, but also on correct timing and placement within the multimedia application.

Authoring software such as Macromedia Director will allow you to pull all of the pieces of your multimedia application together. Using authoring software you can properly incorporate sound files into a multimedia application to enhance any presentation or project.

When incorporating sound into your multimedia application, accurately time narration so it occurs with the appropriate elements, keep background sounds at a volume that complements voices, and remove any unnecessary interruptions.

Delivering Sound

Once a sound has been recorded, digitized, processed, and incorporated into a multimedia application, it is ready to be delivered. So that you can hear it through your speakers, the digital sound is sent through a **digital-to-analog converter (DAC).**

Know how your sound file will be delivered before you save it. A file sampled at 22 KHz will save disk space and is adequate for most multimedia applications.

The delivery system will vary as the intended audience of the multimedia application changes. When considering the delivery of sound, you should consider the number of different sounds that will be delivered, how they will be delivered, where they will be delivered, and to whom they will be delivered. In other words, the application may include one voice and some background music designed for one user in front of a desktop computer or it may be a presentation with various different types of music, narration, and special effects designed for a larger audience to be presented in an auditorium. Regardless, a high quality delivery system will help ensure that the sounds you've worked hard to create make the right impression.

File Formats

There are many different types of digital audio file formats that have resulted from working with different computer platforms and software. Some of the better-known formats include:

WAV

WAV is the Waveform format. It is the most commonly used and supported format on the Windows platform. Developed by Microsoft, the Wave format is a subset of RIFF. RIFF is capable of sampling rates of 8 and 16 bits. With Wave, there are several different encoding methods to choose from including Wave or PCM format. Therefore, when developing sound for the Internet, it is important to make sure you use the encoding method that the player you're recommending supports.

AU

AU is the Sun Audio format. It was developed by Sun Microsystems to be used on UNIX, NeXT & Sun Sparc workstations. It is a 16-bit compressed audio format that is fairly prevalent on the Web. This is probably because it plays on the widest number of platforms.

VOX

VOX is a new proprietary Voxware ToolVox format. It is not the same as the older VOX format that's been around for a while. ToolVox offers the best compression at 53:1; however, the playback quality isn't that great.

RA

RA is Progressive Networks RealAudio format. It is very popular for streaming audio on the Internet because it offers good compression up to a factor of 18. Streaming technology enables a sound file to begin playing before the entire file has been downloaded.

AIFF

AIFF or **AIF** is Apple's Audio Interchange Format. This is the Macintosh waveform format. It is also supported on IBM compatibles and Silicon Graphics machines. The AIFF format supports a large number of sampling rates up to 32 bits.

MPEG

MPEG and **MPEG2** are the Motion Picture Experts Group formats. They are a compressed audio and video format. Some Web sites use these formats for their audio because their compression capabilities offer up to a factor of at least 14:1. These formats will probably become quite widespread as the price of hardware-based MPEG decoders continues to go down and as software decoders and faster processors become more mainstream. In addition, MPEG is a standard format.

MIDI

MIDI (MID, MDI, MFF) is an internationally accepted file format used to store Musical Instrument Digital Interface (MIDI) data. It is a format used to represent electronic music produced by a MIDI device (such as a synthesizer or electronic keyboard). This format provides instructions on how to replay music, but it does not actually record the waveform. For this reason, MIDI files are small and efficient, which is why they are often found used on the Web. On a PC, MIDI files will have a .mid extension.

TSP

TSP is DSP's TrueSpeech format. It offers a good compromise between quality and compression up to a factor of 15, while still maintaining almost original quality. Though optimized for voice, this format can also handle music.

VMF

VMF is Vocaltec's Internet Wave format. It can compress a WAV file up to 10% of the original size while still maintaining pretty good quality.

VOC

VOC is a Voice file format developed by Creative Labs for use with their Sound Blaster audio card. This format supports both compressed and uncompressed 8- and 16-bit sampling rates.

SND

SND is the Sound file format developed by Apple. It is limited to a sampling rate of 8 bits, and is used primarily within the operating system.

LCC

LCC is a fairly new waveform compression scheme from FastMan. It offers from 20:1 to over 70:1 compression for music and other audio recorded at up to 16 bit, 44 kHz, which is considered CD quality. Unfortunately, this format does not support streaming.

SMP

SMP is a format developed by Turtle Beach Systems to be used with their audio recording and editing software.

GSM or GSD

GSM and/or **GSD** are speech compression schemes originally devised for cellular phones. These formats have gained some popularity on the Internet for audio on demand and Internet telephony applications. These are quite common formats in Europe.

ALA

ALA is the AudioLink proprietary audio/video format. It claims audio compression ratios of 12:1 to 70:1.

ASFS

ASFS is a proprietary audio compression algorithm from Eurodat. It offers up to 130:1 compression.

ROL

ROL is the Roll file format. It is a proprietary format developed by AdLib, Inc for use with its sound cards. It stores sound files in a format similar to MIDI.

RIFF

RIFF stands for Resource Interchange File Format. Microsoft developed it. This format can contain a variety of data types including digital audio and MIDI.

DCR

DCR is a Macromedia "Shocked" Director Movie format that can include audio. To play these files from a Web page, the shockwave plug-in must be installed. This technology will be further discussed in Chapter 8.

Sound Designer II

Sound Designer II is an ideal file format for creating CD masters.

If you want your multimedia application to work on Macs as well as PCs, you will probably want to save your files using either the Audio Interchange File Format (AIFF) or the Musical Instrument Digital Interface (MIDI) file format. Though Macromedia Director and most authoring programs support many different sound file formats, if you plan to include sound in your multimedia application (and of course you should), consider using the AIFF format. Not only is it a cross-platform format, it can also reside outside the multimedia application. This means the multimedia file will be smaller and will therefore play faster. In addition, the AIFF format can be used if you plan to burn the multimedia application onto a CD.

Compression

Compression is a technique that mathematically reduces the size of a file. Compression can be beneficial for storing and transferring sound files. There are several different compression rates that can be applied to sound files; however, at this time, there are no standards for compressing and decompressing digital audio. For 8-bit sound, the MACE and MacroMind compression rates are available.

MACE stands for Macintosh Audio Compression/Expansion. The 3:1 MACE compression scheme is useful for music files while 6:1 MACE is adequate for voice only.

The 4:1 MacroMind compression scheme should only be used for voice recordings. An 8:1 MacroMind is also available. It offers the maximum compression permissible for voice only.

When working with 16-bit sound, you can use 2:1 μ-Law, which is often used on Web pages and with .au files, or the 4:1 IMA/ADPCM compression rate. In fact, if you plan to use audio simply to enhance a Web site, rather than to broadcast or serve audio in volume, consider recording the original clip in 11 kHz, 8-bit or 16-bit monotone, and save it in μ-Law AU format. In addition, voice-overs don't need to be any greater than 11 kHz. By doing so, the clip is small in file size and also widely playable. In fact, you should be able to keep most clips below 25 KB in size.

Software

Traditional sound studio equipment used to record, mix, and edit audio costs tens of thousands of dollars. With audio software, you can create sound for your multimedia application for much less money.

FIGURE 5.15
Compression can be used to reduce the file size.

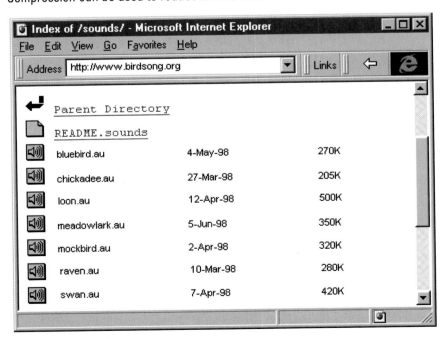

There are many different types of audio tools. The Windows 95 Sound Recorder is free, and other off-the-shelf WAV recorders and converters that allow you to change the audio file format often come with your PC or multimedia package. **Cool Edit** for Windows 95 is considered one of the best shareware packages. Game developers have used it to record the audio for games such as Doom. It provides everything needed to create basic audio files.

If your audio authoring needs are more sophisticated, there are several excellent professional audio-authoring packages available. **Soundry's Sound Forge** for the PC, and **Digidesign's Pro Tools** and **Macromedia SoundEdit 16** for the Mac are some examples of professional audio packages.

SoundEdit 16

Macromedia's SoundEdit 16 is the leading digital audio editor for the Macintosh platform. SoundEdit 16 is ideal for manipulation of single sound files. It also enables you to record, edit, and play back 16-bit, 44kHz multitrack soundtracks. Using SoundEdit 16 you can modify many sound properties including volume, pitch, and tempo. Sounds modified with SoundEdit can be added to any multimedia application, including Web pages and QuickTime® soundtracks.

SoundEdit 16 supports more file formats (SoundEdit 16, SoundEdit Resource, SoundEdit, Instrument, Audio IFF [AIFF], Sound Designer II, System 7 Sound, WAVE [.WAV], QuickTime Movie) than any other audio application. It also enables you to digitally capture music and sound directly from Red Book Audio CDs. **Red Book** is the international storage standard for compact disc audio. It allows audio segments on CDs to be addressed by minutes, seconds, and frames.

When first opened, SoundEdit 16 will appear with an empty, untitled window, a control palette, and a selection window.

The SoundEdit 16 window includes a title bar, track information, rulers that measure time and amplitude, and a waveform area. At the bottom of the window

FIGURE 5.16

SoundEdit 16 opens with an untitled window and a control palette.

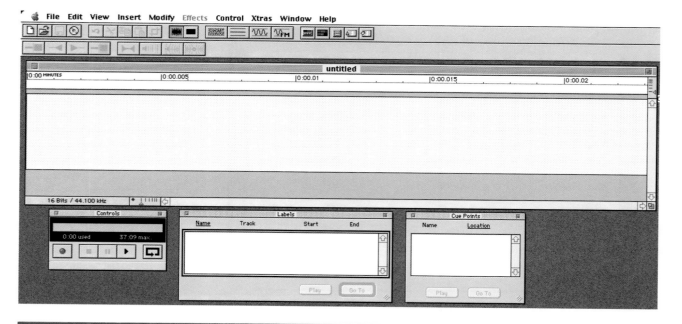

is the CD-quality, default sound format settings of 16 bits / 44 kHz. These settings measure how well SoundEdit 16 will record the audio input.

The Control palette looks like a set of buttons found on a CD player or tape recorder. The Selection window displays the location of the cursor and the portion of the sound file that has been selected.

VISUALLY ANALYZE SOUNDS

Once a sound has been recorded or opened, the sound is displayed in the SoundEdit 16 window. In this window, time displays horizontally from left to right, while amplitude displays vertically from top to bottom.

EDIT AUDIO FILES

SoundEdit allows you to manipulate audio files or portions of audio files by changing the volume, pitch, and tempo.

Portions of the soundfile can be selected by dragging over the sound file or entering numbers into the value boxes in the Selection window. Once selected, portions of the file can be cut, copied, or otherwise modified.

The first value is the time (in milliseconds) where the selection begins, the second value is the time where the selection ends, and the third value is the total amount of time selected.

APPLY SPECIAL EFFECTS

You can add special sound effects from within SoundEdit or from plug-ins developed by third parties. From the Effects Menu, there are many special effects that

FIGURE 5.17

In the SoundEdit 16 window, time displays horizontally while amplitude displays vertically.

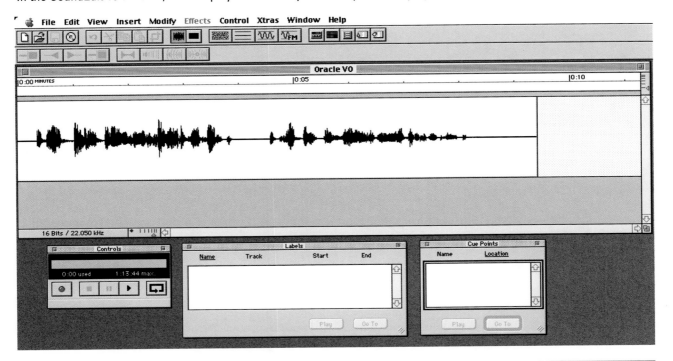

FIGURE 5.18

Clicking the Play button in the Control palette will play the loaded sound.

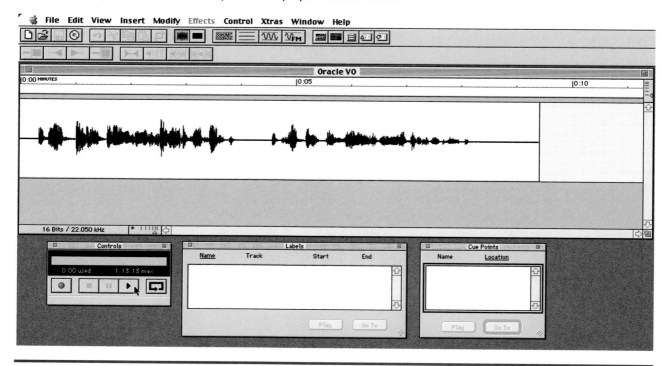

FIGURE 5.19

The Selection palette displays the selected portion of the sound file.

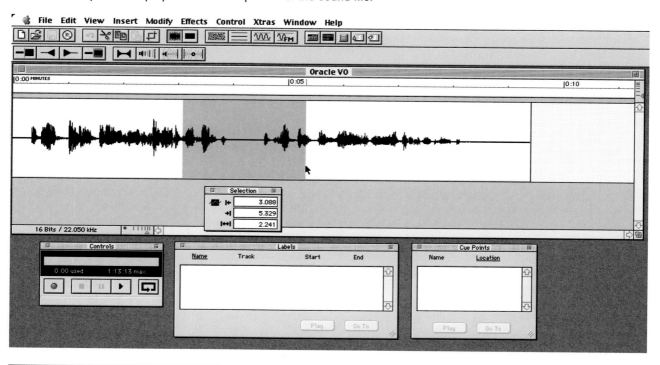

can be applied to a sound file or a portion of a sound to emphasize a point, stimulate emotions, define space, and add realism.

- **Fades**—You can set the file to fade in and out. Fades are effective in providing a professional transition from one sound to another. Generally, fade in is applied at the beginning of the sound file and fade out is applied at the end.

- **Envelopes**—You can apply envelopes to stereo files. Envelopes transmit the sound from the left speaker to the right speaker or from a rear speaker to a front speaker.

- **Equalizer**—By using the equalizer, you can control the bass and treble as well as emphasize and stretch frequencies.

- **Echo and reverberation**—Echo and reverberation effects make audio files sound as if they were recorded in a stadium, a concert hall, or even outer space.

- **Pitch shift**—This effect allows you to actually change the sound. It is particularly effective in altering voices so that they sound entirely different from the original.

- **Normalize**—Normalize amplifies a sound file to its maximum value without distorting the sound.

- **Backward**—You can play a sound file backward with this effect.

- **Tempo**—Change the tempo or speed at which the sound file plays by using the tempo effect.

These are just a few of the many effects that can help you create just the right sound for your multimedia application. With third-party plug-ins, the possibilities are really unlimited. The biggest drawback to using effects and one of SoundEdit 16's few downfalls is the length of time required to process effects.

CREATE MULTITRACK AUDIO FILES

Using SoundEdit 16 you can modify one sound file at a time. In modifying and mixing sound files, you can also cut, copy and paste entire sound files or pieces of sound files from one file to another. Once you have the sound files you want you can add tracks of sound files and then mix them into one mono or stereo file. For example, a sound file that includes narrations or voice-overs can be added with another track that contains background music.

Deck II

Macromedia's DECK II is another powerful desktop audio tool that serves as a software-only recording studio.

CREATE MULTITRACK AUDIO FILES

If you are interested in multitrack recording and complex audio arrangement, DECK II is the tool you need. With Deck II you can listen to and mix multiple tracks, which makes Deck II superior to SoundEdit 16 when you are working with multiple tracks. In addition, unlike SoundEdit 16, Deck II allows you to record a track while playing the audio from other tracks. The number of tracks you can work with at one time is only limited by the memory and storage capacity of your computer system. With a powerful computer system and lots of RAM, you can listen to up to 30 tracks at the same time you are recording up to 500.

FIGURE 5.20
Many different special effects can be applied to your sound file.

USE NON-DESTRUCTIVE SOUND PROCESSING

In general, sound processing in Deck II is non-destructive. The files you record are only changed for screen display. The original files are left unchanged. If a change is destructive, Deck II alerts you with an on-screen warning. Because Deck II saves 16-bit, 44 KHz files, and keeps the original file, you will also want lots of storage space and fast access to take advantage of these features.

RECORD AND PLAY CD-QUALITY AUDIO

Though Deck II offers many of the same features found in SoundEdit 16, it also permits professional-quality audio CD recording without the expensive equipment found in a traditional sound studio.

EDIT WAVEFORM FILES AND CREATE MULTITRACK AUDIO FILES

Along with many of the same editing features found in SoundEdit 16, Deck II offers you superior control by allowing you to set the volume and apply **pan envelopes** to each track independent of the others. Pan envelopes determine how the music will be heard (from the left, right, back, or front) through a stereo system. Because all of these settings are completed digitally, there is no loss of fidelity in the editing process.

After processing, the sound files from each track can be mixed down to create a stereo file that contains pre-set volume and pan settings. This file can then be used in a multimedia application or burned to a track on an audio CD.

MIDI FUNCTIONALITY

Deck II is also MIDI compatible. In addition to processing and editing digital audio files, you can use Deck II to modify sounds created from MIDI instruments including synthesizers and keyboards.

FIGURE 5.21

Deck II can be used to create professional-quality CDs.

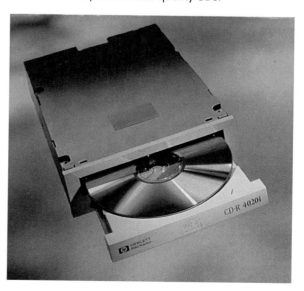

SOPHISTICATED SMPTE SYNCHRONIZATION

Deck II allows you to synchronize a music file to a video clip. By using the professional **SMPTE** code, beats of music are set to match changes in video for all standard video frame rates.

By using both Deck II and SoundEdit 16, you have a comprehensive audio solution for sound editing and synchronization directly from your desktop.

Sound Forge

Soundry's Sound Forge is very similar to SoundEdit 16, however, Sound Forge is designed for the PC platform. Most of the features available in SoundEdit 16 are also available in Sound Forge.

Wave Studio

Wave Studio by Creative Labs is similar to Macromedia's SoundEdit 16 and Sound Forge. It comes with Sound Blaster sound cards and is only available on the PC platform.

Third-Party Plug-ins

There are a number of plug-ins for Macromedia's SoundEdit 16 and Deck II. These plug-ins extend the functionality of audio-editing programs by adding additional sound effects. Some of the common plug-ins include **CyberSoundFX Audio filters** and **InVision Native Power Pack**.

Authoring Software

Once you have sampled and processed the sound, you are ready to incorporate it into your multimedia application. To do this, you need an authoring tool. Simple

FIGURE 5.22

Deck II uses SMPTE code to set the beats of the music to the video.

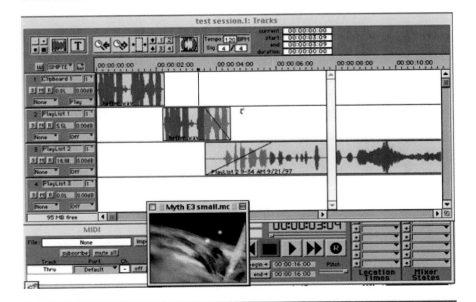

FIGURE 5.23

Microsoft PowerPoint allows you to incorporate sound into simple presentations.

presentation programs such as **Microsoft PowerPoint** or **Adobe Persuasion** allow you to play sounds over a slide or add sounds to bulleted items or transitions that take you from one slide to another.

At the next level are authoring programs that allow you to navigate from card to card in a non-linear fashion. These programs include **HyperCard, HyperStudio,** and **Toolbook.** With these authoring programs, you can program sound to occur when a certain action takes place. For example, a sound may play when the user presses a button or transmits from one card to another.

More advanced multimedia authoring packages offer powerful, but complex features designed for professionals. Included in this category are programs such as **mFactory's mTropolis** and **Macromedia's Authorware** and **Director.** Because these programs are quite extensive, they take a significant amount of time to learn. Many professionals who have used these programs every day for years claim that they still don't know or take advantage of all the features available. Though Director is the industry standard for multimedia development, all of these programs allow you to incorporate sound into a multimedia application created for either the Macintosh or PC platform.

Among other things, when choosing a multimedia authoring tool, you should consider the multimedia application, the audience, how your project will be delivered, your budget, and how much time you have to learn the authoring tool. Once you have selected an authoring tool, there will still be many different ways of incorporating sound into your multimedia application depending upon the content and how you plan to present it. The bottom line is that it takes patience to incorporate sound effectively into a multimedia application.

Because Macromedia Director is the industry standard for incorporating sound into multimedia applications, let's take a look at how you can add sound to your multimedia application using the features in Macromedia Director. Similar features are found in other programs.

FIGURE 5.24

The multimedia elements, including sound, interact on the Director Stage.

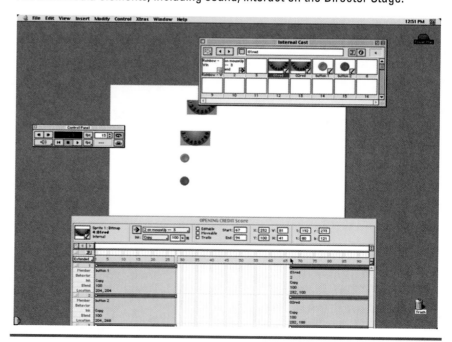

As discussed in Chapter 4, Director uses the theater as a metaphor. Using this metaphor, multimedia elements become **cast members** that are added to the **Stage.** The Stage is where all of the elements interact. In Director, sound files are considered cast members. As cast members, Director allows you to include these internal sound files directly into the multimedia application. Another option is to have Director access external sound files as the multimedia application plays. This keeps the multimedia file size to a minimum.

Before you make a sound file a cast member in Director, the file should be sampled and edited using programs such as Macromedia's SoundEdit 16 or Deck II. In other words, at this stage in the process, the sound should be ready to go.

IMPORTING SOUNDS

Importing is probably the easiest way to get sound into the multimedia application you are creating with Macromedia Director. By choosing Import from the File Menu, you can select the sound file you wish to be a cast member. After you select the file and choose Import, the sound file automatically appears as a cast member in the **Cast window.**

From the Cast window, the sound file will be moved to the **Score.** If you recall from Chapter 4, the Score provides the details of each cast member's location and action at any point within the movie. Once in the Score, the sound file is considered a **Sprite** or image of the original file that is now part of the action in the movie.

In the Score, the sound file or Sprite will be placed into one of two **Audio Channels.** Generally, one of the audio channels is reserved for voice and special sound effects while the other is used for background music. If two different sounds are placed in the same frame on different channels, the sounds will play at the same time. In order to create an appropriate effect, you will want to make sure the

FIGURE 5.25

An imported sound automatically appears as a cast member in the Cast window.

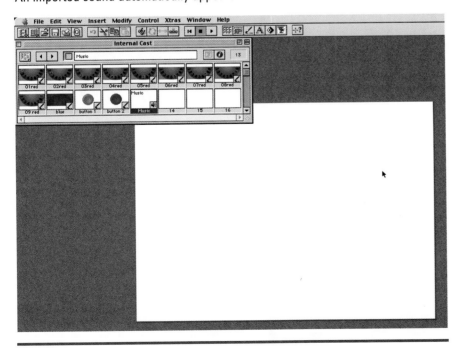

FIGURE 5.26

A Lingo script allows you to adjust the volume of a sound file.

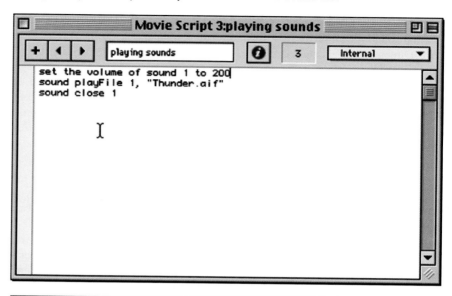

volume is set so that the narration is heard over the background music. The appropriate volume should be set during the recording process; however, if you need to make slight adjustments in the volume level of either sound, you can write a **Lingo** script that instructs Director to take a certain action. From Chapter 4, you'll remember that Lingo is the programming language used in Director. In

FIGURE 5.27

The sound file will be moved to one of two audio channels within the Score.

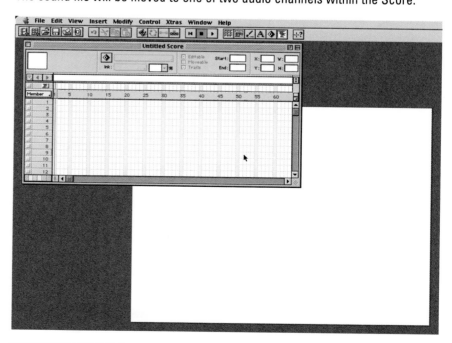

the Score window of the Director movie, you will place the Lingo script in the cell of the **Script Channel** where you want the volume of the sound to be adjusted.

In the Score, the sound file may need to be copied across multiple **frames,** which represent the amount of time that the sound file will play.

Once the sound file or Sprite has been included in cells within the appropriate audio channels across the appropriate number of frames, the Director movie including the sound can be played.

USING EXTERNAL SOUNDS

Importing sounds is the easiest way to include them in a multimedia application, but using external sounds is the easiest way to play sound files that are not included in a multimedia application. If file size is a concern, you should consider keeping sound files external to the multimedia application and only accessing these files when the application is ready to play them. By keeping sound files outside the multimedia application, Macromedia Director is able to process the multimedia application more efficiently.

To use external sounds, save them using the AIFF file format and place them in the same folder or subdirectory where the multimedia application is being stored. In the Score window of the Director movie, place a **Lingo** script in the cell of the **Script channel** where you want the sound to begin playing.

Another advantage of using external sound files, is that you are no longer limited to just two audio channels because Lingo scripts have their own channel.

Players

If an audio file has been created for the Web, a player must be used to hear the file. Many players come standard with the operating system or Web browser, others must be installed. Netscape Navigator and Communicator provide bundled support for playing AIFF, AU, MIDI, and WAV audio formats while the newest

FIGURE 5.28

In the Lingo script you specify which external file Director should access.

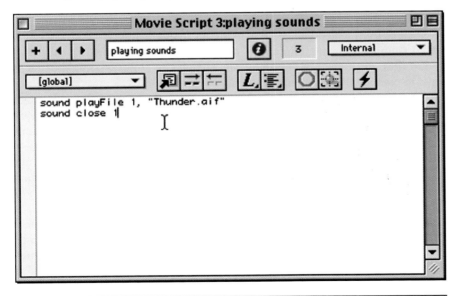

version of Microsoft Internet Explorer provides bundled support for streamed playback of AIFF, AU, MIDI, WAV, and MPEG audio. Some of the common players include the **PCM WAV** player that comes installed with every off-the-shelf PC. **WPLANY** plays AU, WAV, AIFF, and other formats transparently. The **RealAudio** player is needed to play RA formatted files.

SUMMARY

We acquire a great deal of knowledge through our sense of hearing. Sound enhances a multimedia application and today's technology makes it possible for the average person to include sound in multimedia applications.

A sound is a **waveform.** In multimedia applications, sounds are either **content sounds** that supply information or **ambient sounds** such as background music that sets the mood. Sound adds another dimension to a multimedia application. If used well, sound is an extremely powerful element that can be used to get attention, to entertain, to give directions, to personalize an interface, or to convey an educational or persuasive message.

Sound can be effectively added to multimedia applications designed for computer-based training, education, advertising and marketing, entertainment and games, and the Web. On the Web, audio is either **downloaded** or **streamed.** Other applications of sound on the Web include **one-way audio, Internet audio e-mail** or **voice mail,** and **Internet audioconferencing** or **Internet telephony.**

Because sound is so important to a multimedia project, you should consider hiring audio specialists who are responsible for recording and processing quality audio files at the appropriate **rate** and **resolution.** Audio specialists help ensure that the **mono** or **stereo** sound selected creates a multimedia application that is credible and effective.

Analog sound is a continuous stream of sound waves. The process of converting analog sounds into numbers that a computer can understand is called **digitizing** or **sound sampling.** Analog sounds that have been converted to numbers are **digital sounds.** Digital sounds can be **waveform audio, MIDI, compact disc audio,** or **3D.**

Sources from which you can obtain digital sound include creating your own **MIDI sound files,** using **clip audio,** using **CD audio,** or **recording your own sound files.** Regardless of the source and complexity of the recording, you will need to plan your audio carefully.

Once the digitized sound is in the computer, it will need to be processed. There are two types of digital sound processing methods. Processing methods that permanently alter original sounds are considered **destructive** while **nondestructive** sound processing methods maintain the original file.

There are many different types of digital audio file formats. If you want your multimedia application to work on Macs as well as PCs, you will probably want to save your files using either the **Audio Interchange File Format (AIFF)** or the **Musical Instrument Digital Interface (MIDI)** file format.

Different programs are available for recording and processing digital sound. **Macromedia's SoundEdit 16** and **Deck II** are powerful, professional programs that provide a comprehensive audio solution for sound editing and synchronization directly from your desktop. A number of third-party plug-ins are also available for these programs.

Authoring programs used to incorporate sound into a multimedia application range from simple presentation programs such as **Microsoft PowerPoint** to more advanced multimedia authoring packages such as **Macromedia's Authorware** and **Director.** A high quality delivery system will help ensure that the sounds you've worked hard to create make the appropriate impression.

KEY TERMS

Waveform
Frequency
Content sounds
Streamed
Internet audioconferenc-
  ing
Stereo sounds
Analog sound
Waveform audio
Surround sound
CD audio
Scripts
Destructive
SoundEdit 16

Amplitude
Hertz (Hz)
Ambient sounds
One-way audio
Internet telephony
Rate
Digitizing
MIDI
3D sound
Storyboards
Microphones
Non-destructive
Deck II
Decibels

Kilohertz (kHz)
Downloaded
Internet audio e-mail
Mono sounds
Resolution
Sound sampling
Compact disc audio
Clip audio
Flowcharts
Digital audio tape
  (DAT)
AIFF
Multitrack audio files

Matching Questions

a. frequency   **b.** amplitude   **c.** decibel

d. rate   **e.** resolution   **f.** analog sound

g. clip audio   **h.** digital sounds   **i.** destructive

j. compression   **k.** red book   **l.** ambient

_____ **1.** The distance between the valley and the peak of a waveform.

_____ **2.** The number of peaks that occur in one second.

_____ **3.** This is a continuous stream of sound waves.

_____ **4.** The smallest variation in amplitude that can be detected by the human ear.

_____ **5.** Prerecorded digital audio clips of music and sound effects.

_____ **6.** The number of waveform samples per second.

_____ **7.** A technique that mathematically reduces the size of a file.

_____ **8.** Sound processing methods that permanently alter original sounds.

_____ **9.** Analog sounds that have been converted to numbers.

_____ **10.** The number of binary bits processed for each measurement.

_____ **11.** Sounds that reinforce messages and set the mood.

_____ **12.** The international storage standard for compact disc audio.

Fill-In Questions

1. Audio on the Web can either be _____ or _____.

2. _____ _____ are flat and unrealistic compared to _____ _____, which are much more dynamic and lifelike.

3. _____ translate analog signals into electrical impulses. Through the use of an _____, these impulses are converted to numbers that can be stored, understood, and manipulated by a microprocessor.

4. One way to get music or other sound into the computer is to use _____ _____ _____ _____. DAT devices convert analog sound into digital sound. These high-quality digital sounds are then stored on _____ _____ _____, which is then used to get digital sounds into the computer.

5. Progressive Networks _____ format is very popular for streaming audio on the Internet because it offers good compression.

6. _____ _____ is the most commonly used and supported format on the Windows platform. Developed by Microsoft, the _____ _____ is a subset of RIFF that is capable of sampling rates of 8 and 16 bits.

7. The _____ _____ format was developed by Sun Microsystems to be used on UNIX, NeXT and Sun Sparc workstations.

8. _____ _____ determine how the music will be heard (from the left, right, back, or front) through a stereo system.

9. By using the professional _____ code, beats of music are set to match changes in video for all standard video frame rates.

10. _____ _____ _____ is very similar to SoundEdit 16, however, it is designed for the PC platform.

DISCUSSION QUESTIONS

1. When creating multimedia applications, how do content sounds differ from ambient sounds? When are music and special sound effects considered content sound?

2. Why is a high-quality microphone important when you are recording sound for a multimedia application?

3. If you are developing a cross-platform multimedia application, which sound file format should you use? Why?

4. What is the difference between destructive and non-destructive sound processing?

5. Why is it important to edit sound files before incorporating them into your multimedia application?

6. Why are external sounds more efficient than imported sounds?

7. Why shouldn't you use sound files of different resolutions within the same

multimedia application?

8. Why isn't it always best to use the highest sampling rate and highest resolution when recording sound files.

HANDS-ON EXERCISES

1. Visit http://www.mpmusic.com/. If your browser is set up correctly, you should be able to listen to Real Audio files. Choose one and try it. If it doesn't work, follow the instructions to properly set up your browser to play Real Audio files. How long did it take before the sound file began playing? How large was the sound file? How would you rate the sound quality?

2. Visit http://www.wantree.com.au/~richmond/simpsons.htm. Download any sound file and play it. What type of sound files are these? How long did it take to download the sound file? How large was the sound file? How would you rate the sound quality?

3. Visit http://www.prs.net/midi.html#index. Play any MIDI file. How long did it take before the sound file began playing? How would you rate the sound quality? How long did the sound file play?

Case Study Chapter 5

The audio on this Web site needs to follow the same fast-and-fun theme as the graphics and animation. Sean Coleman will be the audio specialist on this project.

Sean will record the sound of revving engines from jet skis, waverunners, and other personal watercraft. Sean needs to record these sounds instead of using a synthesizer to create them. This is because it is difficult for synthesizers to recreate realistic engine sounds. However, he will use the synthesizer and MIDI files to create the sounds of rushing and splashing water.

Once the sounds have been recorded or created and sampled or digitized so that the computer's microprocessor can understand them, Sean will use Macromedia's SoundEdit 16 to process the sounds. In processing the sounds, Sean will trim the sounds, add a fade at the beginning as the engine begins to rev, and modify the volume of the audio as needed. Sean will then work closely with Wendy to synchronize these sounds with the animated personal watercraft GIFs.

As viewers and listeners at the Island Watercraft Web site click on one of the animated watercraft navigation buttons, the watercraft will rev its engine before jumping a wave, completing a 360-degree turn, or speeding off into the sunset. As the watercraft speeds off, viewers and listeners will hear the sound of water splashing from the wake.

In addition to sound effects for the animated watercraft, Sean will also have the background music from the SeaDoo TV commercials playing. As viewers and listeners exit the site, they will hear a final, loud "SeaDoo," followed by a faded soft narration whispering "at Island Watercraft."

Before Sean can use the music from the SeaDoo TV commercials, Digital Design must obtain permission and signatures of release or licensing agreements from SeaDoo. These release agreements will specify how, where, when, and for how long the music can be used on Island Watercraft's site. If the page is modified at a later date and the music is altered in any way, another release form will need to be signed by SeaDoo.

Video

1. Understand the importance of video in a multimedia application
2. Define some of the basic terminology associated with video, including CAV, CLV, DVD, VHS, S-VHS, Hi-8, Betacam SP, DV, and hypervideo
3. List several applications of video
4. Describe the different types of video
5. Define frame rate as it relates to video quality
6. Explain where video should be included in the planning process
7. Describe several methods of recording analog or digital video
8. Describe the roles and responsibilities of the video specialist
9. Explain the difference between destructive and non-destructive video processing
10. Describe how video is incorporated into a multimedia application
11. List the key considerations for delivering high-quality video
12. List and describe several of the more common video file formats
13. Define compression and describe some of the most commonly used compression schemes or CODECs
14. List and describe some of the key features found in Adobe Premiere
15. List and describe some of the key features found in Adobe After Effects
16. List and describe some of the key features found in Macromedia Director that pertain to video

Introduction

Video gives you the power to communicate with motion and sound and serves as a rich resource in multimedia applications. Video is incredibly stimulating. It combines the vibrant colors and interesting shapes of graphics with motion and sound and conveys a realism that can't be found in animation. Video **is** multimedia, and as technology improves, it is becoming more common in multimedia applications including Web pages.

In the past, video-editing equipment was too costly for the average person to purchase. Consequently, producing video used to be limited to professional video production studios. Though this high-cost equipment was not prohibitive for professional facilities that could pass the cost on to clients and amortize investments over a long period of time, it was prohibitive for the masses.

Today, video technology has become more affordable. With the introduction of desktop tools and several other new technologies, users have everything they need to manipulate video and create high quality images at a fraction of the cost of professional equipment. This new, affordable video editing equipment provides unlimited creative control because it puts the power of the technology in the hands of the creative.

Frame Rate

Video is really nothing more than a sequence of individual images or frames displayed fast enough to create the illusion of motion. In other words, because the frames are moving too fast for the brain to register each individual image, video tricks the brain into thinking still images are moving. The **frame rate** is the speed at which individual frames display. Frames displayed at 24 to 30 **frames per second (fps)** appear continuous. Frames displayed at a slower rate appear choppy.

Video Standards

Frame rates vary because there are different video standards used throughout the world.

FIGURE 6.1

When displayed fast enough, this sequence of images tricks the brain into thinking there is motion.

NTSC

NTSC stands for **National Television Standard Committee.** According to the standard established by this organization, video signals have a rate of 30 fps (29.97 to be exact) and a single frame of video consists of 525 horizontal lines. The television and video industries in the United States and Japan have adopted the NTSC standard.

PAL

PAL stands for **phase alternating line.** According to this standard, video signals have a frame rate of 25 fps and a single frame of video consists of 625 horizontal lines. PAL is the most common television and video standard in Europe, South Africa, the United Kingdom, and Australia.

SECAM

SECAM stands for **sequential color and memory.** The basic technology and broadcasting techniques offered by SECAM are different from NTSC and PAL. Unlike NTSC and PAL, SECAM measures the speed of video in Hertz. The standard speed is 50 Hz with 625 horizontal lines per screen. SECAM is used in France, Russia, and several other countries.

HDTV

HDTV stands for **High Definition Television.** This video standard supports a resolution of 1,200 horizontal lines with an aspect ratio (length: width) of 16:9. Japan, Europe, and the United States have all developed different standards for HDTV.

Tracks

Several different tracks are used to store video information. One of the tracks stores the visual images while other tracks are reserved for the audio and time-code

FIGURE 6.2

One track stores the visual images while other tracks store the audio and time code signals.

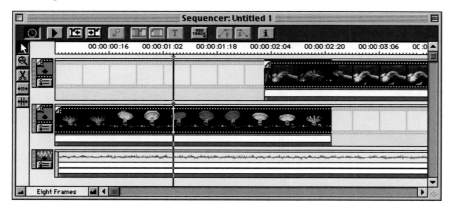

signals. The Time Code track is used to synchronize all of the components. The standard time code is called **SMPTE** because it was developed by the **Society of Motion Picture and Television Engineers.**

SMPTE measures video in hours, minutes, seconds, and frames. This system of measurement enables the audio specialist to synchronize voice, music, and sound effects to the appropriate frames of video based on the frame rate.

Types of Video

There are several different types of video that can either be captured and used as digital video, or accessed while a multimedia application is running.

Videotape

Videotapes can be used in multimedia to capture or deliver video. Multimedia links can be created that access a videotape in a VCR (in the video editing industry you may see VCR referred to as a VTR [video tape recorder]) and enable users to view a video segment directly from videotape.

The biggest advantage to using videotape and VCRs is their abundance. Almost everyone has one. There are, however, some disadvantages to viewing and digitizing video from a VCR. Because videotapes are linear, you must either fast-forward or rewind to get to the video segment you are interested in viewing or digitizing. Though some of the newer videotape players are computer controllable, most of those in existence today are not. This means that in addition to using fast-forward and rewind to get to a video segment, you also have to get there manually. This can be time consuming. It can also be difficult to get the tape to stop at just the right video frame.

Today, videotape is more likely to be used in capturing video than playing video. Provided you have the right computer setup, including a video capture card as discussed in Chapter 2, you can digitize from videotape directly into your computer. If you do use videotape for recording, you'll want a high quality video camera. The following are lists of the most commonly used videotape formats.

FIGURE 6.3

The disadvantage of video tape is that it is linear, so you must rewind or fast-forward to get to the frame you want to view.

THE ANALOG FORMATS INCLUDE:

- **VHS** is the most common video format found on the consumer market. Due to the low quality of this format, VHS isn't really a usable format in video editing.
- **S-VHS** is a higher quality format than VHS, but slightly lower quality than Hi-8. This format can be used for video editing.
- **Hi-8** is the highest quality videotape format found in the consumer market. Tapes from this format are smaller than VHS and S-VHS. For video editing, this format is superior to VHS and S-VHS. It is the best choice for nonprofessionals who want good quality video.
- **Betacam SP** is a high-quality, component video format used in professional video editing. Betacam offers a much higher resolution than the other formats.

THE DIGITAL FORMATS INCLUDE:

- **D1, D2,** and **D3** are three common digital standards. D1 is not suitable for video editing. Professional video editors and television studios use the other digital formats.
- **DV** is Sony's new **Digital Video** recording format that has been set as the standard by the major producers of video camera technologies. DV offers smaller 1/4-inch tapes while delivering higher quality images than Betacam SP.

Videodisk

Videodisks or **laser disks** provide a random access alternative to videotape. In other words, videodisks allow you to access any segment of video without having to fast-forward or rewind to that segment in a linear fashion. This makes using videodisk faster and more accurate than videotape. In addition, the cost of

FIGURE 6.4

Hi-8 is the highest quality video format found in the consumer market.

producing a videodisk has dropped and continues to drop. Consequently, videodisks have become the more effective and more common method of providing video to multimedia applications. However, they are analog technology.

There are three industry formats used for videodisks: **CAV, CLV,** and most recently, **DVD,** which we discussed in Chapter 2. CAV disks store up to 30 minutes (54,000 still frames) of motion video with stereo sound. With CAV, in addition to playing full motion video, you can display each still frame. Each frame has an address from 1 to 54,000.

CLV disks store up to an hour of video on each side of the disk. Though CLV can store twice as much video as CAV, most video players won't allow you to show still frames from the CLV disks.

DVD, "Digital Versatile Disk," will undoubtedly overshadow both CAV and CLV in the next year. If you recall our discussion from Chapter 2, we mentioned that DVDs have tremendous storage capacity ranging from 4.7 GB to 17 GB. DVDs offer up to four hours of digital video. In addition, the quality of video on a DVD is clearer and sharper than any other format.

Live Video Feed

Television and live video camera feed can also be digitized or directly accessed from a multimedia link. As links within multimedia applications, they become real-time objects that can offer surprising and interesting content in a multimedia application. For example, an educational multimedia application may include a direct link to a PBS station, or a specific PBS video segment may be digitized and included in a multimedia application.

Digital Video

Digital video is video that is already in a digital format. It may have been digitized using one of the original video types listed above, or it may have been digitally

FIGURE 6.5

A DVD offers significantly more storage capacity than a CD.

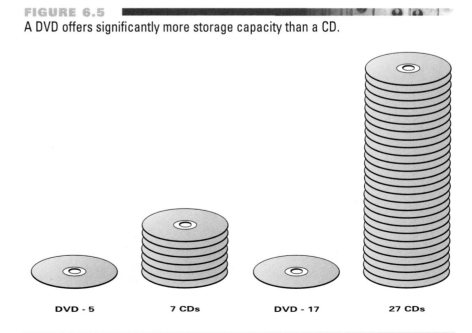

| DVD - 5 | 7 CDs | DVD - 17 | 27 CDs |

recorded using one of the new digital video cameras that have recently appeared. Manufacturers such as Sony and Panasonic are shipping these high quality, professional video cameras under the names **DVCam** and **DVCPro.** Because these cameras use digital storage and some use digital transfer technology, no quality is lost when the media is edited or copied. Because of the high quality images and ease of use, DVC is being rapidly accepted in the professional video market. It is also expected to succeed in the consumer market.

Because it has already been digitized, digital video offers many advantages over videotape, videodisk, and live video feed. Like other forms of non-linear media, frames can be randomly accessed. In addition, digital video can be controlled by the computer and can be transmitted from computer to computer over networks.

When video is included in a multimedia application, it is either synched to run on its own at a given time, or users can choose to play the video at their convenience. When a video clip is set up to trigger another multimedia event, it is called **hypervideo.**

Always remember that video falls under the copyright protection laws. If you intend to use someone else's video segment in a multimedia application, be sure to get permission, and carefully read the licensing agreement.

QuickTime

QuickTime by Apple is a software-based video-delivery system. It is an engine that allows you to deliver multimedia and video on the computer without using additional hardware. QuickTime is an excellent engine for playing most multimedia files, but it is particularly well suited for video. It is **time-based** rather than frame-based. This means that QuickTime has multiple tracks each containing different media that can be played for different periods of time. For example, one track may contain video, another track may contain sound, and a third track may contain text. Multiple tracks are helpful if you have a multimedia application designed to be heard in two different languages. In this case, each language resides on its own track. Because QuickTime is time-based, each event on each track can be played for a variable length of time by storing the data and information denoting its duration in just one frame.

FIGURE 6.6

Digital Video cameras store video in a digital format.

DCR-TRV7 OPEN & CLOSED WITH REMOTE

FIGURE 6.7

QuickTime is time based, which means multiple tracks store different types of data.

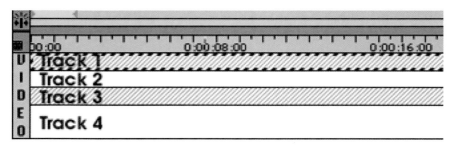

QuickTime supports a wide variety of media file formats and media encodings discussed later in this chapter. Included in this list are **digital audio, MIDI, compact disk,** and digital video including the **MPEG** (Motion Pictures Experts Group) standard. QuickTime also has the ability to work with **AVI** files. This means Windows users can have the power and flexibility of the QuickTime architecture without leaving their existing media content behind. QuickTime is able to work directly with the digital media streams from digital cameras. This means that QuickTime applications are immediately enabled to work with DVC media, including the ability to edit different DVC clips without losing data.

Similarly, QuickTime provides the ability to work with nearly any video compression format through its Image Compression Manager. The QuickTime software architecture has the ability to work with a wide range of digital media file formats and video compression formats. QuickTime even offers built-in support for the newest **DV** standard.

QuickTime Movies can be used to store NTSC, PAL, and film frame rate video. QuickTime Movies can also be used for MPEG, CD-ROM, and Internet video. Furthermore, because there is no upper limit on the frame rate of a QuickTime movie, it is an ideal format for high-frame-rate animation, and it is ready to support future digital video standards, which may enable even higher frame rates. QuickTime can also handle cross-platform video because it is available on Windows machines and as an extension on the Mac.

Early on, QuickTime videos were very tiny, about 1/16 of a screen or the size of a postage stamp. Though you can now deliver full-motion video on the entire screen of a 14" monitor with a resolution of 640×480 pixels, the optimum screen size for multimedia applications is about a quarter of the screen. QuickTime provides a comprehensive, flexible, and integrated set of media services to creators and developers working with video, CD-ROM, or the Internet. The QuickTime Movie format has become the most widely adopted format for publishing digital video on the Internet.

Uses of Video

Incorporating video into a multimedia application requires planning and attention to detail. Because video includes graphics, motion, and sound, it **is** multimedia. Of the multimedia elements, video has the greatest potential to impact the audience. As a multimedia element, video possesses great promise for use in multimedia applications because it adds multiple dimensions to an application.

FIGURE 6.8

At this time, displaying full-motion QuickTime movies at approximately one-quarter of the full screen size is optimum. It is less taxing on your processing, and you can still see the navigation buttons.

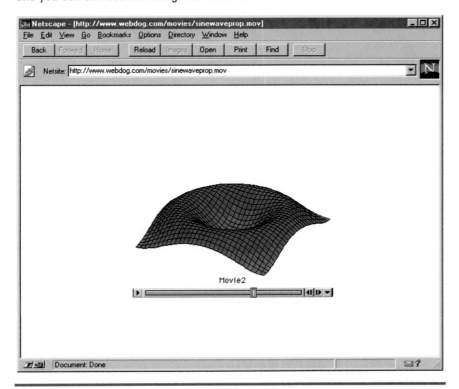

Video can stimulate emotions, convey messages, provide instructions, demonstrate techniques, and relate experiences. However, its appeal is weighted toward emotive rather than cognitive functions. Though it "grabs" attention, users soon become conditioned and inattentive. As always, balance is important. You should use video where it is appropriate. Because the inclusion of video in multimedia applications requires powerful processors and large amounts of storage, you should never use video if it does not add to the application.

Computer-Based Training Programs

Video is very effective in computer-based training programs. With video, both action and narration can be used to demonstrate correct techniques or procedures. Many companies have been using video for quite some time to train and retrain their employees. Video is effective because multiple senses are involved. This enhances learning. By including video in interactive multimedia applications, learning is further enhanced because employees can get involved as they watch and listen. However, because it is photo-realistic, it often gives too much detail. Animation offers less detail and can often simplify a lesson.

Larger companies can provide comprehensive training programs and interactive employee orientation CDs that include video and cover aspects such as company history, goals, procedures, products, and other information. These applications save companies with a large employee base thousands of dollars in time-consuming, resource-intensive training and orientation.

FIGURE 6.9

Because it involves multiple senses, video enhances learning.

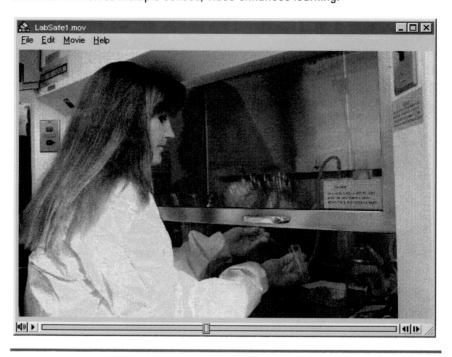

Some complicated and very specific equipment now comes complete with a multimedia application installed within. This multimedia application enables users to choose from a user-friendly interface. If users need information about installation, they press number 1 to watch a video on installation while number 2 offers a demonstration on maintenance and repair. This is a particularly cost-effective method of setting up and maintaining equipment that is shipped to distant or remote locations where it would be difficult or cost prohibitive to send repair personnel should a piece of equipment break down.

Education

Like computer-based training, video has long been used in education because it accommodates different learning styles. Video is particularly effective in reinforcing important points, illustrating difficult concepts, demonstrating processes, and teaching skills. In a multimedia application, video can be used to demonstrate the process of swinging a golf club. Correct and incorrect techniques can be illustrated. For example, a multimedia application designed to improved golf skills could demonstrate proper golf swings. By selecting slight changes in grip, follow through, or stance, students could see a video demonstrating the effect slight changes in any or all of these areas have on the loft of the ball. External factors such as wind conditions and type of grass could also be included.

In this golf example, students not only hear and see what happens, they are also involved in selecting choices that impact the outcome. Giving learners some control helps keep them involved and motivated. For more examples of how video is used in multimedia education titles, check out Educorp's site at http://www.educorp.com.

FIGURE 6.10

Video is an excellent resource for teaching skills.

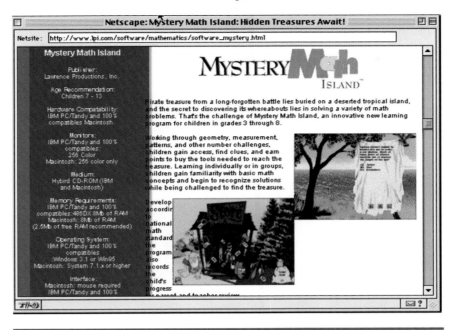

Advertising and Marketing

Television has certainly demonstrated how effective video can be in advertising and marketing. More and more multimedia applications are being created to sell. This is particularly true on the Internet. **Bandwidth** is a measurement of the amount of data that can flow over a channel on a network. An increasing number of Web pages include video, and if bandwidth was not a deterrent, nearly all Web pages designed to market and sell products and services would include video. This is because video catches and holds our attention. If you doubt this, try to get the attention of a 5-year-old involved in his favorite television show.

Video footage of famous people offering their opinions about a product, a service, or a position in a political campaign can be used as testimonials in a multimedia application designed to sell. The gas pumps at newer gas stations now include short video clips designed to entertain you while you pump your gas. These clips alone are a marketing tool, but how long will it be before the clips become commercials? How long will it be before these clips become interactive so that customers can choose the type of advertising they are most interested in viewing? If your goal is to sell a product or service, you will be much more successful if you add video to your multimedia application.

Entertainment and Games

In today's society, video and entertainment are almost synonymous. Though games are more likely to include animation than traditional video clips, some of the flight simulation programs include a video clip at the onset of the game. These video clips explain the mission and provide instructions about the game. MECHADEUS includes video in several of its interactive CD-ROM games including "Critical Path" and "The Daedalus Encounter." Other multimedia applications

FIGURE 6.11
Television has proven the effectiveness of using video in advertising.

FIGURE 6.12
Before beginning many computer games, users may be exposed to a video that describes the mission.

designed to entertain are more likely to include traditional video clips. For example, in addition to including traditional text, graphics, and sound in multimedia applications, some bands are now producing multimedia CDs that include video footage of the band at live concerts or in the recording studio.

The Web

At this time, video is the least common multimedia element found on the Web. This is because video files are really too large to be delivered effectively over the Internet. In Chapter 8, we will discuss the issue of bandwidth, which is the biggest deterrent to video on the Web. As bandwidth becomes less of a concern and compression techniques improve, video will become a more common element on Web pages. In the meantime, small video clips can be used on personal pages to show your buddies your prowess on a skateboard or to extend a "happy holidays" wish to your friends and family in other states and countries.

Video on the Web can either be **downloaded** or **streamed.** Downloadable video files are stored on your computer before they are played. QuickTime and AVI files would be examples of downloadable video files. Streaming is a more advanced process that allows the video to be played as it is downloading. The two most popular streaming video technologies are **VDOLive** from VDOnet (http://www.vdolive.com) and **RealVideo** from Progressive Networks (http://www.realaudio.com). Both of these products are cross-platform and both require software to create the files and players to play them back. Usually, the software needed to create these files must be purchased, although users can download and install the players for free. Downloading and streaming video files will be discussed in greater depth in Chapter 8.

FIGURE 6.13

Due to bandwidth constraints, video files are really too large to be delivered effectively over the Internet.

Desktop Videoconferencing

Desktop videoconferencing enables video conversations to occur over telephone lines or networks. By attaching a small video camera to a multimedia computer with a microphone, speakers, and an appropriate network connection, desktop videoconferencing can take place. Due to the high cost of travel and large distances that are often between people who need to do business or spend time together, desktop videoconferencing is on the rise. In addition to holding conversations, whiteboards allow participants to share and edit documents.

Several companies that offer desktop videoconferencing systems include **PictureTel Corporation, Connectix,** and **White Pine.** PictureTel has been working on videoconferencing systems for years. They manufacture larger systems, while Connectix and White Pine have focused on the lower-end systems called **VideoPhone** and **CU-SeeMe** respectively. Once again, bandwidth issues have deterred the growth of desktop videoconferencing.

The Video Specialist

Because working with video can be complicated, you may find it worthwhile to hire a video specialist. If you are working as part of a multimedia team on a larger project, a video specialist has probably already been assigned to work with you.

FIGURE 6.14

Desktop videoconferencing systems enable participants to hold videophone conversations and share documents.

Video specialists are responsible for working with multimedia directors and videographers to assist with recording and processing digital video files to be used in the multimedia application. They ensure that the video is correctly incorporated into the multimedia application. In some cases, they may also assist the presenter in setting up the equipment for the delivery of video. The services of the video specialist are even more valuable to the project as the video in the multimedia application grows more complicated.

Digital Video File Formats

There are different digital video file formats just as there are different graphics and sound formats.

QuickTime

QuickTime specifies its own file format called a **QuickTime Movie.** Although QuickTime does not require you to store your media as QuickTime Movie files, the QuickTime Movie file format is among the most convenient and powerful formats for storing common digital media types such as audio and video. In addition, QuickTime Movie files are platform neutral, open, and extendable. Because QuickTime Movie files work on any computing platform with a variety of different software, this file format continues to grow in popularity.

The QuickTime Movie file format is also able to store any number of video channels. This is essential for supporting real-time rendering of transitions and

FIGURE 6.15

QuickTime movies have become very popular on the Web.

special effects. QuickTime also provides a set of tools for manipulating digital video.

Video for Windows (AVI)

Video for Windows or **AVI** is by Microsoft. In the Windows 95 and Windows NT environments, Video for Windows is built in. This means that any AVI movie will just play, assuming the multimedia components of the operating system have been installed correctly.

Video for Windows is much less sophisticated than QuickTime. There are no tracks, nor are there any options for modifying time duration for any multimedia elements.

MPEG

MPEG stands for **Motion Picture Experts Group.** The MPEG video standard was developed to provide a format for delivering digital media to the consumer market. Because MPEG provides relatively high quality video and relatively low data rates, it has been successful in some markets and is emerging as the digital video standard. This is true not only in the United States, but also for most of the world.

MPEG has defined several standards for storing audio and video. Original MPEG files had to be decoded with hardware, however, with the advances in processor technologies, it is now feasible to decode these streams with software alone.

FIGURE 6.16

On PCs, AVI files will play without downloading additional software.

A disadvantage of MPEG is that there is a wide range of encoding conventions utilized in different manufacturer encoders. The Internet contains a great deal of MPEG content that is only partially compliant with the MPEG-1 specification. Likewise, early MPEG encoders often generated MPEG streams that were playable only when using specific hardware decoders.

DV

In the last year, most major video camera manufacturers have introduced digital video camcorders based on the **DV** standard. These DV cameras use a new tape format that stores the video and sound in a purely digital format. The video and sound data can be transferred to another DV camera or deck using a new high-speed connector called **FireWire** (also known as **IEEE 1394**). Because the video and sound are transferred through a digital connector, there is virtually no loss of image or sound quality—every copy is identical to the original. The highest possible image quality is maintained because all data are digitally transferred, so no noise is ever introduced into the signal.

OpenDML

The **OpenDML** file format standard extends the AVI format, making it more useful for the professional market.

OMF

To enable media interchange in the high end of the digital video market, Avid created the **Open Media Framework (OMF)** file format. The OMF format is used by many Avid products, as well as products from other developers working in the high-end market. The OMF format is a relatively complex format; therefore, it is not often supported by video editing applications in the desktop/PC markets. There is a software extension to QuickTime that enables direct access to OMF media files from QuickTime-enabled applications.

Compression

As mentioned throughout this chapter, digital video files are huge. One second of high-resolution, full-screen, uncompressed digital video with audio can require upwards of 30 MB of storage space. This means that the average CD-ROMs, which hold about 650 MB of data, can store about 25 seconds of uncompressed digital video. Though laser disks and DVDs offer greater storage capacities, they still can't begin to touch the storage needs of full-motion video in an uncompressed format.

The **data transfer rate (dtr)** is the time it takes for the video to be transferred from the processor and displayed on the monitor. Different delivery systems offer different data transfer rates. Even within the same storage medium, data transfer rates vary depending on technologies such as **bus structures** and bandwidth. If the data transfer rate is too slow, the video will be choppy. For example, using the same computer system, video played from a 12× CD-ROM will offer relatively smooth playback quality while video played from a 4× CD-ROM will probably be choppy.

FIGURE 6.17

This CD can store all of the personal phone numbers in the United States, but it can only hold about 25-30 seconds of digital video.

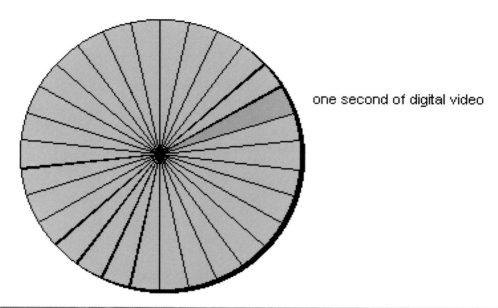

one second of digital video

To be delivered effectively, the video must fit on the delivery medium used to store it, and it must be accessed from this storage medium fast enough to trick our eyes into believing that it is really in motion. One way to improve the data transfer rate and reduce the amount of storage space that video files consume is to compress them. **Compression** reduces the video file size. In addition to improving data transfer and reducing file size, by compressing the files, the processor doesn't have to work as hard to display the video on the monitor.

The compression/decompression algorithms used to compress data are called **CODECs** (Coder Decoder). Depending upon the CODEC used and the ratio employed, compressed video files can be well over 10 times smaller than uncompressed video files. When the video is played back, the processor decompresses the file.

Working with digital video can be confusing because there are dozens of different compression schemes from which to choose. Some of these compression formats are hardware-based while others use software-based playback engines. In addition, with some of the compression schemes image quality is lost. However, these minor losses in quality are usually worth the savings.

QuickTime CODECs:

If you understand some of the different CODECs that work with QuickTime, you'll be better equipped to work effectively with video. The QuickTime formats include:

ANIMATION (RLE)

The **Animation codec** was developed to compress and play QuickTime animated movies. It uses **run length encoding (RLE),** which is great for sequencing single-color frames such as cartoons, but it is not a good choice for compressing real video clips.

APPLE CINEPAK

Apple Cinepak is a compression scheme that works well for CD-ROM video delivery. The Apple Cinepak codec offers excellent image quality at thousands or millions of colors. The playback time is also very fast. In addition, this codec is cross-platform. Hybrid CDs, which play on either Windows or Macintosh computers, can be created using this codec.

DCR

DCR is a cross-platform Macromedia "Shocked" Director Movie format that includes both audio and video. Director movies are "shocked" in order to be played on the Web.

GRAPHICS (SMC)

Like Animation, the **SMC** codec is better for compressing animation than real video. However, it doesn't offer the rendering speed or compressed file size offered by the Animation codec. SMC is often used to compress computer-graphics sequences, which are images that have been created by rendering software instead of being drawn by hand.

INDEO

Indeo is Intel's compression scheme. Indeo is more common on the PC than on the Mac. It is superior to Cinepak in resolution; however, it is inferior to Cinepak with regard to smoothness. For more information on this codec, visit Intel's site at http://www.intel.com.

JPEG

The **JPEG** format is used primarily for archiving QuickTime movies. Without additional hardware, this format usually produces unacceptable video playback. However, if you have a high-end video capture card that uses a **motion JPEG (MJPEG)** compressor to encode and play back video files, the quality will be quite high.

MPEG

MPEG stands for **Motion Picture Experts Group.** MPEG files fall into several different standards designed for different markets. MPEG files are growing in popularity because of their small file size and high quality. However, in the past, this compression scheme has been inferior to some of the others in delivering audio. This will probably change as DVDs become the standard.

RAW

Raw is also called **None** because it doesn't really offer much compression when a file is saved or captured. In fact, the file may actually be uncompressed with no gain in video quality. The primary use for this compression scheme is to transport Macintosh movies to the Windows platform where they can be compressed by a different scheme.

TRUEMOTION-S

TrueMotion-S from **Horizons Technology** is yet another third-party codec. Visit its site at http://www.horizons.com for more information.

AVI CODECs

The **Video for Windows** (VfW or AVI) format has improved since it was first released in 1992. An **AVI** file is really a **Resource Interchange File Format (RIFF)** file. RIFF is a Microsoft standard similar to WAV and BMP files. AVI files don't include track management or time-coded frame duration; however, they play back files just fine. AVI files support some of the same codecs as QuickTime, as well as some different ones.

APPLE CINEPAK

In the Windows platform, **Cinepak** works just as it does on the Mac. You can easily port these files from one platform to the other.

DCR

As was stated earlier, **DCR** is a cross-platform Macromedia "Shocked" Director Movie format to be used on the Web.

INDEO

As mentioned earlier, Intel's **Indeo Video (IVI)** codec is available for the PC and the Mac. The potential of the newer versions of the codec can only be experienced on more powerful desktop computers such as Pentiums and Power Macs.

MPEG

MPEG is another codec supported on both Macintosh and Windows platforms. MPEG files will probably continue to grow in popularity with the rise of Internet activity and DVD technology.

RLE

RLE is lossless data compression. This means no data are lost when the file is compressed. This codec is useful for making animated movies from screen captures. It is similar to the Animation codec on the Mac.

VIDEO 1

Video 1 was the original video compressor for Video for Windows and is rarely used today because compression schemes such as Cinepak are superior for encoding video footage.

Sources of Video

When you work with video for multimedia applications, you will either work with video you have recorded or stock footage video acquired from a third party.

Stock Video Footage

Stock video footage is video footage acquired from a third party. It may or may not already be in a digital format. If it's not, you can digitize it with the proper equipment; if it is, it will be easier to work with because it doesn't have to be sampled before the editing process begins. Unfortunately, video footage is not as abundant as stock photography. Consequently, it is often quite difficult to find video footage of what you want and need for your multimedia application. If you

FIGURE 6.18

Stock footage or clip video is not as common as clip art.

can find stock video footage or **clip video** for your multimedia application, it may or may not be royalty free. Even if it is royalty free, it is still copyright protected. Read all licensing agreements carefully before you agree to the terms. After signing, be sure to follow the licensing agreement strictly.

Create Your Own

If you can't find the video footage you want and need from a third party, or if you don't want to pay the royalties and can't agree to the licensing agreement specified, you may choose to record your own video footage. When you record your own video footage, you will either record it on site or in a studio setting. Regardless of location, video recording requires practice, skill, and artistic talent if you want your video footage to look professional. If you don't have these attributes and can't acquire them by the time you need the video footage for your multimedia application, you may want to consider hiring a professional videographer to shoot the footage for you.

Be aware that video footage of artistic works may still be copyright protected. Also, if your video footage includes people—whether they were just passing by or scripted into your application as actors, interviewees, or narrators—you must have their permission through a signed release if you wish to use them in your multimedia application.

Videographer

Like professional photographers, **videographers** are skilled in the art of video recording. These professionals know which elements to include in video footage. They are also skilled at setting up the location, camera angle, and lighting conditions. Videographers with experience working on multimedia projects or designing video for the computer should also know how to set all of these conditions to design a video image that will fit in one quarter of a standard 14–17" computer monitor.

Many videographers freelance. If you don't feel qualified to capture professional-quality video, it may be worth your time and money to consider finding a skilled videographer to help you obtain the video footage you need for your multimedia application. Be advised, however, that hiring a videographer can be a high budget item.

Planning Video

You should plan your videotaping in advance:
■ **Prepare the location**
■ **Check your equipment**
■ **Confirm appointments with actors and other key personnel.**

Before you include video in your multimedia application, you should plan what, when, where, and how it will be incorporated. Throughout these stages, it is important that you always keep your audience in mind. First you must consider what pieces of the multimedia application could be effectively delivered as video and when they should play. Next, you should include this information in the multimedia planning documents for the application. As you will see in Chapter 9, in the **storyboard** you will specify which screens will include video. Storyboards should also designate where video footage will begin and end in the multimedia application.

FIGURE 6.19

Professional videographers are skilled at setting up the location, lighting, and camera for video.

FIGURE 6.20
Video should be included in the planning documents of a multimedia application.

Scriptwriting 101

THE SIGHT OF COFFEE

INTERIOR DARK COFFEEHOUSE

MEDIUM SHOT:	Poet extends containers toward audience. Slowly pours coffee from both containers onto the stage in front of her.
EXTREME CU:	Ground coffee and beans flow together into a pile on the floor.
CLOSEUP:	Poet's feet in background jump and land on coffee in foreground.
CLOSEUP:	Poet's sad face as she begins poem . . .

The **scripts** are very important to video because they serve as the story that will be told with the video camera. The scripts include details about the narration, voice-overs, dialogs, sound effects, actors, scenes, and video footage that will be used in a multimedia application. Because video footage will also include audio, scripts should be written for listening rather than reading. If actors are involved, each one should have a separate and detailed script. **Flowcharts** will be needed if the multimedia application is interactive. Based on choices selected by the user, the flowchart will specify where video will be included.

As is true with all elements, proper planning for the inclusion of video in a multimedia application is important.

Because the video window in multimedia applications is small, you will get better results by recording close-ups and avoiding long shots of distant landscapes that will be lost in such a small frame.

Recording Video

Provided your equipment is properly connected to your computer and you have appropriate video editing software, you can **capture** or digitize your video from a live-feed, a laser disk player, a VCR, or a video camera. Remember that in addition to recording the video, you will also be capturing the audio.

Before you begin recording you will need to specify settings such as **window size, compression format, source,** and **output.** Many programs include **presets** that allow you to choose default settings from a list of options in case you aren't comfortable setting all of these on your own. However, the more you know about the settings, the more control you will have over the recording process. For example, generally the default setting on the window size will be 160 × 120 pixels. Though this is the standard window size for most multimedia applications, you may need to adjust it under certain circumstances.

Processing Video

After you have captured the video for your multimedia application you are ready to process it. In other words, you may need to **trim it, splice it, add special effects** and **transitions, overlay titles** and **text,** or even **add additional sound tracks.** There are many tools available to help you raise raw video footage from an amateur to a professional level.

FIGURE 6.21

Once you establish the proper settings, you are ready to begin recording.

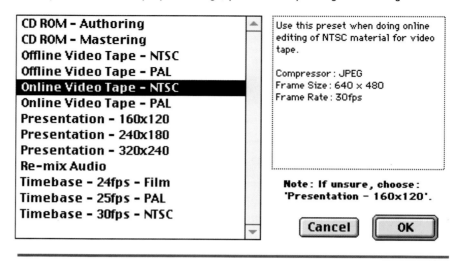

CD ROM - Authoring	Use this preset when doing online editing of NTSC material for video tape.
CD ROM - Mastering	
Offline Video Tape - NTSC	
Offline Video Tape - PAL	Compressor : JPEG
Online Video Tape - NTSC	Frame Size : 640 x 480
Online Video Tape - PAL	Frame Rate : 30fps
Presentation - 160x120	
Presentation - 240x180	
Presentation - 320x240	
Re-mix Audio	**Note : If unsure, choose :**
Timebase - 24fps - Film	**'Presentation - 160x120'.**
Timebase - 25fps - PAL	
Timebase - 30fps - NTSC	Cancel OK

Visual Effects

One of the most time-consuming aspects of working with digital video on a computer workstation is rendering visual effects. Video editors often have to limit their use of **motion, transitions,** and **filters** because of the lengthy rendering times that these effects can require. Hardware vendors have created plug-in boards that can accelerate the rendering of many of these effects, often performing them in real time.

FIGURE 6.22

The Movie Capture Window allows you to view your video as you capture or digitize it.

QuickTime offers a software-based program that will work with any kind of visual effect. In fact, QuickTime includes a set of built-in, software-based effects. These effects include **cross-fade, chroma keying, SMPTE wipes,** and **color adjustments.** By providing a complete set of standard visual effects, QuickTime helps to establish common ground around which greater industry-wide standardization of effects can be achieved.

Delivering Video

After your video has been successfully recorded, digitized, processed, and incorporated into a multimedia application, it is ready to be delivered. The delivery quality of video in multimedia applications is as dependent upon the delivery equipment as it is on the recording and processing equipment. Even if the video appears to be of superior quality running on your computer, it may be ineffective on the end-user's equipment. When planning for delivery, consider the potential delivery system and the intended audience of the multimedia application before you begin.

When considering the delivery of video, you should consider how, where, and to whom the video will be delivered. The application will be designed differently if it is delivered to one individual sitting in front of a desktop computer or for a presentation to a larger audience in an auditorium. Regardless, a high quality delivery system will help ensure that your video achieves its intended purpose.

FIGURE 6.23

The equipment used to deliver the multimedia application is as important as the equipment used to create it.

Video Editing Software

There are several software applications available for editing digital video. Adobe, Avid, and Apple are three of the bigger players offering desktop video editing for both the consumer and professional markets.

Apple Video Player

All **A/V (audio/visual)** Macintosh computers come with a program called the **Apple Video Player.** This program allows you to record QuickTime movies and play them back with the Movie Player application that corresponds with the version of QuickTime installed on your computer system. If you don't have the correct Movie Player you can download it from Apple's Web site at http://www.quicktime.apple.com.

Adobe Premiere

Though the Apple Video Player is an excellent and simple solution for recording, if you wish to do more extensive video processing, you will probably want a more sophisticated application.

Adobe and Avid are the two leaders in digital video software and systems. Both offer mid-range and high-end video editing packages. **Adobe Premiere** is an affordable, highly rated, non-linear video-editing program available for both the Macintosh and PC platforms. With Adobe Premiere, you can capture, edit, and incorporate video into multimedia applications. It allows you to give your ideas life by combining video, audio, animation, and still images without the need for special-effects hardware or expensive production services. You can even create still images from video. In addition to being cross-platform, Adobe Premiere offers extensive recording and processing capabilities. Let's look at some of the key features found in Premiere.

FIGURE 6.24

Adobe Premiere is an excellent non-linear, video editing program.

The power to communicate with motion and sound

FIGURE 6.25

The Adobe Premiere Project Window allows you to import and store clips from a wide range of file formats.

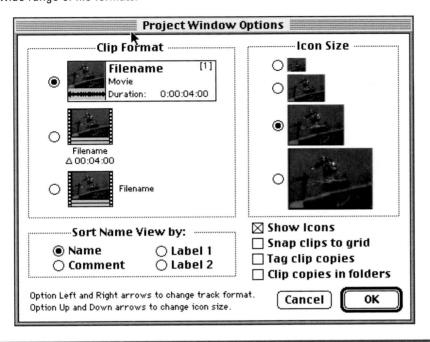

OPEN ARCHITECTURE

In addition to being a cross-platform application, another reason Adobe Premiere is so highly rated is that it is based on an **open architecture.** This means that Adobe Premiere was designed to be compatible with numerous programs, extensions, and file formats. This open architecture increases the functionality of Adobe Premiere and allows third-party developers to create software that extends Adobe Premiere's capabilities.

Adobe Premiere supports Apple QuickTime and Microsoft Video for Windows formats, in addition to multiple still image and sound formats including PICT, PICS, Photoshop Native, Illustrator, Dimension, AIFF, SND, and SoundEdit 16 formats.

IMPORTING VIDEO FILES

In Adobe Premiere, documents or files are referred to as **Projects.** Before you begin a new project, you will need to specify several settings from the presets dialog box. Any of these presets can be changed at a later time.

Any of the file types listed in the previous section, including sound files and still images, can be imported into the **Project window.** Before you import the file, you can preview it. Once the file has been imported into the Project window it will be alphabetized by filename and assigned a number 1. If that same file is imported again, it will be assigned a number 2, and so on. This is how Premiere keeps track of different files. The Premiere project doesn't actually include the files you add; it merely includes a reference or path to where the files are stored.

When working with many files as part of a large project, you will probably want to group your files into a single folder. Other options that will help you organize your files include the ability to apply labels and comments to your files and sort by these options or the filename.

FIGURE 6.26

Presets are similar to style sheets and include predefined settings for output and compression.

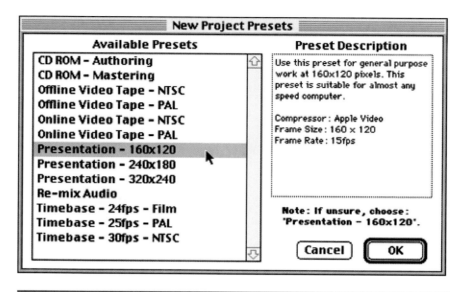

EXTENSIVE VIDEO EDITING

Adobe Premiere allows you to arrange video clips linearly and instantly edit them nonlinearly. You can see your video in **filmstrip style** or zoom in on single frames. In Premiere, you will use the **Construction Window** to assemble, synch, and edit your files. By using **nondestructive editing,** Premiere preserves your original video clips just in case you make a mistake, change your mind, or wish to use them in another application. Because Premiere supports the SMPTE time code, you can position video clips precisely where you want them.

The Construction window includes **transition, video,** and **audio** tracks. It also includes built-in tools such as the **razor tool** for trimming unwanted frames from

FIGURE 6.27

Use the Construction Window to assemble your clips linearly so that you can edit them nonlinearly.

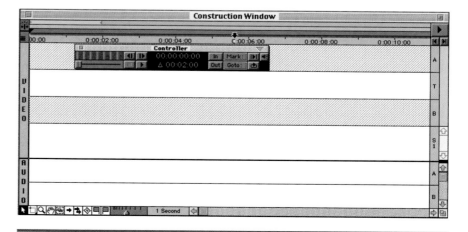

your video clips. A minimum of three video and three audio tracks is included in each file. If you want more, you can have up to 99 of each. Additional video tracks are labeled S2 through S97; the S stands for **Superimpose.** Premiere also includes some rather sophisticated sound-editing features including the ability to apply special effects to audio tracks. The additional audio tracks are labeled X2 through X97. Remember that each additional track you include will require additional storage and computer processing power.

Once you have imported clips into the Project window you can then drag them into the Construction window. When you drag a video clip from the Project window to the Construction window, the audio that accompanies the video clip is automatically placed in the corresponding audio track. The **Time Ruler** and the **Time Selector** allow you to set the duration of the video clip. You can overlap clips and add other transitions between clips. Other editing windows include the **Timeline, Trimming,** and **Playback** windows, and at any time, you can use the **Preview window** to preview your entire movie or a selected section of it.

SPECIAL EFFECTS

With Premiere you will find traditional special effects such as **wipes, dissolves, spins,** and **filters.** In the Title Window, you can create text with **smooth edges, gradient fills, soft shadows,** and **transparent backgrounds.** Text effects including transparent letters can be used for titles and subtitles. You can even create animated titles. In addition, you can design shapes and patterns for transitions and apply **motion paths** such as **twisting, zooming, rotation,** and **distortion.** With 97 superimpose tracks, you can add multiple layers and even animated filters. To add transitions, you simply drag them from the Transitions window to the Construction window.

Plug-in filters and special effects available from other Adobe products such as Adobe Photoshop as well as from third-party developers extend your creative options by allowing you to change the **color, brightness,** and **contrast.** You can

FIGURE 6.28
At any time, you can preview your movie in the Preview window.

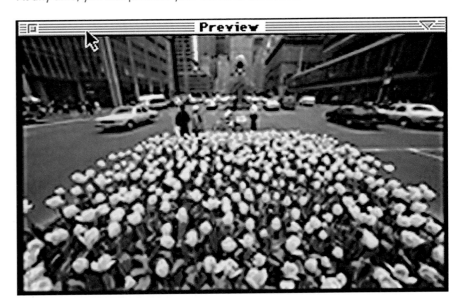

FIGURE 6.29

From the Transistions Window you can apply special effects.

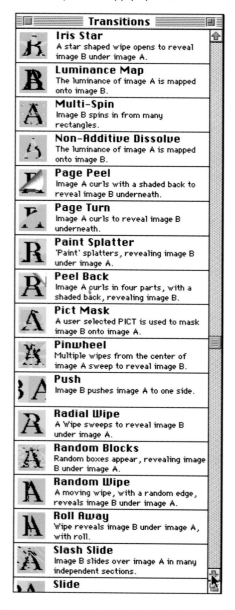

The best transitions are transparent to the user. Try to make your transitions appropriate and consistent with the rest of the multimedia application.

also apply **blurs, distortions,** and **morphing** effects. Built-in and third-party audio processing filters are also available to enhance and change audio characteristics.

ADDED FEATURES

Adobe Premiere offers many additional features and tools to help you create quality, full-motion video. For example, presets establish predefined settings for output, compression, and other tasks, or you can control these settings yourself.

Low-resolution files can be edited and then converted or output to high-resolution versions. This allows you to save disk space and work more efficiently during the editing process. In addition, Premiere comes with **multimedia tutorials** that demo new features and expert techniques. They also include **stock images, video, audio, templates,** and **fonts.**

EXPORTING VIDEO

When you have captured and edited your multimedia movie to your liking, you can produce it for small- or full-screen viewing and export it to another application, videotape, CD-ROM, or as a QuickTime Movie to be viewed on the World Wide Web. To make a movie, you simply choose **Movie** from the **Make** menu, and then select the proper settings from a list of **Output Options.** The **Print to Video** function also allows you to export your movies to professional production equipment.

Output Options that you must select include the **resolution, frame rate, frame size, file format,** and **audio settings.** Premiere supports 24-, 25-, and 30-frame-per-second editing and export. By using the QuickTime format, your Adobe Premiere movie can be played from within any application that supports QuickTime. Most multimedia applications that incorporate video use the QuickTime standard. Adobe Premiere also supports Microsoft Video for Windows and other third-party formats.

Adobe After Effects

Adobe After Effects is a program full of tools that can help you create neat effects for Adobe Premiere projects. It's a wonderful tool for multimedia developers and

FIGURE 6.30
The most frequently used commands are located in the Commands Palette for easy access.

FIGURE 6.31
Adobe Premiere allows you to export to a variety of different formats.

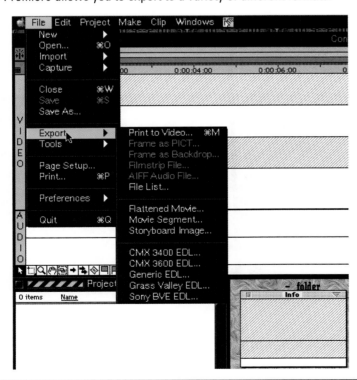

Movies created for the Windows platform must be "flattened" before they are saved. This is because all of the information must be included in one data fork. Macintosh files have two forks. A data fork is used to store the video and sound and the resource fork is used to store descriptive information. Therefore, Macintosh movies do not need to be "flattened" before they are saved.

FIGURE 6.32

When you are ready to finalize your video, simply choose Make Movie and select the appropriate settings.

Project Output Options	
Output: [Work Area ▼] as [QuickTime™ Composite ▼]	

☒ Video
Size: [160] h [120] v ☒ 4:3 Aspect
Type: [Full Size Frame ▼]

☒ Audio
Rate: [22 kHz ▼]
Format: [8 Bit - Mono ▼]
Blocks: [1 sec ▼]

☐ Beep when finished
☒ Open finished movie
☐ Show samples   [Cancel] [OK]

designers because it encourages creativity and experimentation. Let's take a look at some of the tools and features offered in After Effects.

LAYERS

With After Effects, you can use unlimited layers of both moving and still images. In addition, special effects and animation can be applied to each layer. Once this composite of layers has been created, After Effects gives you precise control over adjusting every aspect until you are sure you have everything just right.

MOTION PACK

There are lots of fun tools available with the Motion Pack including the **Motion Sketch** tool, which allows you to draw animation paths and record the velocity of

FIGURE 6.33

Layers can be used to create interesting effects.

these paths. The **Motion Tracker** tool matches the motion on one frame with the motion on another frame. The **Motion Stabilizer** reduces unwanted motion, while the **Wiggler** is used to apply random smooth or jagged changes to color, motion, and other effects over time. **Motion Math** can be used to write scripts that manipulate the properties of one layer in relationship to another.

KEY PACK

The Key Pack tools are used to create high quality mattes. The **Color Difference** key allows you to create combination mattes for difficult-to-create images such as glass and water. The **Matte Choker** creates natural edges between objects and background images, and the **Spill Suppressor** eliminates blue and green colors.

DISTORTION PACK

Time-based special effects can be applied with the Distortion Pack. The **Displacement Map** is used to mirror a pattern from one layer to another. The **Glow** special effect creates a diffused halo around objects. There are many other special effects including **Lightning, Scatter, Ripple, Bulge,** and **Wave Warp.**

POWERFUL COMPOSITING

With After Effects you can combine an unlimited number of layers from files imported from QuickTime, AVI, Illustrator, Photoshop, and a variety of other graphics and animation programs. You can even mix multiple files resolutions and layer very tiny thumbnail graphics to full-screen video.

ANIMATION CONTROL

You can add an unlimited number of keyframes to animate any attribute in any layer down to one sixty-five thousandth of a pixel. You can also edit at the sub-pixel level. You can even use time remapping to create effects such as **slow motion, playback delay, backward playback,** and **freeze frames.**

SPECIAL EFFECTS

In After Effects, the number of effects seems endless because of the precise and powerful tools available. There are more than 60 special effect plug-ins including

FIGURE 6.34

The Glow special effect creates a diffused halo around objects.

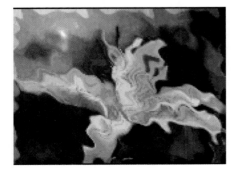

blur & sharpen, channel manipulation, distortion, color correction, perspective, stylize, and **transitions.** Multiple special effects can be applied to each layer. In addition, After Effects is compatible with other third-party plug-ins. This compatibility further enhances its expandability.

PROFESSIONAL QUALITY

With Adobe After Effects, you can produce professional-level output for film, video, multimedia, and the Web. You can perform multiple renders of a composition at various sizes. You can also work with low-resolution layers and then revert to the higher-resolution originals for final output.

IMPORT/EXPORT FORMATS

After Effects supports a wide variety of file formats including QuickTime, Photoshop, Illustrator, TIFF, Targa, PICT, AIFF, BMP, GIF, WAV, and AVI.

Authoring Software

After you have recorded and processed your video, you are ready to incorporate it into your multimedia application. Remember that your video clips should be ready to deliver at this stage in the process. Because video files are huge and require powerful processors, properly incorporating video into your multimedia application will help guarantee that your applications are designed to run quickly and efficiently.

To add the video to your applications, you need an authoring tool. Simple presentation programs such as **Microsoft PowerPoint** or **Adobe Persuasion** allow you to play video from a slide.

Authoring programs that use a card or page theme such as **HyperCard, HyperStudio,** and **Toolbook** also allow you to incorporate video. With these event-driven authoring programs, you can program video to occur at certain times or after a certain event occurs. For example, a video clip may play after the user positions the mouse over an icon.

More advanced multimedia authoring packages offer powerful, but complex features designed for professionals. Included in this category are programs such as **mFactory's mTropolis** and **Macromedia's Authorware** and **Director.** Because these programs are quite extensive, they take a significant amount of time to learn. Because Director is the industry leader for multimedia development, let's look at some of its features for working with video. Keep in mind that the other programs offer similar features.

In Director, video clips become **cast members** that are added to the **Stage.** If you remember from the previous chapter, the Stage is where all of the elements interact. As cast members, video files can be included internally within the multimedia application, or they can remain external and Director can then access them as the multimedia application plays. There are advantages to keeping the video files external to the multimedia application. External video clips keep the multimedia application file size to a minimum and allow your application to run more efficiently and more rapidly. However, the path to the external video clip must be the same on every computer that plays the application.

IMPORTING VIDEO

Importing is probably the easiest way to get frames into your multimedia application. By choosing Import from the File Menu, you can select the video files you wish to be cast members. If you only want a certain portion of your video file to be included, you can specify the number of frames to import from the Options dialog box. After you select the files and choose Import, the video files appear as cast members in the **Cast window.**

Next, you will move the video files to the **Score.** Once in the Score, the video files become **Sprites** and are now part of the action in the Director movie. If you recall from the previous chapters, Director uses the Score to keep details about the location and action of every Sprite at every moment within the movie.

To get the video clip to play all the way through before moving on to the next frame, don't worry about trying to determine how many frames you need to fill in the Score in order to play the entire clip. Instead, from the cell directly above the video clip in the Tempo Channel, select "Wait for End of Digital Video in Channel" and specify the correct channel number.

PROGRAMMING LINGO SCRIPTS

As you will recall from the previous chapters, **Lingo** is Director's programming language. **Lingo scripts** can be used in Director to play video clips when a certain action occurs, such as when a user presses a play button or moves the mouse pointer on top of a graphic. Lingo scripts that reference the Sprite number and Cast Member number of the video can be placed in a **Script Channel.** Because Lingo scripts can be written to include commands that play the entire video clip, you don't need to set this control in the Tempo channel.

Another way to play video clips in a Director movie is to reference Lingo scripts to cast members. Using this method, cast members simply need to be added to the Score to become part of the movie's action. Thus buttons, icons, and other graphics can be set up with accompanying Lingo scripts to play video upon a certain user action such as a mouse click.

Shockwave

Macromedia Shockwave enables Director movies including audio to be played in a Web browser. Though Shockwave files are smaller than QuickTime and AVI files, they still take up lots of storage space. With Shockwave, no server-side software is required. On the client- or user-side, the Shockwave plug-in must be properly set up in the Web browser in order to play shocked movies.

FIGURE 6.35

Shockwave allows you to play Director moves on the Web.

Copyright

Copyright laws affect the video footage you can incorporate into your multimedia application. It is particularly important to follow these laws if you plan to use the video footage in a commercially prepared multimedia application. Because digital video is fairly new, precedents for the laws surrounding issues such as fair use are still being determined.

Also, keep in mind that even if you record the footage yourself, what you have recorded may still be copyright protected. For example, if you record footage of an artistic performance such as a play or choreographed dance, it may be subject to copyright laws. Films, television programs, motion picture videos, documentaries, and other commercially prepared video are also copyright protected.

Don't take chances. If you wish to use video footage within your multimedia application, always get permission from the videographer or publisher. After obtaining a release to use a video file, be sure to read the agreement carefully. Though you can use some video royalty free in any multimedia application you create, with others, you will need to pay the creator a royalty for each application in which the video is used.

SUMMARY

Video serves as a rich resource in multimedia applications. Video-editing technology is now affordable to the masses.

A video file is a sequence of individual images or frames displayed fast enough to create the illusion of motion. The **frame rate** is the speed at which individual frames display. Frames displayed at 24 to 30 **frames per second (fps)** appear continuous, at a slower rate they appear choppy. Frame rates vary because there are different video standards used throughout the world. The most common video standards are **NTSC, PAL, SECAM,** and **HDTV.**

Several different tracks are used to store video information. The Time Code track is used to synchronize all of the components. The standard time code is called **SMPTE (Society of Motion Picture and Television Engineers).** SMPTE measures video in hours, minutes, seconds, and frames.

Videotapes can be used in multimedia to capture or deliver video. The analog formats include **VHS, S-VHS, Hi-8,** and **Betacam SP.** The digital formats include **DV1, DV2, DV3,** and **DV. Videodisks** or **laser disks** provide a random access alternative to videotape. Television and live video camera feed can also be digitized or directly accessed from a multimedia link. **Digital video** is video that is already in a digital format.

QuickTime by Apple is a software-based video-delivery system. It is an engine that allows you to deliver multimedia and video on the computer without using additional hardware. QuickTime supports a wide variety of media file formats and media encodings making it the most widely adopted format for publishing digital video on the Internet.

Of the multimedia elements, video has the greatest potential to impact the audience. It is commonly used in Computer-Based Training, Education, Advertising & Marketing, Entertainment & Games, and the Web. **Desktop video-conferencing** enables video conversations to occur over telephone lines or networks. **Bandwidth** is a measurement of the amount of data that can flow over a channel on a network. Though bandwidth is a deterrent to the growth of video on the Web, more and more Web pages include video.

Video specialists are responsible for working with multimedia directors and videographers to assist with the recording and processing of digital video files to be used in the multimedia application.

There are different digital video file formats, just as there are different graphics and sound formats. Some of the most common include **QuickTime, Video for Windows** or **AVI, MPEG,** and **DV.** A new high speed connector called **FireWire** is now being used to transfer digital video and audio from one device to another.

Digital video files are huge. **Compression** reduces the video file size and improves the data transfer rate. The compression/decompression algorithms used to compress data are called **CODECs.** Different file formats support different codecs. Some of the most common codecs include **Animation, Apple Cinepak,** and **MPEG.**

Sources of video include **stock footage** or **clip video,** creating your own video, or hiring a **videographer** to shoot it for you. Your video should be planned in advance using **storyboards, scripts,** and **flowcharts.** Once you have determined what, where, and how video will be recorded, you can begin the recording process. You can **capture** or digitize your video from a live-feed, a laser disk player, a VCR, or a video camera.

After you have captured the video for your multimedia application, you are ready to process it. In other words, you may need to **trim it, splice it, add special effects** and **transitions, overlay titles** and **text,** and even **add additional sound tracks.** After your video has been successfully recorded, digitized, processed, and incorporated into a multimedia application, it is ready to be delivered.

There are several software applications available for editing digital video. **Apple Video Player** comes with all AV Macintosh computers. **Adobe Premiere** is a step up from Apple Video Player. It is an affordable, highly-rated, non-linear video-editing program available for both the Macintosh and PC platforms. **Adobe After Effects** is a program full of tools that can help you create neat effects for projects created with Adobe Premiere. Finally, you need authoring software to bring all of the video clips and other multimedia elements into your multimedia application. Authoring tools range from simple presentation programs such as **Microsoft PowerPoint** to more advanced programs such as **Macromedia Director.** If you wish to deliver a Macromedia Director movie over the Internet you'll need **Shockwave** to do it.

KEY TERMS

Frame rate	Clip video	Apple Cinepak
PAL	Frames per second (fps)	Videographer
SMPTE	SECAM	Scripts
Hi-8	VHS	Flowcharts
DVD	Betacam SP	NTSC
QuickTime	Digital video	HDTV
Downloaded	Time-based	S-VHS
AVI	Streamed	DV
Data transfer rate (dtr)	MPEG	Hypervideo
Animation	Compression	Bandwidth

Desktop videoconfer- encing	CODEC	Capture
FireWire	Stock footage	
	Storyboards	

Matching Questions

a. frame rate	**b.** NTSC	**c.** PAL
d. SMPTE	**e.** hypervideo	**f.** bandwidth
g. data transfer rate (dtr)	**h.** CODECs	**i.** open architecture
j. Adobe Premiere	**k.** projects	**l.** Shockwave

_____ **1.** A video clip set up to trigger another multimedia event.

_____ **2.** The time it takes for the video to be transferred from the processor and displayed on the monitor.

_____ **3.** The speed at which individual frames display, measured in frames per second (fps).

_____ **4.** This is the time code that measures video in hours, minutes, seconds, and frames.

_____ **5.** This program enables Director movies including audio to be played in a Web browser.

_____ **6.** The common television and video standard used in the United States and Japan.

_____ **7.** These are documents or files in Adobe Premiere.

_____ **8.** A measurement of the amount of data that can flow over a channel on a network.

_____ **9.** An affordable, highly-rated, non-linear video-editing program available for both the Macintosh and PC platforms.

_____ **10.** This means the program is designed to be compatible with numerous programs, extensions, and file formats.

_____ **11.** The most common television and video standard in Europe, South Africa, the United Kingdom, and Australia.

_____ **12.** These are compression/decompression algorithms used to compress data.

Fill-In Questions

1. _____ is the most common video format found on the consumer market.

2. _____ or _____ _____ provide a random access alternative to videotape.

3. Video on the Web can either be _____ or _____.

4. The _____ _____ _____ is the time it takes for the video to be transferred from the processor and displayed on the monitor.

5. _____ _____ is a compression scheme that works well for CD-ROM video delivery.

6. Like professional photographers, _____ are skilled in the art of video recording.

7. All _____ Macintosh computers come with a program called the _____ _____ _____.

8. _____ _____ is an affordable, highly rated, non-linear video-editing program available for both the Macintosh and PC platforms.

9. _____ _____ and special effects available from other Adobe products such as Adobe Photoshop as well as from third-party developers, extend your creative options by allowing you to change the _____, _____, and _____.

10. _____ _____ _____ is a program full of tools that can help you create neat effects for Adobe Premiere projects.

DISCUSSION QUESTIONS

1. What is QuickTime? What are the advantages of using QuickTime?

2. In multimedia applications, what is the most commonly used screen size for video? What are the advantages of using this screen size?

3. In Adobe Premiere, what is accomplished in the Construction window?

4. In Adobe Premiere, what are the Output Options that you must choose from when you are ready to make your movie?

5. What are the advantages of using the Apple Cinepak compression scheme when delivering video from CD-ROMs?

6. What are two ways in which Lingo scripts can be used to play back video in a Director movie?

7. What are some key features found in Adobe Premiere?

8. What are some key features of Adobe After Effects?

9. What are CODECs? What are some of the more common codecs used with QuickTime and AVI files?

10. How do copyright laws affect the use of video in multimedia applications?

HANDS-ON EXERCISES

1. Visit http://www.quicktime.apple.com. If you don't already have QuickTime installed on your computer, download and install it now. Go to Samples and practice editing video clips using QuickTime's editing features such as copy and paste.

2. Visit http://www.msn.com/Cinemania/Reviews/ReviewsHome.htm and http://www.buenavista.com. Download and play back any of your favorite movie clips.

3. Visit Progressive Networks at http://www.realaudio.com. Download the RealVideo player. From the site, there are some pointers to other sites that use RealVideo. Click on one of these sites and check out streaming video.

Case Study: Chapter 6

Seok-Won Noh has been assigned to the multimedia team for the Island Watercraft project. He will be the video specialist. Because video files are so large and hog so much bandwidth, traditional video used on this Web site will be very limited. Most of the movement will come from the animated GIFs created by Wendy Perry, the animation specialist.

In addition to the fast and fun theme presented throughout this Web site, Island Watercraft's owner and president, Luke Scott, would also like to stress the importance of safety. The message is important, but it also needs to remain consistent with the fast and fun theme of the Web site. Therefore, the safety message needs to be short and light. At the same time, it needs to have an impact on the audience.

Noh will recommend to the team that one short, 10-15-second downloadable video clip be placed on the Web site. The purpose of this video clip will be to encourage watersport participants to have fun while staying safe. Users will have the option of downloading the clip or moving on. Because QuickTime formats are cross-platform and relatively small, Noh will use this file format and codec for the video clip.

Because this video footage won't require extensive camera settings and special lighting, Noh has enough experience to serve as the videographer as well as the video specialist on this project. He will use a Sony digital video camera to record Mr. Scott. The recording will take place on water on location at Island Watercraft, which is located right on the water in Friday Harbor. The clip will feature Mr. Scott on a three-person SeaDoo watercraft welcoming viewers to the sport and encouraging viewers to stop by Island Watercraft (IWC). He will then stress the importance of being safe in order to have fun and will end by jetting off into the sunset on the colorful SeaDoo.

CHAPTER SEVEN

Multimedia Authoring

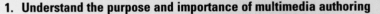

UPON COMPLETION OF THIS CHAPTER, YOU WILL BE ABLE TO:

1. Understand the purpose and importance of multimedia authoring
2. Define some of the basic terminology associated with authoring including layers, navigation, interactivity, linear, non-linear, hierarchical, and combination
3. Describe the four different types of multimedia authoring programs
4. Recognize the differences between the types of multimedia authoring programs
5. Describe the roles and responsibilities of the multimedia director or architect
6. List and describe some of the key features found in Microsoft PowerPoint
7. List and describe some of the key features found in HyperCard
8. List and describe some of the key features found in Macromedia Authorware
9. List and describe some of the key features found in Macromedia Director

Introduction

After you have developed and designed all of the elements that will be included in your multimedia application, you are ready to put it together. Putting together the text, the graphics, the animation, the audio, and the video requires multimedia authoring software.

Most authoring programs are based on one of four metaphors. There are **slide-based** authoring programs, **card-based** authoring programs, **object-based** authoring programs, and **icon-based** authoring programs. All of these authoring programs basically perform the same function. They allow you to integrate all of your multimedia elements into one multimedia application to be delivered to a single individual or a group.

The four functions found in most authoring programs include:

- **Creating Multimedia Elements**—Most authoring programs provide you with tools that allow you to create, design, and edit multimedia elements such as text, graphics, and animation. Oftentimes, however, there are other software tools that are more precise and flexible than those found in authoring programs. In this case, you can create the multimedia element in another program and import and integrate it into the multimedia application using the authoring program.

- **Importing Multimedia Elements**—In addition to creating some multimedia elements with authoring system software, you can also import text, graphics, animations, audio, and video files that have been created, designed, and edited with other application programs.

- **Integrating Multimedia Elements**—Once the multimedia elements have been created or imported, authoring tools can be used to link and sequence them together. Scripts can also be written to access external resources and applications.

FIGURE 7.1

Once you have designed and developed all of the multimedia elements, you are ready to assemble them with authoring software.

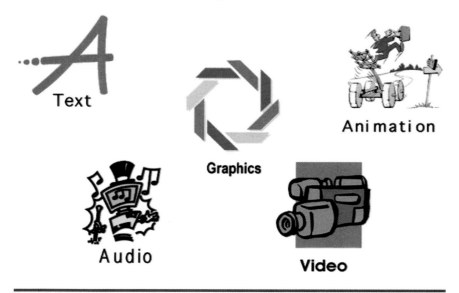

- **Building Interactivity** — Multimedia authoring tools also allow you to add interactivity into your application so that users have control and input into the program.

- **Delivering Multimedia Applications**—The final step is for the authoring tool to make the integrated multimedia elements one self-supported and fully contained multimedia application that either contains or references all of the elements.

Though the goals and functions of each authoring system are basically the same, the features and the ways in which the elements are included vary. In addition, some programs are easier to learn, yet limited, while other programs are more complicated, yet extremely powerful.

Analyzing the features of each type of authoring system should help you determine which one will best meet your needs. Depending upon your computer experience and expertise, you may find it helpful to learn a simple authoring system and progress to the more complicated systems. In addition, keep in mind that you may want to learn several of these programs so that you can use the best tool available as your needs, application, audience, and method of delivery change.

Multimedia Director/Architect

The multimedia director, also called the multimedia architect, is responsible for integrating all of the multimedia elements that have been created by the other media specialists. Using an authoring tool and the planning documents, the multimedia director will develop and design an efficient, cohesive, well-planned

FIGURE 7.2

Authoring system software allows you to create a self-sufficient multimedia application from all of the multimedia elements.

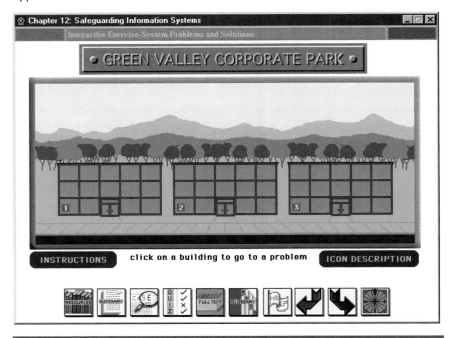

multimedia application. While considering technical and marketing issues, this application must meet the goals established by the multimedia team and the client. Therefore, the multimedia director should possess excellent communication skills.

The Multimedia Director should also be technically competent. This person should thoroughly understand the different multimedia authoring programs and their respective strengths and weaknesses. The Multimedia Director should be an expert in working with the chosen multimedia authoring program and using its programming or scripting language. In addition, this person should have a solid foundation in working with text, graphics, animation, sound, and video.

Authoring the Multimedia Application

Authoring a multimedia application involves planning and pulling everything together into one unified piece. This process requires extensive and ongoing communication between members of the project team, clients, and even external support personnel. The planning documents—including the storyboards, scripts, and flowcharts—are used extensively during this process to make sure that the original goals are achieved in the final application.

Because most multimedia applications permit users to interact with what they see and hear, multimedia authoring tools allow you to design applications that include multiple **layers.** Each of these layers contains different pieces of the multimedia application. To give users access to the different layers, you must incorporate and design intuitive navigation methods such as arrows, buttons, and links.

Structure

While the media specialists are creating the text, graphics, sound, animation, and video for the multimedia application, the structure behind the final product should be evolving. The structure of the multimedia application comes from the planning documents. The **storyboard** is used to prepare the structure of each screen and the sequence of screens in the multimedia application.

In addition to structuring the screens, information from the **scripts** can be used to set up some of the details regarding scenes, interactions among characters, and transitions between screens.

The **flowcharts** should include details about the level of interactivity included in the multimedia application. Some multimedia applications will be much more interactive than others. For example, interactivity is particularly important in multimedia applications designed for computer-based training and education.

Navigation

From the planning documents, you can prepare **navigation structures** or ways by which users maneuver through the multimedia application. There are several different methods of navigating a multimedia application.

- **Linear**—Using this method, users navigate through the multimedia application sequentially. This is the traditional method of navigation used in most slide-based authoring programs. It is also the method of navigation used in analog media. For example, video and printed books generally follow a preset, sequential path established by the producer or author.

- **Non-linear**—Using non-linear navigation, there is no prescribed or sequential path that must be followed. Users can navigate from one topic to another without worrying about missing a step in between.

- **Hierarchical**—Using hierarchical navigation, users maneuver through a multimedia application following a logical, branching structure. Based on their decisions, users are led to an appropriate branch. This branching process continues as long as users continue to make choices. This is a top-down navigation scheme.

- **Combination**—Combinations of the three navigation methods listed above are also quite common. For example, users may use non-linear navigation to move around the multimedia application until they encounter a linear sequence such as a video.

Interactivity

Interactivity is created within the multimedia application when users are given choices. People are more likely to retain information with which they interact. Therefore, interactivity is important to multimedia, particularly to those applications designed to train and educate. The amount of interactivity and its location in the multimedia application should be specified in the planning documents. From these documents, you can use one of the navigation methods listed above to create the interactive pieces of the program. In creating interactivity, intuitive, user-friendly stimuli are important. Methods of interactivity should be obvious to the user.

Multimedia applications such as kiosks and Web pages used for ordering goods, purchasing tickets, or registering information are also interactive. These applications gather information from users. Interactivity individualizes the session and contributes to the participatory nature of a multimedia program. There are many ways to design interactivity into your multimedia applications.

Navigation and interactivity should be simple, user-friendly, and intuitive. Users shouldn't struggle to figure out how to maneuver through your multimedia application.

- **Button & Icons**—A common way for users to interact with a multimedia application is through the use of buttons and icons that appear on the screen. For example, you can have the user respond or interact with a multimedia application by clicking on a navigation button or icon, such as an arrow or stop sign.

- **Menus**—Another option is to have users choose options from a list or a menu. Menu bars and drop-down menus are common design techniques geared toward user interactivity.

- **Keyboard Commands**—Having users press keys or key combinations offers yet another way for users to respond or interact with a multimedia application. Obviously, this method requires that users have access to a list of keyboard commands and what they do.

- **Hypermedia**—An easy way to create links between different parts of a multimedia application, is to use hypermedia. Hypermedia are clickable elements such as text, graphics, sound, animation, or video that are assigned scripts that link users to other locations. In addition to linking

FIGURE 7.3

The shape and design of these navigation buttons make them intuitive and user-friendly.

FIGURE 7.4

Hypermedia can be used to navigate to different locations within and outside of the multimedia application.

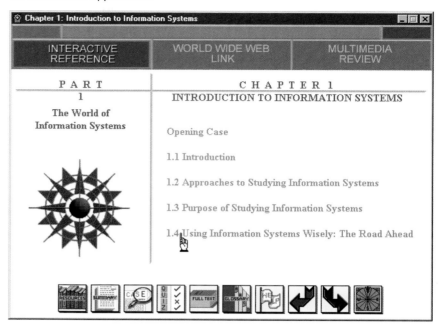

users to other locations within the same multimedia application, hypermedia that link users to other applications or the Internet can also be designated. Hypermedia are often recognizable when the mouse pointer changes to a pointing finger or hand.

FIGURE 7.5

There are a variety of different ways to get a response from users.

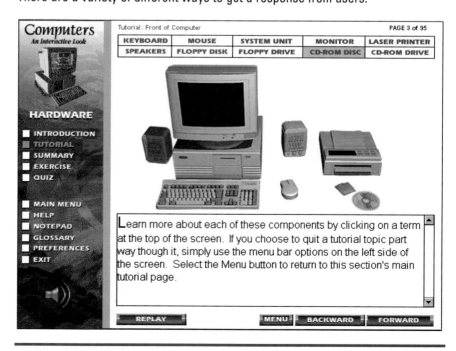

FIGURE 7.6

Feedback enables your multimedia application to communicate with the user.

- **Text Boxes**—Text boxes or record fields are necessary if you want users to provide alphanumeric information. For example, to personalize your application, you may ask users to input their first name. You can then use their names throughout the multimedia application. Text boxes are also quite common in CBT and education where users are required to input answers and make decisions.

- **Check Boxes**—If you want to give users a chance to select more than one option from a group, you can use check boxes. Users simply check off those options that apply. Users have the choice of choosing zero, one, or multiple options.

- **Radio or Option Buttons**—If you want users to discriminate between choices, you can use radio buttons. Radio buttons force users to select only one option from a group.

- **Drop-Down List Boxes**—Another way of providing users with options is to use a drop-down list box. Like radio buttons, users are usually permitted only one choice; however, all of the choices are displayed on the screen at one time. Users have to click on the drop-down arrow to view the options.

- **Drag & Drop**—The mouse can also be used to interact with the multimedia application. For example, users may respond to a multimedia application by dragging and dropping an icon, button, or other object from one location to another on the screen.

No matter which method or methods of interactivity you design into your multimedia application, you will need to provide **feedback** to the user's response. Your multimedia application has to communicate. In other words, for each choice that a user makes, you will need to determine how the multimedia application will recognize and interpret the user's response to the choice. The multimedia application must be able to analyze the response or access an application that can analyze it.

Before you select a multimedia authoring program, analyze the goals of the multimedia application, the amount of interactivity to be included, the audience, and the method of delivering the multimedia application when it is completed.

Multimedia applications must analyze the user's response and provide appropriate feedback. Appropriate feedback may mean displaying the word "Congratulations," on the screen, it may be using a synthesized voice that says, "Try Again," or it may simply take users to another screen within the multimedia application. The feedback can be almost anything as long as it is appropriate to the choice and the goals of the multimedia application.

Once the structure has been built, and the interactivity and navigation methods have been established, you can import or reference all of the other multimedia elements that have been created. Including these elements in the multimedia application requires proper placement, timing, and synchronization to ensure a smooth flowing application.

Four Types of Authoring Programs

1. Slide-Based Authoring Programs

Slide-based authoring programs use the slide-show as a metaphor. For the most part, these programs are linear **presentation packages** that generally don't allow you to include much, if any, interactivity into your application. However, they do make it very easy for you to create professional-looking presentations made up of slides that include text, graphics, animations, sound, and even full-motion video.

The time it takes to learn these programs is short compared to the other three types of authoring systems. Though these programs are simple to learn, the control and power they offer is usually quite limited.

Common slide-based authoring systems include **Microsoft PowerPoint, Adobe Persuasion, Corel's WP Presentation,** and **Claris Impact.** Let's take a

FIGURE 7.7

Microsoft PowerPoint is a slide-based multimedia authoring program.

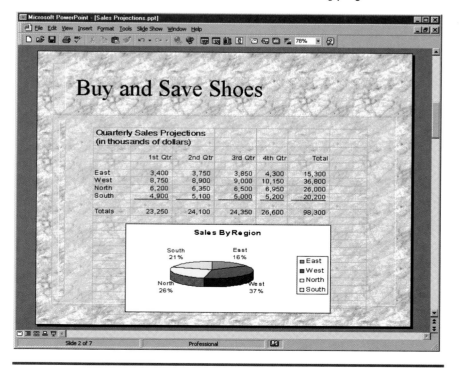

look at some of the key features found in Microsoft PowerPoint. This will give you a general understanding of some of the features found in slide-based authoring programs.

MICROSOFT POWERPOINT

With **Microsoft PowerPoint** you can create professional-looking presentations in a very short time. PowerPoint offers many features that make it easy to learn and easy to use.

Views PowerPoint offers several views from which you can create, work with, and display your presentation.

- **Outline View**—You can design a professional multimedia presentation by simply creating an outline in the outline view.
- **Slide View**—From slide view you can see what each slide will look like. The vertical scroll bar offers a tool tip that tells you the slide on which you are positioned as you move from slide to slide within the presentation.
- **Slide Sorter View**—Slide sorter view gives you a thumbnail view of each slide in your presentation. In this view it is easy to rearrange the slides in your presentation.
- **Slide Show View**—Slide show view allows you to run your slide show. In this view, each slide takes up the entire computer screen. To move from slide to slide, simply click the mouse.

Design Templates If you don't feel comfortable designing your own color schemes and choosing appropriate fonts, PowerPoint offers many **templates** that you can apply to your presentation to give it a professional and consistent feel.

Transitions & Builds **Transitions** are special effects that are applied between slides. **Animation** is special effects applied to the elements on the slides. PowerPoint comes with a variety of special effects including **wipes,**

FIGURE 7.8

MS PowerPoint offers different views from which you can work with and display your presentation.

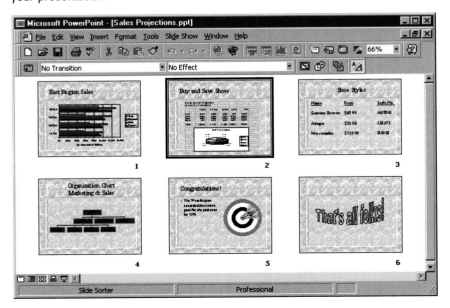

FIGURE 7.9
From PowerPoint you can access the Microsoft Clipart gallery.

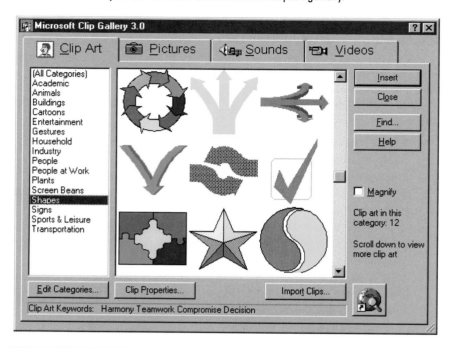

checkerboards, and **dissolves.** You can even add **animated** special effects to titles and objects.

Clip Art & Photos Within PowerPoint you have access to the entire **Microsoft Clipart Gallery.** Included in this library are **line drawings, buttons, icons, photographs,** and other graphics. In addition, you can import clip art and clip photographs that have common graphic file formats such as BMP and TIFF.

Object Linking & Embedding As a multimedia authoring program, PowerPoint also allows you to **link** to other applications and external resources or you can **embed** these resources directly into the slide. Objects that you may wish to include in a slide include **graphs, charts, equations, sound,** and **video.**

Output Options When you have completed your slide-show presentation, you can output the slide show to the screen using projection equipment. Other output options include **overhead transparencies, printouts,** and **35mm slides.**

2. Card-Based Authoring Programs

Card-based authoring programs use stacks of cards or pages as a metaphor. The cards are actually databases that store the multimedia elements. On each card you may find text, graphics, animations, sound, full-motion video, or references to these objects.

Unlike slide-based authoring systems, these authoring systems allow you to move throughout the multimedia application in a **non-linear** fashion. In other words, there is no sequence of cards that has to be followed. Instead, all of the cards are cross-referenced so that you can jump from one related card to the next.

To create a unified feel throughout the multimedia application, you can create common navigation buttons and backgrounds. These items that remain constant from card to card can be placed in a background layer. Items that are unique to each card can then be placed in the foreground layer.

Though these programs have a slightly greater learning curve than slide-based authoring systems, they also offer greater flexibility, control, and power. Common card-based authoring systems include **Apple Computer's HyperCard,** and **Asymmetrix's ToolBook.** The metaphor used in ToolBook is pages in a book rather than cards in a stack. However, the basic idea and method of manipulating pages is the same. By looking at some of the key features found in Apple's HyperCard, you should get a general understanding of how these authoring systems work.

HYPERCARD

HyperCard is Apple's authoring program for creating custom, interactive multimedia applications. You can use HyperCard to create multimedia presentations, CD-ROM titles, courseware and computer-based training materials. HyperCard organizes information into "stacks" of cards. Users can use these stacks to navigate and search for information, view related text and graphics, hear sounds, watch a QuickTime movie, or listen to spoken words.

User Friendly Because no scripting experience is required, beginners can start creating stacks immediately. HyperCard also offers ready-to-use stacks, templates, and elements. At the same time, HyperCard provides a powerful and flexible development environment complete with powerful scripting tools, debugging tools, external commands, and many other features for professionals.

As an added bonus, thousands of HyperCard stacks are available as freeware or shareware. Though these already created multimedia applications may not be exactly what you want, they often provide a foundation from which you can build. For beginners, working with already created stacks is an excellent way to learn.

Powerful Development Features HyperTalk is HyperCard's programming language. It is a powerful, English-like scripting language. **AppleScript** is another scripting language available with the program. You can write scripts that launch, control, and exchange data with other applications or create and customize menus and tool palettes. You can create simple stacks or applications without learning any scripting languages. However, to set up more complex relationships within a multimedia application you'll need to know these scripting languages.

You can use **LiveCard** software to share your HyperCard projects over an Intranet or Internet Web site. In addition, HyperCard's functionality can be further extended with third-party add-on products. Other development tools include a **debugging menu** that lets you step through a HyperTalk script while it's running, and background processing that lets you continue working in other applications while complex scripts are running, compacting, or sorting. The **Variable Watcher** shows how variables are used and changed. It also lets you edit variables while debugging your script. The **Message Watcher** lets you view HyperTalk messages as they're sent. This way you can see how the logic of your script is working.

Support for Global Application Development WorldScript system extensions can be used to create multilingual HyperCard solutions. You can mix different character sets in a single field or script in French, Japanese, or other languages using international dialects of AppleScript software.

Multimedia Features With HyperCard you can choose from 256 colors that you can assign to multimedia elements such as buttons, fields, and backgrounds. You can use 24-bit color painting tools to create color images and to import and edit graphics. You can even have HyperCard read text aloud or add QuickTime movies, sounds, and graphics to your stacks.

Automated Tasks HyperCard offers many automated tasks. For example, you can assign tasks to buttons without writing scripts. You can navigate to other cards or launch applications. You can also add transitions between cards.

Flexible Formatting and Reporting With HyperCard you can design multiple report layouts for each stack. You can also copy and paste report formats between stacks. You can control the content, appearance and placement of text elements in reports, and you can create card sizes ranging from 1 by 1 inch to 18 by 18 inches.

Stand-Alone Application Capability You can save any HyperCard stack as a stand-alone, double-clickable multimedia application that can be distributed without software and royalty fees. This means users don't have to have HyperCard software to view your applications.

Using HyperCard HyperCard stacks come in a variety of shapes and sizes. However, there are many common elements. For example, arrow-shaped buttons are used to navigate through the cards in a stack while fields serve as containers for text.

Buttons usually include icons that indicate the type of command or activity they perform. For example, a button with a printer icon will print something.

At the top of the screen you'll find the **HyperCard Menu bar.** Commands from each menu give the user many options.

Keyboard Shortcuts are also available. You can find these to the right of each of the menu items. Menus can also be customized.

HyperCard has impressive search capabilities. To perform a search, use the find command and type in your text.

If HyperCard finds the string typed between the quotation marks, it stops searching and puts a box around the search string within the stack.

HyperCard offers five different **user levels.** You can set the user level by going to the home stack (type <Command H>) and setting the level on the **User Preference** card. The lowest level is **Browsing.** This is where most users will work with a multimedia application.

FIGURE 7.10

Icons indicate the type of command they perform.

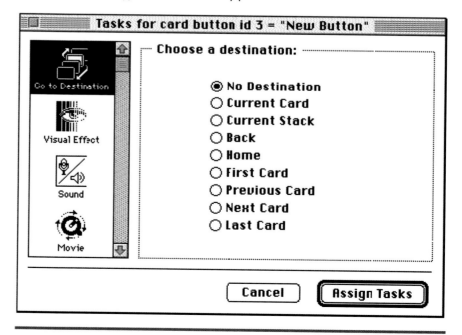

By setting the user level to 5 or **Scripting** you gain access to scripts and are able to make permanent changes to a stack.

3. Object-Based Authoring Programs

Object-based authoring programs use an object as a metaphor. These programs are powerful, non-linear authoring tools. Like card-based authoring systems, objects within these systems serve as object-oriented databases that store the many multimedia elements included in an application. With these programs you can create professional-level multimedia applications made up of objects that include text, graphics, animations, sound, full-motion video, as well as references to other elements and applications. In addition, programming languages within these authoring systems allow you to extend their capabilities further, making the possibilities seem almost endless.

Because these programs are significantly more sophisticated and powerful than slide-based and card-based authoring systems, they take more time to learn. In fact, they offer so many features that many professionals, who work with these programs every day and have for years, claim that they still don't know everything there is to know about them.

Common object-based authoring systems include the industry-leading **Macromedia Director,** as well as a powerful program by Oracle called **Oracle Media Objects.** Because Director is the industry leader for developing multimedia applications, we're going to look at how it works. If you would like more information on Oracle Media Objects, visit Oracle's site at http://www.oracle.com.

DIRECTOR

The object that Director uses as a metaphor is the theater. All of the windows and elements used in this program follow this theatrical metaphor. For example, multimedia elements such as text, graphics, animation, sound and video, become **cast members** on a **stage.** These cast members can then act out **scripts** in the **score.** To help you include interactivity and more complex references in your multimedia application, you can use Director's scripting language, **Lingo.**

All projects and presentations created in Director are called **movies.** Director gives you all the tools you need to assemble a wide variety of multimedia movies. In addition, Director can be used to edit existing movies. Let's explore the fundamentals of this powerful authoring program.

The Stage When you begin working with Director, try to think in terms of producing a theater performance. Using this parallel, the stage is a place where all of the props and actors interact. In Director, the **Stage** is the container for the multimedia elements and other objects that constitute the multimedia application.

When you first open Director, you will see an empty stage. Though there may be open windows lying on top of the stage, the stage is not a window. This distinction is important because many of the techniques you are comfortable using in a window do not apply on the stage. For example, you cannot paste objects onto the stage from the clipboard. The empty windows lying on top of the stage will be filled with the multimedia elements you intend to use to create your application.

You can change the size, location, and color of the stage. The size of the stage is particularly important when you are creating multimedia applications with Macromedia Director. This is because every computer monitor has a different resolution, and it is important that you pick a stage size that is easily displayed on many different types of computer monitors. At this time, a stage size of 640×480 will probably enable most people to view the animation you create for standard applications. For Internet movies, the stage size will be smaller and will vary depending upon bandwidth.

FIGURE 7.11

The Director stage serves as a container for the multimedia elements.

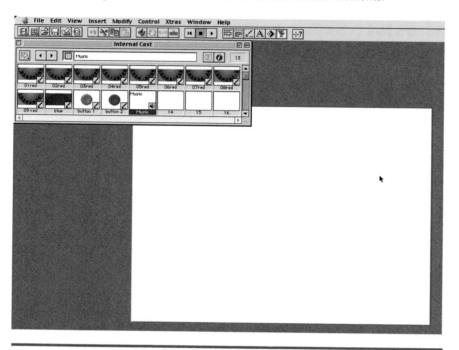

The Cast In Director, the **Cast window** will contain all of the **cast members.** These are the basic elements of any Director movie. In other words, all of the actors, scripts, directions, backgrounds, and props will become cast members and will be placed in the Cast window. Applying this metaphor to the actual creation of a multimedia application, all of the multimedia elements including text, graphics, animation, sound, and video will become cast members.

Within a single cast, Director allows you up to 32,000 cast members. However, because you can have multiple casts, the number of potential cast members is actually greater than 32,000. Multiple casts make it possible to better manage large numbers of cast members because the cast members are divided into smaller units.

To keep your Director movie files as small as possible, get rid of any cast members that aren't being used.

Cast members can be **internal** or **external.** Internal cast members are stored with the movie file. External cast members are stored outside. From the previous chapters, you will recall that keeping elements external to the multimedia application is often more efficient because it creates a smaller-sized application that requires less storage and processing power. In addition, by using external casts, you can create libraries of commonly used cast members that can be shared by multiple applications.

Cast members such as graphics, text, and scripts can be created in Director using the **tool palettes** from the **Text** and **Paint windows.** The graphics tool palettes in Director are very similar to those found in other paint programs. You will find the pencil, eraser, paint bucket, paintbrush, airbrush, rectangle, oval, polygon, and line tools. You will also have the ability to rotate, skew, and distort the image just as you can in other paint programs.

In the Text window you'll find text tools for creating and editing text. Using these features, you can change the font, point size, line spacing, alignment, and style of text without worrying about jaggies or staircasing that would result if the text were a bitmap image. These features make it easy to create the buttons that are often found in interactive animated movies.

FIGURE 7.12

In Director, you can have up to 32,000 cast members per cast.

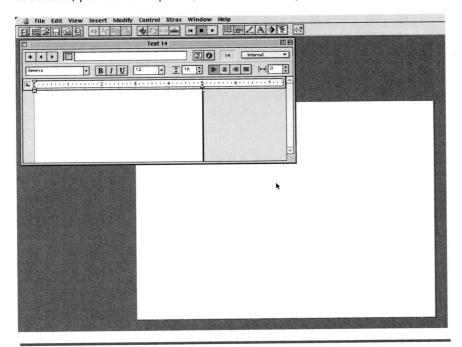

Cast members can also be imported from other applications. Macromedia Director supports a large number of file formats, so you can import graphics, text, sound, animation sequences, and digital video from many different types of image, sound, and video creation and editing programs.

FIGURE 7.13

Director supports a large number of file formats.

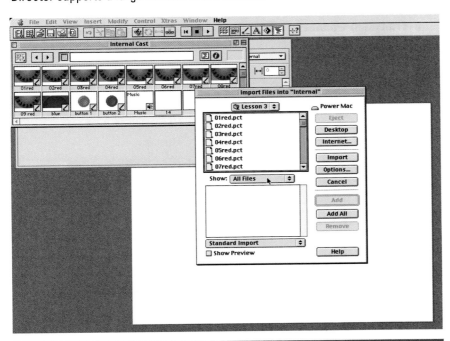

Cast members are varied file types, and all cast members have properties that vary with the file type. Typical properties include the cast member name, number, file size, color depth, and storage location.

The Score The **score** provides the Director movie with information about which cast members are on stage and where they are located. The score also holds information that determines the tempo of the movie, the transitions that will occur, the sounds that will play, and the scripts that will be followed. In other words, the score is the blueprint for the action in the theater production.

The score consists of columns and rows that divide it into a grid of cells. A **cell** occurs where the rows and columns meet. A cell is the smallest unit in the score and contains information about a cast member at a particular moment in the Director movie.

Each column represents a **frame.** A frame is a single moment (approximately one-third of a second in full motion) in a Director movie. It is a snapshot of the cast member at any point in the movie. Cast members include all of the elements that you can see, such as the text and graphics, as well as those that you can't see but are just as important to the movie, such as programmed scripts that access applications or control interactivity.

Each row represents a **channel,** which represents a specific type of information. In other words, channels represent the different activities that will take place in the animated movie. Think of channels as layers stacked on top of one another. There are channels designated to control transitions, those that control the tempo and others than control the script. The following channels are used in Macromedia Director:

- **Tempo Channel**—This channel allows you to change the tempo and insert pauses. It is this channel that determines the speed at which the movie will run. With this channel, you can also pause for a set amount of time, until a mouse or key action occurs, or while another movie or sound finishes playing.

- **Color Palette Channel**—Colors can be selected from special color palettes such as metallic or pastels, or you can create your own custom colors. Changes to the color palette of the movie appear in the Color Palette Channel at the point where the change takes effect.

- **Transition Channel**—Effects that occur as the movie moves from frame to frame are set in the Transition Channel. Common effects include fade,

FIGURE 7.14

The score is divided into a grid of cells.

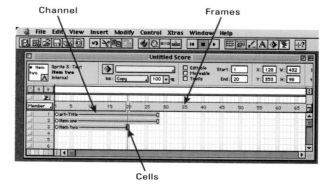

cover, wipe, strip, dissolve, and reveal. Third-party transitions can also be purchased and used with Director.

- **Sound Channels**—These channels contain the sound effects, voice-overs, and music for a movie. Director makes it possible to play music and voices at the same time by giving you more than one audio channel. All Macintosh computers and most PC compatibles support multichannel sound.

- **Script Channels**—The programming language included in Director is called **Lingo.** Lingo allows multimedia developers to extend Director's built-in capabilities to more fully customize a movie. Lingo scripts can be quite simple or extremely complex. The script channels contain the Lingo programming scripts for the different cast members.

- **Sprite Channels**—The sprite channel displays all of the cast members that have been added to the score. Sprites can be bitmaps, buttons, text, or shapes.

The score uses frames and channels to tie all of the multimedia elements together. When you are ready to add a cast member to the Director movie, you drag it to the score. Once a cast member has been placed in the score, it is called a **sprite.**

Sprites can be set up with different properties. For example, you can use an **ink effect** to give a sprite or range of sprites a particular appearance. The **transparent ink** effect can be set so that another sprite on another channel can show through or you can establish various shades of opacity by using the **blend ink** effect. Three other attributes or properties that can be set for a sprite or range of sprites include **trails, moveable,** and **editable.** With the trails property, a trail of layered images of the sprite remains along the sprite's path of movement. The moveable property enables users to interact with the sprite. As the movie is played back, the user can reposition moveable sprites. Similar to the moveable property, editable sprites can be edited by the user as the movie is being played.

In addition to all the cast members, the score also contains controls for the movie. These controls include scripts that expand the capabilities of the program. For example, a script might instruct the movie to open an external application when the mouse is positioned on top of a navigation button. Scripts allow you to include interactivity and more complex activity within your multimedia application.

FIGURE 7.15
Different properties can be set for each sprite.

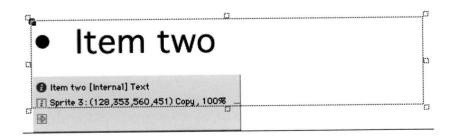

The score can be displayed using a number of different views.

- **Member**—The cast member view is the default. In this view, all of the cast members are identified by number or name.

- **Script**—In the script view, a notation is displayed to distinguish sprites that have an associated script from those that have none.

- **Motion**—The motion view uses arrows to denote the direction a sprite is moving across the stage. The introduction of new cast members is also noted in this view.

- **Ink**—The ink view indicates which ink effect has been applied to a sprite. For example, if a transparency ink effect has been applied to a sprite, this will be indicated by the letter "T."

- **Blend**—If a blend has been applied, this view displays the percentage of blend.

- **Extended**—The extended view enlarges the score. It displays all of the sprite information based on the settings checked in preferences.

Control Panel The **Control Panel** allows you to play the movies you create. The Control Panel buttons are very similar to those found on your VCR with some additional buttons for added control.

- **Step Backward** moves the movie back one frame at a time.

- **Step Forward** moves the movie forward one frame at a time.

- **Frames Per Second (fps) Button** is a toggle button. Actually, there are two frames per second (fps) buttons on the control panel. The top button indicates the speed of the movie. The bottom button allows you to monitor the speed of an individual frame. If you click the arrow in the lower corner of either button, it changes to seconds per frame.

- **Loop Playback** causes the movie to keep repeating through the entire range of selected frames.

- **Selected Frames Only** plays only the selected frames.

- **Play** starts the playback head through the movie or selected range of frames.

FIGURE 7.16

From the Control Panel, you can check the elements of your movie as they will appear when it is complete.

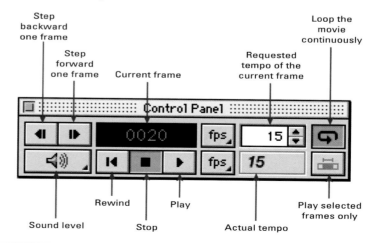

- **Stop** stops the movie on the frame the playback head was located on when the button was selected.

- **Rewind** takes the playback head back to the first frame.

- **Frame Counter** displays the currently active frame as the movie plays.

- **Frames Per Second (fps) Indicator** shows the current speed of the movie. Clicking the spin box will reset the speed.

- **Disable Sounds** toggles the sound on and off. Clicking the down arrow in the lower right corner allows you to control the volume.

Lingo Lingo is Director's scripting or programming language. Lingo gives you the ability to control the action in a movie more precisely. In addition, with Lingo you can assign additional attributes to cast members so that they can perform more than one job. It is Lingo that allows you to add interactivity to your multimedia application. In other words, by including **Lingo scripts** in your multimedia application, you can evaluate and respond to user actions, control sprites, navigate to new locations within or outside of the multimedia application, access and control external files and applications, create common interfaces, and evaluate math operations.

Lingo scripts are simply programming commands written in simple English-like word combinations that Director interprets and executes. Scripts are written in the script window and can consist of simple statements or extensive lines of code.

Lingo can be intimidating if you have never done any programming. However, the basics are actually quite simple to learn. Before you begin, however, you should have a basic understanding of how programming within Director works.

Object-oriented programming within multimedia authoring tools is event driven. When a certain **event** takes place, Director sends messages to the movie elements. These messages have been programmed in Lingo to be sent as a result of a user clicking the mouse on a particular button, a sprite reaching a particular destination on the screen, or some other activity that takes place within the movie. The set of instructions or program that determines what should occur when an event takes place is known as an **event handler.** For example, two of the most commonly used event handlers in Director are **on mouseUp** and **on exitFrame. On mouseUp** tells Director what action should occur if a mouse click is detected and **on exitFrame** tells Director what should occur as soon as the playback head leaves the current frame.

FIGURE 7.17

Scripts can be very basic or extremely complex lines of code.

```
on mouseUp
    set the movieRate of sprite theDVSprite = 0
    set the visible of sprite theDVSprite = FALSE
    — set the controller of member "myVideo" = FALSE
    — unloadMember "myVideo"
    updateStage
    set the visible of sprite theDVSprite = TRUE
    go to frame "myMarker" — (or whatever)
end
```

(from Macromedia Web page at http://www-euro.macromedia.com/support/director/ts/documents/video_tt_direct_to_stage.htm)

Scripts can be placed in different locations in a Director movie. The placement of the script determines its type. There are different types of scripts, each of which handles and processes Lingo commands differently.

- **Score Scripts** are assigned to cells in the score. Within the score, you will find **sprite scripts,** which are scripts assigned to a sprite cell. These scripts tell Director what to do should a certain event occur that involves the sprite. Sprite scripts only affect the specific sprite in the specific frame. For example, you can animate sprites and control their location and appearance based on changes that occur within the movie. You will also find **frame scripts** within the score. These scripts tell Director what to do when entering or leaving a particular frame. These scripts are assigned to frames rather than to cast members or sprites. Consequently, these scripts are only active when the movie is in the designated frame.

- **Cast Member Scripts** are assigned directly to cast members. The difference between sprite scripts and cast member scripts is that cast member scripts are performed no matter where and when the cast member is placed in the score, while sprite scripts are only applied to a specific sprite in a specific frame. For example, scripts could be written and assigned to cast members that are buttons. Whenever and wherever a user clicks the button (the cast member) the **on mouseUp** script will be triggered.

- **Movie Scripts** are assigned to the entire movie. These are the most basic scripts. The code in movie scripts is active whenever the movie is playing. For example, a script that tells Director to pause the movie until the user clicks a button is assigned to the entire movie.

- **Parent Scripts** are used to create **child objects.** Child objects are objects that have all of the same properties assigned to the parent, but behave differently. In other words, the parent script contains all of the variables that are assigned to the child objects.

Score, movie, and parent scripts all become cast members. However, because cast member scripts are already assigned to cast members, they are not cast members themselves.

Lingo scripts can be attached to objects or edited in the following locations:

- **Cast window**—In the Cast window, scripts can be attached to any cast member except other scripts. Scripts can also be edited in the Cast window.

- **Paint window**—Cast member scripts can be attached to bitmapped objects in the Paint window. Scripts can also be edited in the Paint window.

- **Text window**—Cast member scripts can be created or edited in the Text window.

- **Score window**—In the score window, a score script can be created. A script can also be added to or removed from a sprite or frame in the score window.

- **Script window**—Movie scripts can be added in the script window. Any script can be edited in the Script window.

With Lingo, the possibilities for creating multimedia applications full of interactivity and action are almost endless. Lingo is one of the primary reasons Director is such a versatile and powerful multimedia authoring tool.

Links There are several ways to create links within your multimedia application.

- **Specific Frames**—You can write scripts that go to a specific frame once a particular action has been completed. Though these scripts are easy to write and include in your multimedia application, they aren't automatically updated as your multimedia application is modified. In other words, if you write a script that tells the multimedia application to go to frame 10 upon exiting frame 3, and then you later add or delete frames before frame 10, the link no longer takes the user to the correct frame.

■ **Markers**—This type of linking system uses markers that are placed in the destination frame. These markers are assigned names. Instead of specifying a specific frame number in the script, the script references the name of the marker. Markers are the preferred method of setting links because frames can be added or deleted from the multimedia application without affecting the links.

4. Icon-Based Authoring Programs

Icon-based authoring programs use icons to give you a visual outline of your multimedia application. These authoring tools use a visual approach to programming and sequencing multimedia elements and events to create a multimedia application.

Because these programs tend to be very comprehensive, the learning curve to mastering them is steep. Two common icon-based authoring programs are **Macromedia Authorware** and **AimTech IconAuthor.** Let's take a look at the features found in Authorware.

AUTHORWARE

Authorware is a professional-level authoring program by Macromedia. With Authorware, multimedia applications are built with **icons.** Icons contain the different objects that will be included in your multimedia application. Different icons contain different multimedia elements such as text, graphics, animation, sound, and video.

First you create a logic sequence for your multimedia application. Next, you simply select from 15 different icons that you then drag and drop in the appropriate location on a **flowline.** These icons can be labeled so that they are easier to identify. The flowline organizes the icons and determines the sequence in which they will be played in the multimedia application. The flowline also provides a visual outline of the project and allows you to quickly assemble complex interactive applications without writing scripts or programs. After the structure has been developed, the content including text, graphics, animations, sound, and video, is referenced as the application plays.

Authorware was built with interactivity in mind. It provides a wide array of choices for including interactivity within your multimedia application. For example, you can design multimedia applications that have users click buttons, select objects, enter text, and move objects. In Authorware, it is also easy to design multimedia applications that can be navigated in a non-linear fashion by users.

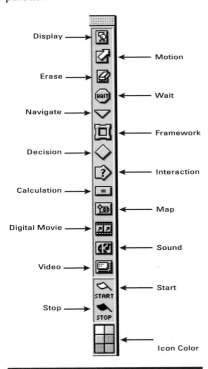

FIGURE 7.18

Macromedia Authorware icon palette.

Display — Motion
Erase — Wait
Navigate — Framework
Decision — Interaction
Calculation — Map
Digital Movie — Sound
Video — Start
Stop — Icon Color

Director vs. Authorware

Both Director and Authorware are extremely powerful multimedia authoring programs. While they are basically similar in that they allow you to create multimedia applications, there are some rather significant differences between the two. Director is the industry standard. Director is particularly good in its image manipulation and basic animation capabilities. It is the program of choice for people who want to create consumer multimedia applications. Well over half of all "entertainment" titles on the market today were created with Director.

Those people who wish to create business applications such as computer-based training (CBT) products more commonly use Authorware. Consequently, Authorware places less emphasis on creative magic and more emphasis on data handling. Authorware is better designed for handling interactive question and answer sessions. It is also better at keeping scores, records, and evaluations.

The approach used in each of these applications is also different. Once again, Director takes a more "creative" theatrical approach to its metaphor, while Authorware uses flowcharts, icons, and a timeline for a much more "logical" approach. As a direct result of its scripting language, Lingo, Director offers greater freedom and flexibility while Authorware is more formal and rigid. At the same time, Authorware generally has a steeper learning curve than Director.

SUMMARY

After you have developed and designed all of the elements that will be included in your multimedia application, you are ready to put it together using multimedia authoring software. Authoring programs are based on one of four metaphors—**slide-based, card-based, object-based,** and **icon-based.** These programs allow you to create, import, and integrate your multimedia elements into one multimedia application.

The **multimedia director,** also called the **multimedia architect,** is responsible for integrating all of the multimedia elements that have been created by the other media specialists. Using an authoring tool and the planning documents, the multimedia director will develop and design an efficient, cohesive, well-planned multimedia application. The multimedia director should possess excellent communication and technical skills.

Authoring a multimedia application involves planning and pulling everything together into one unified piece. The planning documents, including the **storyboards, scripts,** and **flowcharts,** are used to make sure that the original goals are achieved in the final application. While the media specialists are creating the text, graphics, sound, animation, and video for the multimedia application, the structure behind the final product should be evolving.

From the planning documents, **navigation structures** can be prepared. Several different methods of navigating a multimedia application include **linear, non-linear, hierarchical,** and **combination.**

Interactivity is created within the multimedia application when users are given choices or allowed to input individualized data. In creating interactivity, intuitive, user-friendly stimuli are important. Methods of interactivity should be obvious to the users. Ways of designing interactivity into your multimedia application include using **button & icons, menus, keyboard commands, hypermedia, text boxes, check boxes, radio buttons, drop-down list boxes,** and **drag & drop.**

When interactivity is included, multimedia applications must analyze the user's response and provide appropriate **feedback.** Appropriate feedback can be almost anything as long as it is appropriate to the choice and the goals of the multimedia application.

Slide-based authoring programs use the slide-show as a metaphor. These programs are linear **presentation packages** that generally don't allow you to include much interactivity in your application. These programs are simple to learn, but the control and power they offer is usually quite limited. Common slide-based authoring systems include **Microsoft PowerPoint, Adobe Persuasion, Corel's WP Presentation, and Claris Impact.**

Card-based authoring programs use stacks of cards or pages as a metaphor. The cards are actually databases that store the multimedia elements. On each card you may find text, graphics, animations, sound, full-motion video, or references to these objects. These programs permit **non-linear** navigation. Though they are more difficult to learn than slide-based programs, they offer greater flexibility, control, and power. Common card-based authoring systems include **Apple Computer's HyperCard, and Asymmetrix's ToolBook.**

Object-based authoring programs use an object as a metaphor. These programs are powerful, non-linear authoring tools. With these programs you can create professional-level multimedia applications. Programming languages within these authoring systems allow you to further extend their capabilities making the possibilities seem almost endless. Because these programs are significantly more sophisticated and powerful than slide-based and card-based authoring systems, they take more time to learn. Common object-based authoring systems include **Macromedia Director** and **Oracle Media Objects.**

Icon-based authoring programs use icons to give you a visual outline of your multimedia application. These authoring tools use a visual approach to programming and sequencing multimedia elements and events to create a multimedia application. Because these programs tend to be very comprehensive, the learning curve to mastering them is steep. Two common icon-based authoring programs are **Macromedia Authorware** and **AimTech IconAuthor.**

KEY TERMS

Slide-based	Card-based	Object-based
Icon-based	Multimedia director	Multimedia architect
Storyboards	Scripts	Flowcharts
Navigation structures	Linear	Non-linear
Hierarchical	Combination	Interactivity
Feedback	Presentation packages	PowerPoint
Persuasion	Presentation	Impact
HyperCard	ToolBook	Director
Media Objects	Authorware	IconAuthor

Matching Questions

a. linear	**b.** hierarchical	**c.** interactivity
d. hypermedia	**e.** radio	**f.** slide-based
g. templates	**h.** HyperTalk	**i.** score
j. control panel	**k.** Lingo	**l.** icons

_____ **1.** These are predesigned color schemes and designs that you can apply to your presentation to give it a professional and consistent feel.

_____ **2.** Using this navigation method, users maneuver through a multimedia application following a logical, branching structure.

_____ **3.** This allows you to play the Director movies you create.

_____ **4.** This window provides the Director movie with information about which cast members are on stage and where they are located.

_____ **5.** Navigation method where users navigate through the multimedia application sequentially.

_____ **6.** These buttons force users to select only one option from a list.

_____ **7.** This is Director's scripting or programming language.

_____ **8.** This occurs whenever users are given choices.

_____ **9.** This is what Authorware uses to build multimedia applications.

_____ **10.** Generally, this type of multimedia authoring program doesn't allow you to include much interactivity within your application.

_____ **11.** This is HyperCard's programming or scripting language.

_____ **12.** These are clickable elements such as text, graphics, sound, animation, or video that are assigned scripts that link users to other locations.

Fill-In Questions

1. From the planning documents, you can prepare _____ _____ or ways by which users maneuver through the multimedia application.

2. Using _____ _____, there is no prescribed or sequential path that must be followed.

3. No matter which method or methods of interactivity you design into your multimedia application, you will need to provide _____ to the user's response.

4. _____ are special effects that are applied between slides. _____ are special effects applied between bulleted items.

5. Common card-based authoring systems include _____ _____ _____, and _____ _____.

6. In Director, the _____ _____ will contain all of the _____ _____. These are the basic elements of any Director movie.

7. Cast members can be _____ or _____. _____ cast members are stored with the movie file while _____ cast members are stored outside.

8. The _____ _____ effect can be set so that another sprite on another channel can show through or you can establish various shades of opacity by using the _____ _____ effect.

9. The process of putting content into an icon is referred to as _____ ____ _____.

DISCUSSION QUESTIONS

1. What are the four functions found in most multimedia authoring systems?

2. What are the four categories of multimedia authoring systems? How do they differ?

3. What are the roles and responsibilities of the multimedia director or architect?

4. How does interactivity enhance a multimedia application?

5. What are some of the elements of interactivity and how are they used in interactive multimedia applications?

6. What are some key features found in Microsoft PowerPoint?

7. What are some key features found in HyperCard?

8. What are some key features found in Macromedia Director?

9. How can Lingo be used to extend Director's functionality?

10. What are some key features found in Macromedia Authorware?

HANDS-ON EXERCISES

1. Describe a multimedia application you would like to create. In your description, include the type of graphics, animation, sound, and video you would use. List the specific multimedia authoring program you would use to create your application and justify your reason for choosing this tool.

2. Using the multimedia application you created in Exercise 1, describe the type of navigational structure you would use to get users through your multimedia application. Draw a diagram illustrating this structure.

3. Using the multimedia application you created in Exercise 1, describe other stimuli you would use in your multimedia application to promote interaction. Describe the feedback users would receive as a result of their interactions or responses to the stimuli included in the multimedia application.

Case Study: Chapter 7

This past week, the president of Island WaterCraft, Luke Scott, contacted Jamie Hunt, production manager at Digital Design, to inquire about the possibility of creating a second multimedia application using the same content found on the Web page currently under construction. Mr. Scott would like to include the multimedia application on a kiosk located at SeaTac airport.

Because the content and multimedia elements for the multimedia application are basically complete, Jamie doesn't think it will be too difficult to design a second, touch-screen interface using multimedia-authoring software. However, before she agrees to proceed with a second multimedia application, she will discuss the possibility with Walt Stevens, multimedia director.

Walt concurs. Because the content and multimedia elements are done, creating a second multimedia application for a touch-screen will involve designing a new interface, navigation structure, and interactivity using multimedia-authoring software.

Walt must first decide which multimedia-authoring tool he will use to design this application. In making his decision, Walt considers the navigational structure, the amount of interactivity, and the method and medium of delivery.

The navigational structure will be combination. For the most part, non-linear navigation will allow users to jump from one topic of interest to another without following a sequential path. The only linear or sequential element will be the video clip of Mr. Scott welcoming viewers and encouraging safety and fun.

Users will interact with the multimedia application by clicking on the animated personal watercraft that serve as hypermedia links. The feedback users get as a result of clicking on the personal watercraft will include watching these clickable animated watercraft jump a wave, complete a 360-degree turn, or speed off into the sunset as they hear revving engines, rushing water, and the SeaDoo music in the background. Users will then be transported to different screens within the multimedia application.

Walt knows that this multimedia application will only reside on the computer supporting the kiosk; therefore, it probably does not need to be cross-platform compatible. However, using tools that support either platform will be to the company's advantage just in case the computer platform supporting the kiosk changes or Mr. Scott decides to place it on other kiosks. Walt will be able to save the multimedia application to an Iomega Jaz disk to be transported to the hard drive of computer at SeaTac airport supporting the kiosk.

A slide-based multimedia-authoring program is too simplistic for this project because of the non-linear navigation and degree of interactivity needed. Any of the other three types of authoring programs would work, but Walt believes Macromedia Director will be the best choice. Lingo scripts that link users to other areas of the multimedia application can easily be assigned to the animated personal watercraft. In addition, the multiple audio channels available in Director will make it easy for Walt to include both background music and content sound. Director also makes it easy to synchronize all of the elements.

Multimedia and the Internet

1. Relate the general history and background of the Internet and the World Wide Web

2. Understand the purpose and importance of multimedia technology on the Web

3. Define some of the basic terminology associated with the Internet including Internet, Intranet, hypertext, World Wide Web, bandwidth, transmission speed, modem, ISDN, T1, cable modems, browsers, applets, plug-ins, helper applications, zine, push technology, and electronic agents

4. Discuss the multimedia elements as they relate to the Web

5. Describe the purpose of the following software programs: GIF Construction Set, GIFBuilder, RealAudio, QuickTime, Shockwave, and Flash

6. Explain the Set, GIFBuilder, RealAudio, QuickTime, Shockwave, and Flash

7. Explain the advantages of using Web-based multimedia applications

8. Describe some of the uses of Web-based multimedia applications

9. Describe the roles and responsibilities of the Web master

10. Describe the four different methods of creating Web-based multimedia applications

11. Provide examples of HTML markup tags and explain how they are used

12. Recognize the names of common HTML converters and editors

13. List and describe some of the key features found in converters

14. List and describe some of the key features found in editors

15. Explain how Portable Document Software is used to create Web pages

16. Identify some of the advantages and disadvantages of using PDF files on the Web

17. List and describe the primary programming and scripting languages used to create interactivity on Web pages

Introduction

The Internet grew out of a project called **ARPANET** started by the military in the 1960s to create a decentralized communication network. Today, the **Internet** is a network of networks that connects millions of computers and people around the globe. **Intranets** are also quite common today. **Intranets** are private networks accessible only by the people within the organization or people with proper authorization to access the internal network. Intranets are distinguished from LANs (local area networks) in that the environment is browser-based just like the WWW. Through Intranets, corporations can make information that was once spread across the organization accessible to anyone in any department within the organization. Though Intranets may provide access to the Internet, most companies protect their Intranets from access by outsiders.

In March of 1989, Tim Berners-Lee of the European Particle Physics Center (CERN) in Switzerland proposed a standardized hyperlinking system that would permit the distribution and sharing of information around the world. This hyperlinking system was called the **World Wide Web.** It came into existence in May of 1991.

Mosaic was the first cross-platform Web browser that fully exploited the Web's **hypermedia** capability. The Mac and Windows versions of Mosaic were released in the fall of 1993 and were available for free from the University of Illinois supercomputer. Because it put a friendly graphical-user interface browser in the hands of millions of users, Mosaic played a key role in influencing the explosive growth of the Web. Although newer browsers such as **Netscape Navigate Communicator** and **Microsoft Internet Explorer** have surpassed Mosaic's original capabilities, it was the development of this first multimedia browser that popularized multimedia on the Web and also led to the Web's rapidly growing popularity.

FIGURE 8.1

The Web allowed the distribution and sharing of information around the world.

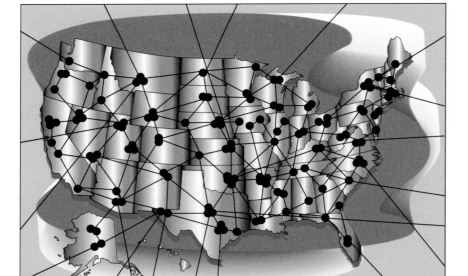

FIGURE 8.2

Graphical-user interface browsers played a key role in the explosive growth of the Web.

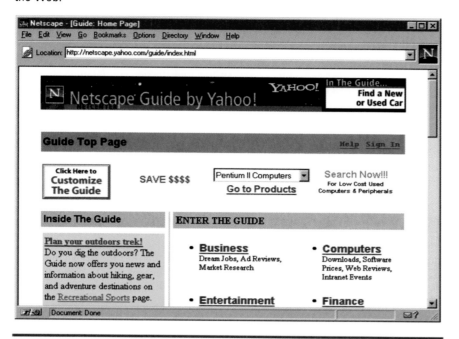

By the summer of 1994, the Web had grown far beyond anyone's wildest expectations. There were literally millions of new users on the Web, and to many of them, the Web was the Internet. Today there are literally billions of Web sites through which people share information around the world. **Web pages** are hypermedia documents that can contain text, graphics, photographs, animation, sound, video, software, applications, and data forms. It is becoming easier to include multimedia on Web pages. Because most of the underlying principles of multimedia technology are the same for the Internet, in this chapter we will attempt to address only the differences.

Bandwidth

It is impossible to write accurately about changing technology. By the time you read this, something or everything will have changed. That's part of the challenge and excitement of this industry. At this time, however, the biggest obstacle to delivering multimedia over the Internet is **bandwidth.** Bandwidth is the amount of data that can be transferred across some physical channel in a given period of time. Channels with a larger bandwidth can transmit more data at one time. Like most technologies, transmission rates are improving, but they have not yet matched the development of multimedia technology.

Text files are generally small. Simple graphic files are much larger than text files. Audio files are even larger than graphics and video files are larger still. Though multimedia is becoming increasingly more common on the Internet, multimedia files are much larger than text alone. This large file size makes them difficult to transmit across channels.

This large file size also means that multimedia applications can clog the lines connecting the Internet. There are several places where bottlenecks can occur — the speed of the modem, the bandwidth of the phone line or cable connection, the server connection, the number of users, and of course, the volume of data being sent and received.

Bandwidth suppliers are trying to make more bandwidth available and content providers are trying to improve the way data is compressed. This combination will create greater possibilities for delivering multimedia applications over the Web. Everything will continue to improve. It's only a matter of time before these multimedia delivery obstacles are surmounted, and in the technology industry, improvements occur in no time.

In the meantime, when we include multimedia on our Web pages, we have to work hard to keep our files small. If we make them too large and it takes them too long to download, viewers will be long gone and off to another site before they have even seen our site.

Transmission Standards

In working with Web-based multimedia applications, **transmission speed** is the time it takes for the data to be sent from the Web server to the user's computer. Transmission speed is usually measured in **bits per second (bps).** As mentioned above, there are many factors that influence the data's transmission speed. One of the most important is the data channel.

MODEMS

Modem stands for modulate/demodulate. A modem converts a computer's digital signals to analog signals that can be transmitted along standard telephone lines. Once the signals have been transmitted, a modem on the other end converts the analog signal back to a digital signal for the computer to interpret. Today's modems are limited by the telephone lines they are connected to.

ISDN

ISDN stands for **Integrated Services Digital Network.** ISDN can deliver almost four times greater performance than most modems. Depending on where you live, you may be able to get dial-up ISDN service for as low as $30 per month. However, despite its relatively low cost and obvious improvement over modems, many people already consider this technology outdated.

T1

A **T1 line** delivers bandwidth approximately equal to the bandwidth delivery of 12 ISDN lines or 50 standard modems. The transmission speed is slightly over 1.5 Mbps (megabits per second). The cost of a T1 line varies depending upon location, but they generally range in price from about $500 to $1,500 per month. In addition, T1 lines require additional equipment, including a router that will cost about $3,000. The logistics of installing a T1 line can also be quite complicated.

CABLE MODEMS

Hybrid Fiber Coax (HFC) is the latest projected cabling scheme. It is projected that it will permit transmission of 10 to 40 Mbps for a cost of approximately $30 per month. This technology will also require additional equipment. Though this technology would deliver about 26 times more than T1 lines and about 1,300 times more than standard modems, it would probably mean sharing bandwidth with a variety of subscribers, each of whom gets a slice of bandwidth. Depending on how many other subscribers are working at the same time, it may not provide anything more than current modem bandwidth. In addition, cable modems still are not standardized.

Despite the fact that we are somewhat crippled by limited bandwidth, the Internet and Intranets still offer vast storage devices and excellent distribution vehicles. Though the ultimate potential of multimedia over the Internet will not be reached until we have fiber optic cable delivering full virtual reality information environments to every home, many individuals and organizations are still using Web-based multimedia applications with great success.

Browsers

The primary purpose of the **browser** is to display Web pages. More specifically, the browser provides the front-end interface that translates and displays downloaded **hypertext markup language (HTML)** documents and the media files and **applets,** or mini-applications, that accompany these documents.

Browser software is getting more and more sophisticated. The newest versions of **Microsoft Internet Explorer** and **Netscape Communicator** now include active channels that feed you information that you request and subscriptions to Web sites that monitor changes in Web pages to which you subscribe. Though all browsers use similar technology, making it easy for users to interface with your multimedia application, each browser may display Web pages differently. It is the browser and the user's hardware that ultimately determine how a Web page will look.

FIGURE 8.3

The primary purpose of the browser is to translate HTML and display the Web page.

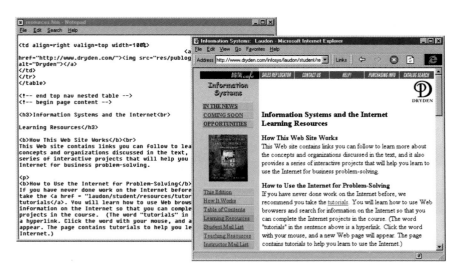

Advantages of the Web for Multimedia Delivery

The Web offers many advantages for delivering multimedia applications. In addition, most computer applications can be improved by adding multimedia elements to them.

Cross-Platform

The features and capabilities of HTML are evolving. Some browsers will support proposed HTML standards before others. This means some HTML features will work just fine when using one browser, but they won't work at all when using another. For this reason, it is important to test your Web-based multimedia application using different browsers and different versions of the same browser.

For the most part, Web pages are **cross-platform** multimedia applications. This means users can view Web pages equally well from a Macintosh; a PC running DOS, Windows, Windows 95, or Windows NT; or even a high-end Sun Workstation running UNIX. Cross-platform compatibility makes it much easier for developers to serve a wider audience because they only have to create one application that will run on any platform instead of creating multiple versions of the same application.

Also, unlike a multimedia application distributed via CD-ROM, a Web-based multimedia application doesn't require one program to play it from beginning to end. Instead, many applets are accessed from within the browser to play the different multimedia elements as needed.

In addition, **plug-ins** and **helper applications** extend the capabilities of the browser software. These programs are installed on the user's computer system and the browser is set up to access them as needed. Like most software, plug-ins and helper applications are constantly being upgraded and improved.

Because some multimedia features require plug-ins and helper applications that may only be available for certain platforms or operating systems, some Web-based multimedia applications may no longer be cross-platform compatible. To ensure cross-platform compatibility, choose formats for your multimedia elements that offer plug-ins for multiple platforms.

When you are creating a multimedia application to be delivered via the Web, cross-platform compatibility allows you to concentrate on the browser, plug-ins, and helper applications instead of the platform. This way, you can focus more on content and less on the user's hardware and operating system. Provided the user has a browser with the appropriate plug-ins and helper applications, the platform isn't a concern.

FIGURE 8.4

Plug-ins and helper applications extend the capabilities of the browser.

User-Friendly

Because browsers are basically the same and are designed to be extremely intuitive, users don't have to learn to use a new interface to use Web-based multimedia applications. In addition, multimedia interfaces in general are much more user-friendly than menu-driver or text-based interfaces. Both of these items reduce the time it takes users to begin making productive use of multimedia applications.

Enhanced Access to Information

By using multimedia in a Web page, you enhance the user's attention, understanding, and retention of the material presented. In addition, multimedia makes Web pages more interesting and more fun.

Cost Effective

Delivering multimedia over the Web is inexpensive. Anyone with average equipment can create multimedia Web pages, and most Internet service providers allow you a certain amount of storage space on their servers as part of your monthly subscription fee.

Dynamic

Unlike multimedia applications delivered via mediums such as CD-ROM, multimedia applications delivered via the Web can be updated and changed at a moment's notice. This makes them extremely **dynamic.** Consequently, Web pages don't need to be scrapped. When information is outdated or a new look is in order, they merely need to be updated.

FIGURE 8.5

Unlike many other mediums, Web pages are dynamic.

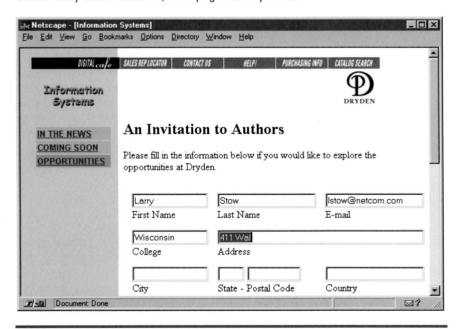

Uses of Multimedia on the Web

Because there are literally billions of Web pages on the Internet, one way to make your Web page stand out from the rest is to liven it up with multimedia. In addition to making your Web page stand out, multimedia is an excellent way to convey information. People notice and retain more when they involve multiple senses. New and exciting Web-based multimedia applications appear every day. Here are some ways multimedia is being used to enhance Web sites.

Education and Computer-Based Training

More and more training programs are being offered online using Web-based multimedia applications. Corporations are including computer-based training modules on their Intranets or at corporate Web sites. This method of disseminating training is inexpensive and available to employees on demand and independent of time, trainer, or location.

For these same reasons, the number of educational institutions offering courses via the Web is growing tremendously. Tools used to enhance these courses include slide-based authoring programs that allow linear slide shows to be saved as HTML files. Instructors can easily create presentations that include multimedia elements and then place these on the Web. Students can view these Web-based multimedia presentations at any time, on any computer that has Internet access.

Because tools like this are becoming more common and online education is becoming more popular, many institutions now offer certificates and degrees using only the Web. In fact, virtual universities are being created that have no buildings or classrooms. All of the courses are offered online.

Intranets

Web-based multimedia applications provide an excellent way for corporations to share information at the same site or around the world. Because Web pages are non-platform specific, corporations can use them to disseminate information throughout the world without worrying about which platform the employee or client will use to view the site. In addition, because the front-end interface of the browser is common and intuitive, the time required to train employees to use Intranet multimedia applications is very short.

Most Intranets provide access to the Internet. However, to keep outsiders from accessing confidential information on a company Intranet, most corporations have set up **firewalls.** Firewalls are separate hardware and software that lie between the Intranet Web server and the Internet to monitor connections, encrypt and protect data, and generally maintain the security of the internal network.

Electronic Periodicals, References, and Books

Many newsletters, newspapers, magazines, books, encyclopedias, and other reference materials are being offered as Web-based multimedia applications. These applications include interactive multimedia features such as full-text search capabilities, graphics, audio, and video.

Zine and **digizine,** which are digital magazines targeted to specific and broader audiences respectively, usually include access to an expanded set of information and multimedia features. Some advantages of offering online publications with multimedia features include hypermedia cross-referencing, advanced online-search capabilities, ability to listen to actual interviews, ability to view video and animation, and other increased multisensory experiences that are more enjoyable and memorable than viewing text and graphics alone.

Push Technology

There is a growing trend on the Internet toward **push technology** and **electronic agents.** These two technologies are extremely interactive. Push technology allows you to make advanced requests for specific information. When new information on the requested topic is available, the server delivers the information to your computer. In other words, as Web sites are added and new information becomes available, you aren't required to search for it; instead, it is automatically delivered to you. Like push technology, electronic agents conduct searches for information while you continue working. They free you from performing tedious, ongoing searches for information you want and need.

PointCast Network (PCN) and Marimba's Castanet are two Web-based multimedia applications that employ push technology. You can visit PointCast's site at http://www.pointcast.com.

Advertising, Marketing and Virtual Shopping

Multimedia captivates and is therefore employed extensively in advertising and marketing. Many Web-based multimedia applications designed to sell products and services include attention-getting graphics, animation, sound, and video. In addition, interactive forms are available for ordering products or requesting additional information via snail mail or e-mail.

FIGURE 8.6

Electronic agents conduct your searches for you.

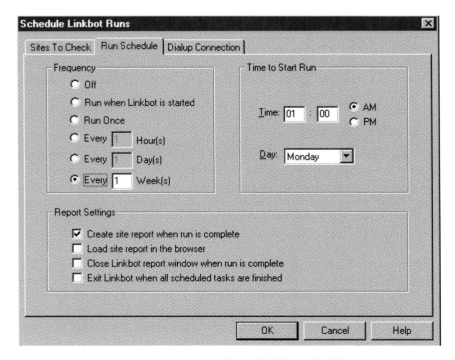

Animated logos and banners advertising products, services, and links to other sites are common on the Web. Multimedia advertising pays for Web sites so that most of these sites can remain free to users.

Record numbers of businesses are using multimedia Web pages to market their goods and services online. **Electronic catalogs** and **malls** offer virtual shopping experiences with thousands of storefronts to choose from. If you'd like to experience virtual shopping, visit the Internet Mall at http://www.internet-mall.com.

Interactive forms even make it possible for users to order online. At this time, the biggest obstacle to online purchasing is the perceived insecurity of supplying a credit card number. However, Web-based purchases will rise as security improves and people feel more comfortable ordering online with credit cards and **electronic cash (e-cash).** With e-cash you "make a deposit" with a third party, such as a bank, which then electronically pays the online vendor after you authorize a request for payment.

Entertainment and Games

Entertainment and games have promoted the growth of multimedia everywhere including the Internet. The Web is now being used to disseminate online games that can be played by the user alone or with players around the world. Web-based games come complete with 3D graphics and animation, sound, and video. Other interactive entertainment is also available on the Web.

Virtual Reality (VR)

Multimedia can also be used to create artificial environments complete with 3D images that can be explored and manipulated. This is called **virtual reality (VR).** VR on the Web is created using **VRML (virtual reality modeling language)** or the **QuickTime VR (QTVR)** authoring tool. VRML enables Web page developers to create 3D objects that users can manipulate with a pointing device such as a mouse, trackball, or joystick. QTVR allows developers to create entire 3D interactive environments for the Web. These environments include 3D objects and full panoramic views of objects and locations. To see some of these 3D interactive environments and find out more about the tools used to create them, you can visit Apple Computer's QuickTime City site at http://quicktime.apple.com/qt-city.

Communication

Using the Internet for alternative methods of communication other than common e-mail, newsgroups, and chat are also on the rise. For example, the Internet can now be used to send and receive sound in real time. This means users can make long-distance phone calls without using a long-distance phone company. In other words, for the price of an **Internet phone** and the monthly fee for an Internet connection, users can place calls all over the world. At this time, the quality is quite poor, but this too shall improve.

Similarly, **desktop video conferencing** over the Internet permits low-cost, cross-platform visual communication around the world. In addition to seeing each other, participants can also share and edit documents via a common whiteboard. With desktop videoconferencing, corporations no longer need to spend huge sums of money on employee travel to conferences, seminars, and other meetings.

FIGURE 8.7

VRML is the programming language used to create 3D worlds on the Web.

The Multimedia Elements on the Web

The same multimedia elements used in other multimedia applications can be used on the Web. Because Chapters 3–6 specifically address the creation and design of these elements, we won't do that again in this chapter. However, we will quickly revisit the elements and describe those attributes that are unique to using them in Web-based multimedia applications. It is important to understand the requirements of the multimedia elements that you want to include in your multimedia Web site. Before you begin, make sure you have the tools to create them as well as the system to support them. Also, don't forget your audience's computer system. If your audience can't benefit from what you've created, you're wasting your time.

Text

Text is still a very important element used extensively to convey information on Web pages. Fonts, color, style, and special effects can enhance text. Remember, use serif fonts for large bodies of textual information because they are easier to read and use sans serif fonts for headings and titles.

On Web pages, less text is usually better. Don't include text that users don't want or need. Hypertext extends the capabilities of Web pages by allowing users

FIGURE 8.8

Hypertext allows you to keep the text on each page to a minimum.

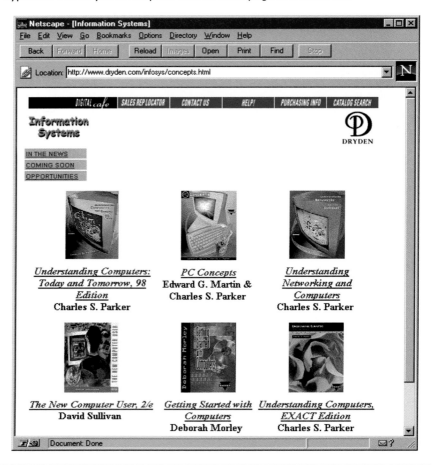

to link to related topics. Hypertext can allow you to keep text on each page to a minimum. By setting up hyperlinks, users can link to another page if they want to read more on those topics that interest them.

Position text carefully to achieve a good balance with the other multimedia elements. For example, you can wrap text around a related graphic to create an attractive, well-balanced paragraph with visual appeal.

Graphics

Whenever you can, use graphics to communicate. Graphics are important elements on Web pages. They can be used as backgrounds where the image is simply **tiled** or repeated over and over behind the other elements on a Web page. Graphics can also be used as navigation buttons, toolbars, icons, or content.

The graphic file formats supported on the Internet include GIF, JPEG, and PDF files. There are advantages and disadvantages to each format.

GIF files only support 256 colors. GIF files permit transparent colors to be displayed. This means that background colors and images can show through. GIF files also allow greater creativity because you can use them to display irregular shaped images. GIF files can also be **interlaced.** When downloaded, interlaced images appear blurry and then gradually increase in detail until they are completely clear.

Using this method, viewers can usually determine what the image will be before it is entirely downloaded.

JPEG files support millions of colors. JPEG files are usually smaller than GIF files, however, JPEG files are restricted to rectangular images with straight edges. JPEG images load in a non-interlaced manner from top to bottom. Users must patiently wait to see the entire picture.

PDF stands for **portable document format.** Though PDF files require a viewer to be displayed, this is the only way that vector-based images can be viewed on Web pages. In addition to the fact that they could not be viewed online without this format, there are other advantages to using the PDF format for vector-based images. Hyperlinks can be included directly into PDF images, and vector-based images can also be scaled or zoomed.

Many traditional document file formats such as Microsoft Word or Adobe Pagemaker files can also be easily converted to a PDF format so that they can be viewed on Web pages. **Adobe Acrobat** is probably the most common portable document application and reader used on the Web. Other popular portable document programs include **Envoy** and **Common Ground.**

Remember that graphic files should be small so that the Web page can download as quickly as possible. The recommended file size for graphics on the Internet is no larger than about 30K.

Animation

Animation on the Web can be accomplished in several ways. The easiest way is to use **animated GIF files.** As you may recall from Chapter 4, animated GIF files store an entire sequence of still images in one file. The entire sequence is replayed when the file is downloaded.

The **GIF Construction Set for Windows/Windows 95** is a powerful collection of tools for working with multiple-block GIF files. This program is incredibly easy to use. The program's "Animation Wizard" will have you creating nifty little animation in no time. About the only thing you need to supply is some images to work with and a bit of artistic talent. Visit the Alchemy Mindworks Web page at http://www.mindworkshop.com for up-to-date information on this software. A powerful tool for building animated GIFs on the Macintosh is **GIFBuilder.**

Another way to create animation is to program it using Java. **Java** is a non-platform specific programming language that is becoming increasingly popular on the Web. With Java, tiny little programs called **applets** can be written to extend the capabilities of Web pages. **Java applets** can program images to move or display sequential frames thus creating animation. Java animation is more sophisticated than animated GIF files because interaction can be built into the applet.

A third way to create animation on the Web is to use **Shockwave.** Shockwave by Macromedia is a set of compression tools that enable graphics, sound, and

FIGURE 8.9

One animated GIF file stores an entire sequence of images.

FIGURE 8.10

This Java applet allows you to change the position of lines in the graph by moving the sliding controls for tax, supply and demand.

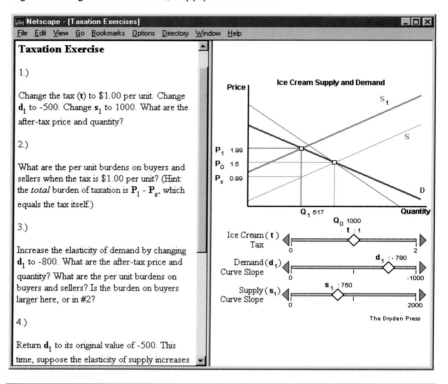

animation to be converted into a format appropriate for delivery via the Web. Shockwave allows you to run Director and Authorware movies through a utility called **AfterBurner** that converts the files to Web-ready Shockwave applications. Once a file has been prepared using one of Macromedia's products, it can easily be exported to the Shockwave format for delivery over the Internet. In order to view the files, Internet users must have the appropriate Shockwave plugs-ins setup on their browser. Shockwave plug-ins allow files created with Authorware or Director to be viewed over the Internet or Intranets.

Because you can basically use the features available in Director or Authorware to create your animations, Shockwave applications can also be quite sophisticated. For example, your Shockwave animations can include interaction and sound.

More recently, Macromedia **Flash** is being touted as the Web page tool of choice. Flash is a full-featured package for creating vector-based graphical elements including buttons and animation. Because Flash works with vector-based images, which are more flexible and require less storage capacity than comparable bitmapped images, it appears to have a bright future for creating Web page elements. Flash is also capable of integrating sound, interactivity, and transitions into Web pages. Predominantly, Flash is being used to create static, but zoomable illustrations; interactive interfaces; and vector-based animations.

Sound

Sound can greatly enhance a Web page. On a Web page, sound can be played as background music, as a specific sound effect that can be heard when you click on a button or drag an object, or as a live broadcast interview.

There are several audio file formats supported on the Internet, and several ways of delivering audio on the Web.

DIGITAL AUDIO

Digital audio files are actual sounds that have been recorded and digitized. Among the downloadable digital audio formats that you can use on the Web are WAVE, AIFF, and AU. You can also serve streaming audio files in formats such as RealAudio. These sound file formats can also be included with video.

MIDI

As you will recall from Chapter 5, unlike digital audio files, **MIDI** files or digital music files are synthesized instead of recorded. MIDI files can also be used to control musical instruments connected to the computer. MIDI files aren't as rich and realistic as digital audio file formats; however, they are much smaller and definitely quite suitable for use in some applications.

DOWNLOADABLE AUDIO

Downloadable audio is a method of delivering audio where the sound file is transferred from the Web server to the user's computer before it is played. In order to be played, the entire file must be transferred. Download time varies depending on the length, quality, and file format of the audio clip. With downloadable audio, visitors download an audio file from a Web page to their own personal computers. Once downloaded, the audio file must then be decompressed before it can be played. To be played, an audio player compatible with the audio file format used to store the file must be used.

When you embed downloadable sound files on your Web pages, be sure to label clearly the size and type of audio files so that users can determine whether or not they wish to wait for the sound files to download. By labeling files, you also enable users to choose only those files that are compatible with their system. Unfortunately, labeling your files doesn't guarantee that users won't have problems, but it helps.

STREAMING AUDIO

Streaming audio is a method of delivering audio where a continuous stream of uninterrupted audio is transmitted from the Web server to the user's computer. The entire file does not need to be transferred before the sound begins to play. Instead, as portions of the audio are received, they are played. Therefore, the download time for streaming audio is insignificant. Although streaming audio doesn't offer the quality found in downloadable clips, the sound is more immediate.

RealAudio by Progressive Networks is one of the most popular programs for streaming audio from a Web page. To convert a sound file to the RealAudio (RA) format you need the RealAudio encoder. To serve the sound from your Web server, you need the RealAudio Server software. For users to play the RealAudio sound you are serving, they need the RealAudio player plug-in for use with their browser. The encoder and player are free. After all of the pieces are in place, audio can be streamed from a recording or broadcast from pre-recorded audio by feeding the signal from an external source such as a VCR, CD player, or tape deck.

Shockwave and **QuickTime** can also be used to provide audio on Web pages. Though these formats store video as well as sound, you don't have to include the video. Therefore, you can use either one of these formats without the video to provide quality sound to your users.

Downloadable audio files are better if you are concerned with short clips of higher quality, although streamed audio is better for lower-quality, longer clips such as a speech or interview.

Make sure your audio can be served through a firewall. This is primarily dependent upon the player. If the player is a feature of the browser, this won't be a problem. If, however, the player is simply launched by the browser and then makes its own connection to some non-HTTP server, it may not play. If it doesn't play, a significant portion of your audience may be lost. RealAudio works through some, but not all firewalls.

FIGURE 8.11

RealAudio is a popular program for streaming audio on the Web.

Video

Like animation, digital video files store a sequence of still images. Unlike animation, these still images are generally real photographs. Using software, digital video files can be edited and processed to include special effects. Two commonly supported video file formats found on the Internet are AVI and QuickTime. As you will recall from Chapter 6, **CODECs** (compression/decompression schemes) must also be applied to digital video to achieve a level of compression that creates the smallest possible file with the highest possible quality.

RealVideo, a new technology by Progressive Networks allows you to use encoders and players to stream video files just as you stream audio files. **QuickTime** is an Apple technology that is quite entrenched on all computer platforms. It can be found on Macintosh computers as well as PCs running Windows 3.x, Windows 95, and Windows NT. QuickTime movies can be viewed over the Internet and can display animation, video, audio, and 3D interactive QuickTime Virtual Reality environments. Another common video format found on the Internet is AVI.

The Web Master

Depending upon the size of the project and to whom you talk, the Web page designer and the Web master may be two different people filling two different positions. If this is the case, the Web page designer is responsible for creating the Web site while the Web master is responsible for managing the files on the Web site. In this context, we are assuming that the Web master will design and manage the Web pages on the site. The Web master is the foundation of any multimedia project on the Internet.

In addition to creating and maintaining Internet Web pages, the Web master is also responsible for converting multimedia applications to Web pages or creating

FIGURE 8.12

QuickTime movies can be included on Web pages.

Web pages with multimedia elements. The Web master is responsible for understanding and becoming skilled in new Web page creation tools and technologies and for writing scripts using Lingo, Java, JavaScript, VRML, and other scripting languages used to include interactivity in a multimedia Web site. The Web master will also ensure that the Web page is technically correct and functional on the Web server.

Planning the Multimedia Web Site

The planning phase is the most important phase in developing any multimedia application because this stage sets the precedents for all other phases of the project. A poor plan or no plan can waste time, money, and effort. Like all other multimedia applications, multimedia Web sites require careful planning to be successful. A plan must be created and the layout and preparation of a Web site must be mapped out. Time spent planning and preparing will pay off in the long run.

Purpose

Step number one is to have a clear understanding of the Web site's goals and purpose. If an entire team of people will create the Web site, everyone should share the same vision for the site. This shared vision can only come from communication and the development and use of planning documents including storyboards, scripts, and flowcharts. To determine the purpose of a Web site, try to imagine why users would visit the site and what they would gain once they got there.

The Web can be a fairly complex development environment. Chapter 9 addresses the planning and design process for mulitmedia applications including Web pages. In addition to using storyboards, scripts, and flowcharts for a Web site, you will also need to develop a **site map** and **link map.** The site map provides the developer or Web master with a complete overview of the site. It illustrates the structure of the contents and their relationship to one another. The link map serves as a schematic that illustrates the interconnectivity of Web pages within the site as well as the links to the various multimedia elements and external Web pages.

Audience

In order to design an effective multimedia Web site with an intuitive user interface, you should visualize and understand your potential audience. You need to know your audience so you can design a site that appeals to their unique interests and beliefs. The more clearly you can see your site through the eyes of your users, the more successful your site will be. This becomes even more crucial as your site becomes more interactive. Because your users will be interacting with your site as well as viewing it, try to imagine how your audience might view and use your site.

Creating the Multimedia Web Site

Once you know the purpose of your Web site and you have developed a thorough plan including a site map and a link map, you are ready to create your Web-based multimedia application. In Chapters 3–6 we discussed the creation and design of each of the multimedia elements. Obviously, these items will need to be developed before they can be included in your Web-based multimedia application. However, because we have already discussed the development of the multimedia elements, in this chapter we will focus on the different methods that can be used to create Web pages.

HTML

HTML stands for **hypertext markup language.** This is the standard language used to create Web pages or hypermedia documents for the Web. HTML was designed to be platform-independent language so that different computers running different operating systems and using different browsers would be able to display the exact same page. Every Web page is written in HTML. There are different versions of HTML. Each new version has supported increased Web page functionality. For example, HTML 1.0 was created primarily to support hyperlinks, HTML 2.0 added support to display online images and interactive forms, HTML 3.0 included support for tables and extended formatting capabilities, and HTML 4.0 focuses on style sheets.

Markup tags specify how the browser will display text and other multimedia elements. Most tags are paired and consist of a beginning tag that specifies the application of the effect and an ending tag that marks the end of the effect. Ending tags are basically the same as beginning tags except they include a slash (/) in

FIGURE 8.13
Browsers display Web pages based on markup tags and associated attributes.

```
<P>
<a href="larsen/"><img src="book.jpg" border=0 height=112 width=83></a>

<table border=0 cellpadding=2 cellspacing=2 width=120>

<tr><td align=left bgcolor="#ff9900"><font size=-1 face="Helvetica">
      <a href="larsen/authors.html">About the Authors</a></td></tr>
<tr><td align=left bgcolor="#ff9900"><font size=-1 face="Helvetica">
      <a href="larsen/features.html">Features of the Book</a></td></tr>
<tr><td align=left bgcolor="#ff9900"><font size=-1 face="Helvetica">
      <a href="larsen/toc.html">Table of Contents</a></td></tr>

</table>
```

front of the tag name. Between two tags you will often find the text that will be affected. For example, in the following container, <B>This text will be bold</B>, the beginning tag is <B>, the ending tag is </B>. These tags will cause "This text will be bold" to display in boldface on a Web page.

Attributes or **extensions** can also be included with the tags to add a slight modification to the effect. To create a Web page, you simply type these tags and attributes into a document using any text editor.

All HTML documents are basically formatted using markup tags. There are HTML tags to include most anything you can imagine on your Web pages; however, as a designer, you have limited control over what your pages will look like. It is ultimately the configuration of the browser and the user's equipment that will determine what the Web page looks like.

As the formatting becomes more complex and frames, graphics, tables, and applets are included in interactive multimedia Web pages, the HTML coding also becomes more complex. Converters and Editors can be used to simplify this process. These tools allow you to design your multimedia Web pages visually using graphical user interface applications that generate the HTML code for you.

Converters

Converters translate your existing document format into HTML. In other words, these programs make it possible for you to publish your existing documents on the Web without knowing a single HTML tag. In fact, the conversion process for your document is very simple and straightforward. Generally, it is as simple as changing the file type from the Save As dialog box to HTML document.

Though converters make it very easy for you to publish your existing pages to the Internet as well as use familiar features to create new Web pages, they do have limitations. They are not "What You See Is What You Get" (WYSIWYG). In other words, the initial formatting you included in your document will be altered. Fonts, margins, and indentations may be changed. This is because when your document is converted to HTML, all of the HTML markup tags are automatically added. If there is no HTML markup tag to exactly match the formatting you have specified with another application, your document will look different.

FIGURE 8.14

To convert a file to HTML, simply choose HTML from the file type drop-down list box.

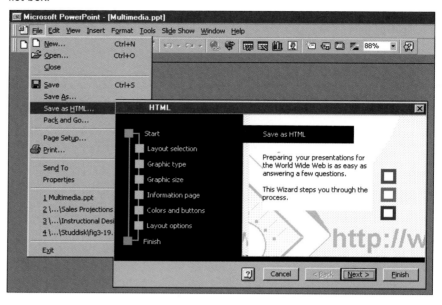

Though it is possible to create an incredibly complex HTML document using nothing more than a text editor, it is also extremely laborious and time-consuming. For this reason, more and more developers are creating software applications that are Internet-aware or Web-ready. This means that many programs now include converters that allow Web page creation and publishing capabilities within these programs. For example, all of the applications within Microsoft Office 97 are Web-ready.

Web Page Editors

Like converters, **Web page authoring programs** and **editors** make designing Web pages simple and practical. Editors allow you to create and design Web pages using menus and buttons on toolbars that represent HTML tags. Web page

FIGURE 8.15

Web Page Editors allow you to create and design Web pages without using HTML.

authoring programs use a graphical interface instead of forcing you to type or even choose HTML markup. Web page editors make it extremely easy for you to format your documents. For example, if you want text to be bold, you don't have to use the <B> and </B> tags around it, you simply highlight it and select Bold. Editors are very similar to working with word processing and desktop publishing applications such as Microsoft Word and Adobe PageMaker.

Some of the more common Web page editors and authoring programs include **HomeSite, Microsoft FrontPage 98, Adobe PageMill, Claris HomePage, BBEdit, HoTMetal** and **HoTMetal Pro, HotDog** and **HotDog Pro.** In addition, Web page creation features are now included in some browsers. Netscape first included Web page creation tools in its **Navigator Gold** version and has extended these capabilities in **Composer.**

Despite all of the new tools available for creating Web pages without knowing or using any HTML markup tags, all Web pages are HTML documents. Therefore, it is to your advantage to learn some HTML in order to understand the placement and use of tags in existing documents as well as edit documents you have created using other Web page design tools.

Portable Document Software

Portable Document Software is a set of electronic publishing tools used to work with **Portable Document Format (PDF)** files. These tools allow you to create, edit, and read PDF documents. It's also very easy to change an existing document into a PDF file. Because PDF files require PDF readers in order to be displayed, these files always look as they were designed to look. They handle any font, any layout, and can be viewed from any type of computer. This makes this file format extremely versatile.

There are several advantages to using PDF files on the Web. They are the only way to create WYSIWYG Web pages because they are guaranteed to look as they were designed. With HTML, there are no guarantees that your page will appear as you designed it. In addition, creating and managing a PDF file is often easier because there are no separate graphic files to manage.

There are also disadvantages to using PDF files on the Web. PDF readers are required to view these pages. Though most browsers are now properly configured to read PDF files automatically, PDF readers still aren't universal. They can be downloaded and installed, but this process can be time consuming and confusing for the beginner.

Common portable document software tools include **Adobe Acrobat, Common Ground,** and **Envoy.**

Testing the Multimedia Web Site

The importance of testing your Web-based multimedia application cannot be overemphasized. It is crucial. Once your multimedia Web site is complete, pretend to be the user and test your site on multiple platforms with multiple browsers. You should even find out what your Web-based multimedia application looks like on different computer monitors.

In addition to testing the Web site yourself, have other people test it for you. The more testers you can get, the better. Choose testers who have nothing to do with the Web site's creation, design, or purpose. Find out how other people view your site and how they interact with it.

Web-Based Programming Languages

There are many programming and scripting tools available for creating Web pages and multimedia elements to be used on Web pages. To create simple applets to be used on Web pages, you don't have to be a computer programmer. However, as these applets get more complicated, some programming experience is helpful.

Java

Java is Sun Microsystems' programming language. Whenever the computer downloads a Java application, the Java interpreter or virtual machine runs the Java application. This **Java interpreter** is capable of coping with the differences that are encountered on each platform; however, it is only available **for 32-bit operating systems** such as Windows 95 and Windows NT. Computers still using older operating systems like Windows 3.x cannot use the Java interpreter or **virtual machine.**

Java is one of the programming languages most often used to create animation for the Internet. It allows developers to create tiny little applications called **applets** that are platform-independent. Because they are usually quite small, applets are able to travel across networks easier than most other programs. In addition, because these applets can function on any computer platform with any operating system, they are extremely versatile. Java is appealing to developers because they can write one program that will run on a PC, a Mac, and a high-end UNIX workstation. These features make Java ideal for use on the Internet. Even nonprogrammers are learning Java because of its potential benefits and applications.

FIGURE 8.16

Java applets can be used to create animation. In this applet, the hand will simulate American Sign Language to spell the word you type.

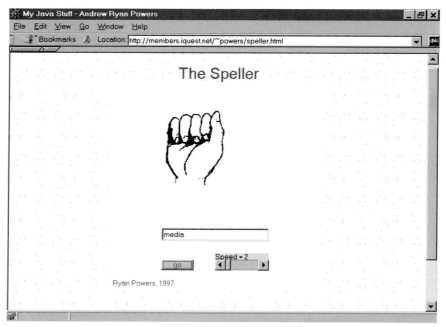

Java is also highly effective in creating more advanced animated objects. This is because, in addition to the benefits listed above, animation created with Java is computational. **Computational animation** can react to outside forces or external input. For example, some developers are including plug-ins with Java applets. This means the applet can be viewed on the Web even if the viewers don't have the proper configurations setup on their computers.

JAVASCRIPT

JavaScript is Netscape's scripting language. Other than sharing the Java name through a licensing agreement from Sun, JavaScript and Java really don't have anything else in common.

JavaScript is also used to create animated objects for Web pages. You may see it used to create animated text or buttons. One of the advantages of JavaScript is that it doesn't get compiled until it ends up on the user's computer. This means that as a user, you can usually see and reuse the source code just as you can with HTML.

ACTIVEX

Another program used to enable animation on the Web is **Microsoft's ActiveX.** ActiveX is an extension of **object linking and embedding (OLE).** Within a Web page that is ActiveX-enabled, you can link or embed objects from any application that supports ActiveX. In essence, the ActiveX component allows you to link to documents or applications and then drop them into your Web page.

Unlike Java, ActiveX is not platform independent. ActiveX works best in a Windows environment. Therefore, it isn't as versatile as Java. Though ActiveX is fine for Intranets where the platform is likely to be more consistent or at least more controllable, Java is a more adaptable language for the Internet.

FIGURE 8.17

Microsoft's ActiveX can enable animation on the Web.

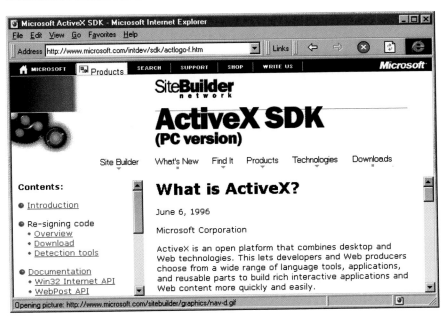

More and more applications are being created with Java and the trend toward Java applications will probably continue to grow. In fact, tools are now available that allow nonprogrammers to develop Java applications without learning the Java programming language.

CGI

CGI stands for **common gateway interface.** Programming languages like C++, AppleScript, and Perl can be used to write CGIs that provide interactivity to HTML documents. Most Web server software includes a set of common CGIs. CGIs are stored and accessed on the Web server and the Web server software accesses them when requested by the end user. For example, counters, online forms, and database communication is often enabled through CGIs. Unfortunately, CGIs pose a security threat to networks by creating a window of opportunity for hackers.

FIGURE 8.18
New authoring tools generate code for you

VRML

VRML stands for **virtual reality modeling language.** VRML is the language used to create and view 3D environments that enable users to view objects on the Internet in a three-dimensional fashion. In other words, with VRML, users can literally view the inside, the front, the outside, and the top of any 3D object. To work effectively, VRML requires quite powerful processing capabilities because the computer has to calculate every position of every object in the VRML environment. This enables users to walk through or fly through 3D worlds. This technology holds great promise for multimedia over the Internet and along with other technologies will be one to behold over the next few years.

In addition to writing code, there are now authoring tools that allow you to design the applet visually using familiar graphical user interface icons and menus. These programs then generate the program code for you. Some of the more popular code-generating applications available at this time include **Radja, Random Noise's Coda, Hyperwire, Jamba, Symantec's Visual Café,** and **Webburst.** To generate VRML code, you can use **3Space Publisher, Caligari's Pioneer, Virtus' 3D Website Builder,** and **Paragraph's Vitual Home Space Builder.**

Basic Principles of Good Web Page Design

To a large extent, the user's Web browser and hardware determine what the final Web-based multimedia application will look like. Though you don't have complete control over the final appearance of the multimedia application on a Web page, there are some steps you can take to help ensure the delivery of a professional-level multimedia Web site. As a designer, your role is to organize information for the most effective communication, guide reader's eyes through the information, and make the document distinct and eye-catching

Simplicity

Truly unique and exciting Web pages pop up every day, but a good multimedia Web page doesn't need to be complicated to be well done. Use the menu option View Source to discover how designers do what they do, but don't overdo it. A simple site can be an elegant site.

Consistency

Just like other multimedia applications, Web sites should have a consistent look and feel. There should be an obvious and related theme or metaphor throughout the site. This will give the site unity instead of the appearance of an eclectic collection of misapportioned elements thrown together on a whim.

Multimedia Elements

Generally, people are most interested in information. Keep this in mind when designing your site and focus on content. Use topics that give your viewer information. Graphics, animation and sound should complement the content of a Web page.

Because it is content that most viewers are interested in, make sure the content is accessible. Your text must be readable. Be careful of tiled backgrounds and light text on a dark background. Keep backgrounds pale or pastel colors and only use faint details on background images. Always test your color and background combinations.

Plan the inclusion of multimedia elements into your Web site by recording the goals and purpose of the multimedia elements within the Web site. Refer to this goal often to stay focused as you become more entrenched in the development process. Make sure your multimedia elements are appropriate and consistent with the goals of your site.

When you include multimedia elements on your Web page, find a good balance between quality and performance. Compress your multimedia elements and files as much as possible without sacrificing too much quality from the final application. Keep your graphics small by limiting the number of colors in your graphic files. In addition, you can significantly reduce the file size by using smaller graphics and lowering their resolution. Smaller files will take much less time to transmit from the Web server. Therefore, these smaller file sizes are almost always preferable when designing for the Web. A general rule of thumb is to keep multimedia elements to about 30K and Web pages including multimedia elements to about 100K.

The Audience

Be considerate of your users. Design your site with your audience in mind. Consider their interests and needs. Also, design your site for the least powerful computer system. By doing so, you'll reach a wider audience and you'll also maximize performance for those users with more sophisticated computer systems.

When designing your Web-based multimedia application, always think about your audience and their potential computer system. Try to imagine which browser they will be using, the type of Internet connection they may have, and their need for plug-ins or helper applications to view your project.

When you include either embedded or external files in a Web page, be sure to tell your users which plug-in or player they will need to view the multimedia application. Better yet, provide a link to the Web site where they can download the necessary utility.

Estimate the connection and system speed of your average user's system before you include animation, video, applets, or other bandwidth intensive multimedia elements on your Web page.

The User Interface

The best interfaces are those that seem transparent to the user. Transparent interfaces appeal to a wider audience. They also allow users to focus more time and attention on using and enjoying the application rather than trying to figure out how it works.

By giving users information in the form of text, graphics, animation, sound, and video, users are better able to assimilate the data, retain the information, and enjoy using the application. Because multimedia interfaces employ more than just text, they tend to be more user-friendly and intuitive. Well-designed multimedia interfaces encourage users to use the application correctly.

Navigation

Make your Web site easy to navigate. Create a text or toolbar so that your viewer can quickly and easily access any page within your site, particularly your home page.

Including a site map or graphical representation of your site on the first Web page will provide your users with a helpful overview of your site. A site map will enable them to go exactly where they need to go instead of searching page by page. The site map also provides users with a feel for what is included at the site and how everything is interconnected and interrelated. A good Web site map should offer a logical structure that intuitively guides your users around your Web site.

Minimize scrolling by using links to pages within your site. Make sure your Web site has an appropriate number of links. Too many hyperlinks become confusing while too few are boring. As always, balance is important. Remember, whenever a page gets too big or confusing, split it into several pages that you can link together. Use relative links in Web documents. Relative links point to links that are relative to the current page's location, while absolute links point to specific locations.

File Organization

Organize your files into common directories and folders. This structure and organization will prove increasingly helpful as your Web site grows. For example, you may want to keep all of your graphics in one folder and all of your audio files in another.

FIGURE 8.19

Site maps provide users with a helpful overview of the Web site.

Testing

Because it is ultimately the browser that determines how a page will look, you should test your site on as many browsers and platforms as possible. Testing is crucial because what may appear to be a masterpiece on one browser may appear quite unreadable on another.

A Final Note

The Internet is fast becoming a vast virtual disk of infinite digital data attached to your computer. Internet-ready, network-only computers are being marketed. The idea behind these computers is that the server should hold and process almost everything, and that there is really no need for many of the features found on full-scale multimedia computers.

Internet-aware applications that include links to Internet Web sites from within the application are also on the rise. For example, applications can link users to Web sites where users can register a new software application, get online technical support, or receive data for an application. In essence, these software applications become a front-end application to the developer's Web site and its data. In fact, the application can access its own Web site and update itself. This means companies no longer have to send out updates on disk or CD.

The opportunity to develop Web-based multimedia applications is huge and growing!

SUMMARY

The **Internet** is a network of networks that connects millions of computers and people around the globe. **Intranets** are private networks accessible only by the people within the organization. The **World Wide Web** is a hypertext system that permits the distribution and sharing of information around the world.

Mosaic was the first cross-platform Web browser that fully exploited the Web's **hypermedia** capability and played a key role in influencing the explosive growth of the Web. Today, there are literally millions of users on the Web and billions of Web sites with **Web pages** or hypermedia documents that can contain text, graphics, photographs, animation, sound, video, software, applications, and data forms.

The biggest obstacle to delivering multimedia over the Internet is **bandwidth.** Bandwidth is the amount of data that can be transferred across some physical channel in a given period of time. Though multimedia is becoming increasingly more common on the Internet, multimedia files are much larger than text alone. This large file size makes them difficult to transmit across channels. There are different transmission media including **modems, ISDN, T1 line** and **Hybrid Fiber Coax (HFC).**

Browsers provide the front-end interface that translates and displays downloaded **hypertext markup language (HTML)** documents. Browser software is getting more and more sophisticated. The newest versions of **Microsoft Internet Explorer** and **Netscape Communicator** now include active channels that feed you information that you request and subscriptions to Web sites that monitor changes in Web pages to which you subscribe.

The Web offers many advantages for delivering multimedia. Web pages are **cross-platform** multimedia applications. This makes it easier for developers to serve a wider audience because they only have to create one application. Because browsers are intuitive, users don't have to learn to use a new interface to use Web-based multimedia applications. By using multimedia in a Web page, you enhance the user's attention, understanding, and retention of the material presented. In addition, multimedia makes Web pages more interesting and more fun! Delivering multimedia over the Web is inexpensive, and unlike multimedia applications delivered via mediums such as CD-ROM, multimedia applications delivered via the Web are dynamic—they can be updated and changed at a moment's notice.

There are literally billions of Web pages on the Internet. More and more of these pages include multimedia for education and computer-based training; Intranets; electronic periodicals, references, and books; push technology; advertising, marketing, and virtual shopping; entertainment and games; virtual reality; and communication.

The same elements used in other multimedia applications can be used on the Web. Text is still a very important element used extensively to convey information on Web pages, and Hypertext extends the capabilities of Web pages by allowing users to link to related topics. Graphics can be used as backgrounds, navigation buttons, toolbars, icons, and content. The graphic file formats supported on the Internet include **GIF, JPEG,** and **PDF.** Animation on the Web can be accomplished using **animated GIF** files, **Java** and other scripting languages, **Shockwave** or **Flash.** Sound and Video can also greatly enhance a Web page. Both digital audio formats including **WAVE, AIFF,** and **AU** are supported on the Web, as are **MIDI** files. Common video formats on the Internet include **QuickTime** and **AVI.** Both audio and video files can either be **downloaded** or **streamed** using technologies such as **RealAudio** and **RealVideo.**

The Web master designs and manages the Web pages on the site using Web page creation tools and scripting languages. The planning phase is the most important phase in developing any multimedia application. The planning documents should provide a clear understanding of the goals and purpose of the Web-based multimedia application. In addition, a **site map** and **link map** will be needed to provide an overview of the site and a schematic of the links. Because your users will be interacting with your site as well as viewing it, design your Web-based multimedia application with your audience in mind.

There are different ways to create Web pages. **HTML** uses **markup tags** to specify how the browser will display text and other multimedia elements. **Attributes** or **extensions** can also be included with the tags to add a slight modification to the effect. To create a Web page you simply type these tags and attributes into a document using any text editor.

Converters and editors allow you to create Web pages without using HTML tags. **Converters** translate existing document formats into HTML. Many programs such as **Microsoft Office 97** are also Web-ready. **Web page authoring programs** and **editors** allow you to create and design Web pages using a graphical interface. Common editors include **HomeSite, Microsoft FrontPage 98** and **Adobe PageMill.** You can also use **Portable Document Software** to create and publish **PDF** files to the Web. Because PDF files need a reader to be viewed, they are guaranteed to look as they were designed.

Once your multimedia Web site is completed, it should be tested on multiple platforms with multiple browsers by many people who have nothing to do with the application.

There are also programming and scripting tools available for creating Web pages and multimedia elements to be used on Web pages. These programs also extend the capabilities of existing Web page creation tools. Some of the more common languages used are **Java, JavaScript, ActiveX,** and **VRML.**

When designing for the Web, follow a few simple guidelines. Keep your Web-based multimedia applications simple and use techniques that give it a consistent look and feel. There should be an obvious and related theme or metaphor throughout the site. There should also be a consistent and balanced feel among all of the multimedia elements. Always consider the needs, wants, interests, and experience of your audience. You must also keep the capabilities of their computer system in mind so that you don't waste your time creating features they can't access. Create a user-friendly or transparent interface along with simplistic navigation methods. Finally, organize your files in related folders and test your site extensively.

Opportunities to develop Web-based multimedia applications abound!

KEY TERMS

Internet	Intranet	World Wide Web
Mosaic	Hypermedia	(WWW)
Bandwidth	Transmission speed	Web pages
Modem	ISDN	Bits per second (bps)
Hybrid Fiber Coax	Browser	T1
Internet Explorer	Netscape	HTML
Animated GIF files	Communicator	Cross-platform
Flash	Java	Shockwave
MIDI	QuickTime	AVI
RealVideo	Streamed	RealAudio
Markup tags	Site map	Link map
Web page authoring	Attributes	Converters
programs	Editors	PDF
JavaScript	ActiveX	VRML

Matching Questions

a. Intranets	**b.** bandwidth	**c.** plug-ins
d. firewalls	**e.** tiled	**f.** interlaced
g. Java	**h.** AfterBurner	**i.** site map
j. animated GIF	**k.** converters	**l.** markup tags

_____ **1.** Programs that extend the capabilities of the browser.

_____ **2.** These images appear blurry and then gradually increase in detail until they are completely clear.

_____ **3.** A non-platform specific programming language used to create applets that extend the capabilities of Web pages.

_____ **4.** Separate hardware and software that lies between the Intranet Web server and the Internet to monitor connections, encrypt and protect data, and generally maintain the security of the internal network.

_____ **5.** This document provides the developer or Web master with a complete overview of a Web site by illustrating the structure of the contents and their relationship to one another.

_____ **6.** Private networks accessible only by the people within the organization or people with proper authorization to access the internal network.

_____ **7.** Codes that specify how the browser will display text and other multimedia elements.

_____ **8.** When an image is repeated over and over behind the other elements on a Web page to create a background.

_____ **9.** These programs translate existing document formats into HTML.

_____ **10.** The amount of data that can be transferred across some physical channel in a given period of time.

_____ **11.** These files store an entire sequence of still images that are replayed when the file is downloaded.

_____ **12.** A utility that converts Authorware and Director movies to Web-ready Shockwave applications

Fill-In Questions

1. In working with Web-based multimedia applications, _____ _____ is the time it takes for the data to be sent from the Web server to the user's computer. Transmission speed is usually measured in _____ _____ _____.

2. A _____ _____ delivers bandwidth approximately equal to the bandwidth delivery of 12 ISDN lines or 50 standard modems. The transmission speed is slightly over 1.5 Mbps.

3. The primary purpose of the _____ is to display Web pages. More specifically, the browser provides the front-end interface that translates and displays downloaded _____ _____ _____ documents and the media files and _____ that accompany these documents.

4. There is a growing trend on the Internet toward _____ _____ and _____ _____. These two technologies are extremely interactive.

5. Web-based purchases will rise as security improves and people feel more comfortable ordering online with credit cards and _____ _____. With _____ you "make a deposit" with a third party such as a bank that then electronically pays the online vendor after you authorize a request for payment.

6. _____ _____ is a method of delivering audio where the sound file is transferred from the Web server to the user's computer before it is played. _____ _____ is a method of delivering audio where a continuous stream of uninterrupted audio is transmitted from the Web server to the user's computer.

7. _____ by Progressive Networks is one of the most popular programs for streaming audio from a Web page.

8. HTML stands for _____ _____ _____. This is the standard language used to create Web pages or hypermedia documents for the Web.

9. _____ stands for _____ _____ _____ _____. This is the language used to create and view 3D environments, which enable users to view objects on the Internet in a three-dimensional fashion.

10. _____ _____ _____ is a set of electronic publishing tools used to work with _____ _____ _____ files.

DISCUSSION QUESTIONS

1. How did the Internet and Web evolve into what they are today?

2. What is the biggest obstacle to delivering multimedia over the Internet? How is this obstacle being resolved?

3. What are some of the different transmission mediums available today and how do they differ from one another?

4. What are the advantages of using Web-based multimedia applications?

5. What are some uses of Web-based multimedia applications?

6. When creating a multimedia Web site, what is the most important phase? What documents should be created during this phase and how are these documents used?

7. What are some different ways of creating Web-based multimedia applications? What are the advantages and disadvantages of each of these methods?

8. What are some examples of HTML tags used for multimedia applications? What do these tags instruct the browser to do?

9. What are several of the most commonly used Web-based programming or scripting languages used today? What is one of their primary functions?

10. What are some of the primary design principles and how do they impact your Web-based multimedia application?

HANDS-ON EXERCISES

1. Describe a Web-based multimedia application you would like to create. In your description, include the type of graphics, animation, sound, and video you would use. List the method or methods you would use to create your application and justify your reason for choosing these tools or programming languages.

2. Using the Web-based multimedia application you created in Exercise 1, create a site map that could be included on the first page of your site to provide an overview to your viewers.

3. Using the multimedia application you created in Exercise 1, create a link map that illustrates the internal and external links within your Web site.

LouEllen Ramos will serve as the Web master for the Island WaterCraft project. LouEllen has been with Digital Design for five years and has been working on Web pages for the past three years. From the storyboards, scripts, and flowcharts, LouEllen will first create a site map for the Island WaterCraft Web site. The site map will provide LouEllen and the team with an overview of the structure of the site. In addition, LouEllen will include this site map on the Island WaterCraft home page. The site map to be placed on the home page will follow the fast and fun water theme established for the project.

Most of the links at this site will be internal. LouEllen hopes to keep users at the Island WaterCraft site until they have explored it all and made a decision to request more information, rent or buy a personal watercraft, or visit the store in person. Several external links will be located on a separate "Links" page. By putting external links on a separate page, LouEllen hopes users will wait until they are finished at the Island WaterCraft site before they link outside. When they do link externally, they will realize that they are no longer at the Island WaterCraft Web site. Based on these considerations, LouEllen will develop a link map to help her manage and set up a user-friendly means of navigating this site.

To keep the mood and feel of the site consistent from page to page, LouEllen has designed an interface for each page that consists of the Island WaterCraft logo in the top left corner; a tiled background of a very faint, pale yellow waverunner; a navigation bar across the top that consists of watercraft buttons such as buoys, personal flotation devices, and jet skis that are representative of the links; and contact information at the bottom of each page. This interface will ensure that users know they are at the Island WaterCraft site at all times.

Within the site, LouEllen will include several interactive forms. One of the forms will allow users to request additional information via snail mail while the other will allow users to reserve and rent a personal watercraft device from the comfort of their own home. To submit information to Island WaterCraft, LouEllen will set up a CGI (common gateway interface) application on the Web server. This application will dump the information submitted from these forms directly into a database located at Island WaterCraft.

To create the Web site, LouEllen will start setting up the structure of the site and the individual pages using Adobe Pagemill. Pagemill is a graphical Web page editor. LouEllen will use it to set up the Home page with the site map. She will also use it to create tables that include thumbnail photographs, descriptions, pricing, and availability for each personal watercraft. If users want to see a larger photograph or a longer description, they can click on a link that takes them to a separate page. Each personal watercraft will be included in the main table and will also have a link to a separate page. This will keep the page sizes smaller, which will make them easier to download.

LouEllen will use Director to create tiny Shockwave movies that incorporate the animated personal watercraft GIFs created by Wendy Perry and

(continued)

(Case Study continued)

synch them with the sound effects created by Sean Coleman. She will save these as QuickTime files to keep them consistent with the video clip of Mr. Scott, which is already in QuickTime format. These will be easy to drop into pages on the site using Pagemill. LouEllen will then write Java scripts that instruct the QuickTime movies to serve as interactive media that link users to a new location within the Island WaterCraft Web site.

When she is finished, LouEllen will test the Web-based multimedia application on different platforms and monitors using different browsers. She will edit and clean up the pages using PageMill as well as the HTML source code. She will then have the team and Mr. Scott test it before it is viewed by a selected group from the potential audience for further testing. Because this is a Web-based multimedia application, once it has been tested and revised, it will be stored on a Web server where it will be immediately available for delivery.

Planning and Designing the Multimedia Application

UPON COMPLETION OF THIS CHAPTER, YOU WILL BE ABLE TO:

1. Explain how the planning process and documents are important to the design phase
2. Describe the design strategy
3. Identify the factors that should be considered in developing a design strategy for a multimedia application
4. List some of the questions that should be answered in defining the purpose of the multimedia application
5. List some of the questions that should be answered when defining the potential audience of the multimedia application
6. Describe some of the hardware limitations that must be considered when designing a multimedia application
7. Describe the design factors that must be considered when creating a multimedia application
8. List and describe the design factors that apply to text, graphics, animation, sound and video
9. List and describe the design principles that should be incorporated into Web-based multimedia applications
10. Describe the process and importance of testing and delivering a multimedia application
11. Explain how copyright laws apply to the elements used in a multimedia application

Planning and Designing

The planning phase is the most important phase in developing and designing any multimedia application. A plan provides the structure for the other phases of the project. This includes the design phase. As mentioned earlier, the multimedia team should meet at the onset of the project to develop a sense of shared vision surrounding the project. Team members should discuss the intended audience of the application and clarify the purpose of the project.

The **storyboard, flowchart,** and **scripts** will serve as the foundation for the design of the project. Though these documents may need to be altered as work on the project progresses, they serve as a beginning point and a point of departure for the multimedia team. These planning documents also provide the multimedia team with a perpetual reference guide that will help it maintain a focus so that the goal of the project doesn't get lost in the creative design process.

Storyboards

A **storyboard** is a diagram that describes the content and sequence of each screen in a multimedia application. Though the information contained in a storyboard will vary, each screen usually includes the following key items: a sketch and description of the elements (text, graphics, animation, audio, video), time allotted for each element, a screen number, transitions, tools to be used, budget information, method of navigation, and comments.

Storyboards are extremely important when planning a multimedia application. Multimedia team members refer to storyboards many times as they design elements for a multimedia product. Using a storyboard helps the multimedia specialist visualize the application and work out problems before the application is developed. Consequently, design changes can be made before money is spent on development. In addition, storyboards keep the project moving because most potential problems have been anticipated and resolved through the planning process. This keeps the creative process from being halted in order to work out a problem that should have been resolved before production began.

Scripts

Scripts are also part of the planning process for a multimedia application. **Scripts** are complete blueprints of a multimedia application. They contain all of the text and narration for a project. The program script will assist the multimedia team in understanding the application's general direction. The scene scripts detail the scenes, screen conditions, transitions, and interactions among characters.

When working with a multimedia team, professional writers, with input from members of the team, generally prepare scripts. Like storyboards, scripts help solve potential problems and identify missing elements before the development process is underway. The animation multimedia team will continually refer to the script in order to design multimedia elements that are audience-specific and applicable to the product being created.

FIGURE 9.1

The storyboard helps guide the animation specialist.

Multimedia Storyboard

Project Name: _____ Page Number _____ of _____

Prepared by: _____ Scene Number: _____

Desc. of Text: _____ Transition: _____

Desc. of Graphics: _____ Transition: _____

Desc. of Animation: _____ Transition: _____

Desc. of Audio: _____ Transition: _____

Desc. of Video: _____ Transition: _____

Time Required: _____

Notes: _____

_____

_____

_____

_____

Flowcharts

In Chapter 1, we said interactive multimedia applications were those that allow users to make decisions. These applications are more difficult to create because there are multiple possibilities that result from these choices. To keep all of these possibilities organized, the multimedia team relies on flowcharts.

Flowcharts illustrate the decision-making process that results as users make choices. For example, a game may require that a player choose between door

FIGURE 9.2

Flowcharts are particularly helpful in keeping track of which animation should result from a choice made by the user of an interactive multimedia application.

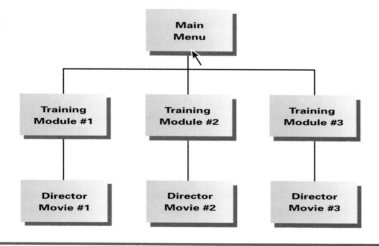

number 1 and door number 2. The flowchart will illustrate two branches of this decision. If door 1 is selected, the player may "Proceed Directly to Go and Collect $200." If door 2 is selected, the player may "Return to Start." Animation must be created and correctly sequenced regardless of whether the player chooses door 1 or door 2. Thus multimedia teams depend on flowcharts to assist them as they prepare animation for the multitude of possibilities that often exist within a multimedia application.

Without a good plan, time, money, and effort will all be wasted. A well-designed plan will lead to a well-designed and successful multimedia application. Time spent planning and preparing will pay off in the long run.

The Design Strategy

In order to ensure the success of a multimedia application, the multimedia team members should develop a **design strategy.** The design strategy will help them design a multimedia application that effectively achieves the purpose of the product for the intended audience.

Purpose

Step number one is to have a clear understanding of the multimedia application's purpose. The purpose of the application should be clearly stated and pervasive in the planning documents. To determine the purpose of a multimedia application, try to imagine why users would want or need to access the multimedia application. Attempt to answer these questions:

- How will users be using this multimedia application?
- Why will users be using this multimedia application?
- What will users gain from this multimedia application?
- What medium and platform will users use to access this multimedia application?
- What types of features will be most useful to the users of this multimedia application?

If the multimedia application is being designed for a client, the client should also help determine the purpose of the multimedia application. In essence, the client is the dreamer of the piece. If the client is struggling with the dream, the multimedia team can help. In the end, however, everyone should have a fairly definitive picture of the dream. At this point, the dream should be articulated into a stated purpose.

Audience

A multimedia application must be designed with the audience always in mind. As a designer, you should attempt to visualize and understand the potential audience. The more you know about your audience, the better you can design a multimedia application that appeals to its unique interests and beliefs.

When designing multimedia applications, you absolutely must make it your goal to create a product that represents what the audience wants and needs. If you have prepared any type of public presentation, you know how important it is to consider your audience in planning the presentation. If you don't consider your audience, your presentation will be a flop. The same holds true when preparing a multimedia application.

Your users should be the reason you create and design a multimedia application; they are the key to your project's success. Therefore, the more you can define your audience, the more you can tailor your application to meet audience members' needs and wants. In defining your audience, find answers to the following questions:

- Who is my audience?
- What is the age range of my audience?
- What gender is my audience?
- How computer literate is my audience?
- What particular interests do my audience members have in common?
- What particular beliefs do my audience members have in common?
- What particular values do my audience members have in common?

The more clearly you can see your application through the eyes of your users, the more successful your application will be. This becomes even more crucial in interactive multimedia applications. Because your users will be interacting with your application as well as viewing it, try to imagine how your audience might expect to use your project, and then attempt to exceed their expectations. If you do this, your multimedia application will be a success.

Giving your users the opportunity to choose or create their own experience is also a plus. For example, on the Web, you can design multiple sites. Your users can then choose whether or not they want to experience the site as a Baby Boomer, Generation Xer, or Old Fogy. People like choices. They like to feel as if they are in control or in charge. So design your multimedia application to give the users the control they want.

Testing your multimedia application cannot be overemphasized. It is crucial throughout the development phase of the application. As you are developing the multimedia application, and before you package and distribute your final piece, have a group of users who are representative of your audience test your multimedia application. Find out from impartial users how your multimedia application will be viewed and used.

Method of Distribution

In addition to your audience and the project's purpose, you must also consider the method of distribution when creating and designing multimedia applications. In other words, you must consider the kind of hardware and software that will be used to store and play back the final product.

USER PLATFORM

As mentioned in Chapter 2, the two major platforms found in the mass market are the Macintosh and the PC. These two platforms have slight differences. For example, they differ in the file formats they will display, in the way they handle color, and in their method of playing sound. These are just a few of the differences.

If a multimedia application will be distributed as a **hybrid CD,** one that will work on either platform, or if the multimedia application will be designed for the Web to be played on both platforms, the multimedia application may need to be produced differently. In addition, it will need to be tested thoroughly on both platforms.

PROCESSOR

The processor of the computer running the multimedia application must be powerful enough and fast enough to effectively play back the multimedia elements included in the application. If the processor is too slow, animation and video may appear choppy. Consider minimum and optimal processor requirements during the planning phase of the multimedia application. If certain minimums need to be specified, then include this information when the multimedia application is distributed.

BANDWIDTH

Bandwidth also plays an important role if the multimedia application is Web-based. Bandwidth must be considered when designing an application for the Web. If files on Web-based multimedia applications take too long to download, users simply will not wait. If you ignore this fact, you might as well not waste your time reading the rest of this chapter because no one will be viewing your application.

MEMORY

RAM (random access memory) should also be considered when designing the elements to be included in a multimedia application. Minimum memory requirements should be stated when the application is distributed. Though most computers sold today come with a minimum of 32 megabytes of RAM, if you want your application to be available to the widest possible audience, it is a good idea to design multimedia applications that will run on systems with 16 megabytes of RAM.

STORAGE

Efficiency
Try to keep the file size of your multimedia applications as small as possible. Smaller files require less storage space and offer improved playback performance. There are several ways you can create smaller file sizes:
- Use external sound and video files whenever possible.
- Keep video files small by trimming unnecessary footage and removing unused cast members.
- Create movies to be displayed in a smaller video playback screen so the file size will be smaller.

Different distribution methods offer different storage capacities. In designing multimedia applications, you must know how much space has been allotted for the media elements. If the multimedia application has been created for distribution via CD or DVD, you will have much more storage space to work with than if the application is being distributed via the Web.

FIGURE 9.3

The minimum requirements to run a multimedia application should be specified when the application is distributed.

Computers:
An Interactive Look

to Accompany The New Computer User by David Sullivan
Copyright © 1997 by Harcourt Brace & Company

AUTHORWARE® COPYRIGHT
© 1993, 1996 Macromedia, Inc.

Minimum System Requirements:
486-66MHz processor with 16 Mb RAM
Microsoft® Windows® 95
SVGA Monitor with 256 color (8 bit)
Multimedia capable system with 2x CD-ROM player
16 bit Sound Card
Produced in the United States of America. All rights Reserved.
For support call 1-800-447-9457 from 7am to 6pm centrl time on
business days or visit our web site at
http://www.hbtechsupport.com/ anytime.
ISBN 0-03-020258-2 Contains one CD-ROM Version 1.1a

Designing the User Interface

Putting together and designing the interface for the final multimedia application is crucial. When you design the **user interface,** you are setting up the foundation of the multimedia application. You are establishing the means through which the user will navigate and interact with your multimedia application.

Even if all of the other multimedia elements have been exquisitely created and designed, if the final application is not well designed, the work done by the other media specialists will be wasted. If the user-interface is not well designed, none of the other multimedia elements matter.

Consistency

Unless you are trying to achieve some special effect, all of the multimedia elements used within a multimedia application should be consistent. They should all play a role in achieving the purpose of your multimedia application. They should also appeal to the audience and match the mood of the project.

Your users will appreciate the help of a common metaphor, color scheme, and navigation method as they move from screen to screen. By changing the look and feel of your application from screen to screen, you will only frustrate your users.

Color Scheme

Don't use too many colors. Generally, multimedia applications created with a **monochromatic color scheme** look better. The idea is to use a color scheme that

FIGURE 9.4

Users appreciate the help of a common metaphor, color scheme, and method of navigating your multimedia application.

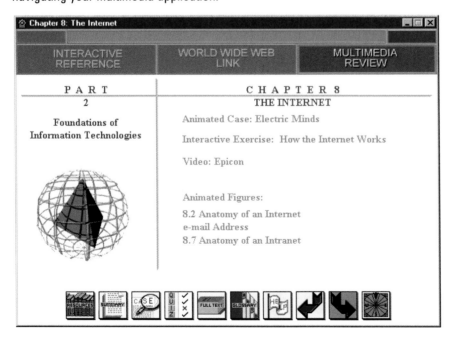

FIGURE 9.5
Different color schemes convey different messages and moods.

> White is associated with the words *innocent, clean,* and *good.*
> **Black** is associated with the words *evil, fear,* and *death.*
> **Brown** is associated with the words *dirty* and *earthy.*
> Yellow is associated with the words *warm, coward,* and *caution.*
> Red is associated with the words *hot, passion,* and *stop.*
> **Green** is associated with the words *envy, nature,* and *go.*
> Blue is associated with the words *cold, sad,* and *sky.*

is appealing to your audience and conveys the desired mood. Therefore, to keep your multimedia application from disappearing in all of the clutter, keep colors to a minimum. The overall look will be cleaner and more pleasing to the eye.

One technique that may help you design an effective color scheme is to limit yourself to black and white when you begin the design. Because black holds the highest contrast to white, it is easy to see black text or elements on a white background. Once you feel you have achieved a nice design concept in black and white, then you can begin adding one or two colors. As a general rule, it is easier to work with dark objects on a light background than it is to work with light objects on dark backgrounds. As a beginning designer, consider using dark on light instead of light on dark.

Different color schemes convey different messages and moods. For example, black and white splashed with a bit of red and yellow is a very traditional, yet classy color scheme. This color scheme would probably be effective for the Web site of a zine for an investment company or perhaps a customer-service computer-based training program for an upscale department store.

Before you choose a color scheme for your multimedia application, conduct some research on the mood the colors you are considering might convey. Is this what you want to convey? Test the color scheme on a group of users who are representative of your audience. What do they think?

Layout

Screens in multimedia applications may include text, graphics, hypermedia, buttons, and icons. Attempting to balance all of these elements on the background of your multimedia screen makes laying out multimedia applications quite challenging.

In laying out the screen for your multimedia application, you want to design it so that it is balanced, but not boring. If you want people to pay attention to your screens, you need to surprise them. Though you do want a consistent method of navigation, you don't want to develop a monotonous rhythm of graphic, text, animation, and sound, in the same place on every screen. You want to grab the user's attention but still maintain a balanced feel on the screen.

One way to achieve balance without monotony is to use elements of different sizes on your screens and to rearrange the order of the elements from screen to screen. You should also consider how the elements work together. For example, make sure text flows around the appropriate graphic.

FIGURE 9.6

Analyze the screen layout carefully to ensure that hypermedia correctly links users to the appropriate screen.

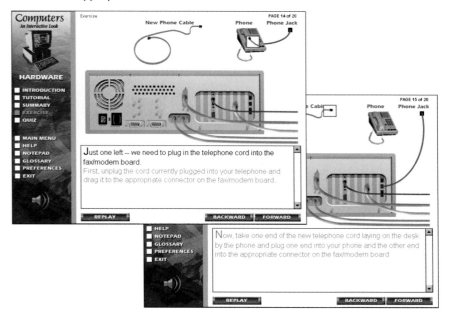

Because your screens will undoubtedly contain **hypermedia** or **hotspots,** each screen layout will need to be closely analyzed and programmed for these triggers. In essence, you must design a layout for the background screen with the programmable links and a layout for the foreground screen with which the user will interact. By designing both, you will ensure that users will be correctly linked when they click on these hotspots.

Navigation

In many ways, the way you arrange the content of your multimedia application is the most important part of the design. It doesn't matter if you have really cool-looking graphics and animation if nobody can find them. A clearly structured multimedia application should offer simple and consistent navigation.

You can't assume that users will grasp the structure of your multimedia application. You must make it easy for them to find their way around and go where they want to go. At all times, users should know exactly where they are and how to get back to where they were. At the same time, you shouldn't have to provide them with a complex set of instructions to help them **navigate.** In essence, if the multimedia application is well designed, the navigation structure should be almost transparent.

To create an application that is easy to navigate, you must first develop an overall structure or map of the multimedia application. This should be specified in the storyboards and flowcharts of the application. You should have determined at the onset of the planning process whether or not your users will navigate your application linearly, non-linearly, hierarchically, or using a combination of these structures. Once you have determined how your users will navigate through your multimedia, you should set up a simple navigation bar.

FIGURE 9.7

The navigation bar should make it simple for users to get around the multimedia application.

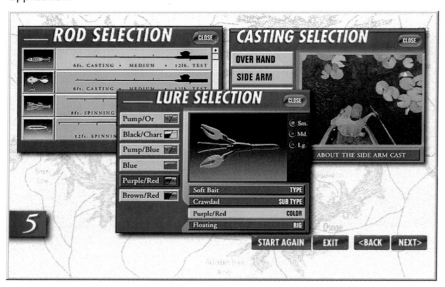

The **navigation bar** should serve as a friendly helper to the user. Keep the navigation bar simple, functional, and most importantly, consistent. On the navigation bar, images or combinations of text and images tend to be better than text alone. Text alone tends to be dull. Navigation bars with images tend to look better. It doesn't take users long to familiarize themselves with a good navigation bar.

In addition to a simple navigation bar, keep the number of navigation links to a minimum. By doing so, users will be able to navigate quickly to their starting point. Because navigability is a vital part of a multimedia application, keep it simple and intuitive for all users.

Transitions

Transition effects are included in most presentation software as well as authoring tools. **Transitions** apply special effects as users move from slide to slide, scene to scene, or object to object. For example, one image may fade into another; or a wipe may be applied to transition from screen to screen. Transitions should be clean, smooth, and appropriate to the goals, theme, and mood of the multimedia application. The transitions you select for the multimedia should not detract from the goals of the project, nor should they interfere with the smooth playback of the application.

Unity

The final multimedia application must be presented as a unified piece. All of the multimedia elements created for this application must come together and complement one another in the final application. Consider the goals of the multimedia application, and keep the underlying theme and mood of the piece obvious and well established.

Sequence and synchronize your multimedia elements so that the multimedia application flows smoothly. Poorly timed sound is particularly obvious and makes the multimedia application appear unprofessional.

Timing

Timing refers to the speed with which the sequential images will appear on the screen. Timing the sequence of activities is essential. The amount of time the multimedia elements remain on the screen is dependent upon the interface, the navigation, the interactivity, the user, and the other elements including potential sound and music. All of the multimedia elements should be properly sequenced and synchronized to create a clean, smooth, unified application.

Designing the Media Elements

All of the multimedia elements should be designed to work with one another and the multimedia application in its entirety. Consequently, none of the following elements can be designed without considering the entire piece.

Text

Text is still an incredibly useful and viable component in multimedia applications. There are many instances in which text is the best alternative for achieving the purpose of the multimedia application. Design isn't merely decoration, it is also used to convey information. Text conveys information very effectively and can be used creatively.

At the same time, in a multimedia application, less text is usually better. People are too busy and impatient to read a treatise online. In multimedia applications, people generally skim and surf. Consequently, text has to be quick and easy to read. Don't try to crowd too much text onto a screen. The six-by-six rule is a good guide: no more than six points per screen and no more than six words per point. In multimedia applications, you must break information into smaller bits.

Readability should be a concern as you design your multimedia application. Never set large bodies of text in all capital letters. All caps are much harder to read. Fonts were not intended to be set in all caps. They were intended to be upper- and lowercase because the descenders and ascenders make it easier for us to read.

Don't use more than a couple of typefaces in your multimedia application. The best combination is to choose a light serif font and a bold sans serif font. Reserve **sans serif** fonts for callouts, pull quotes, titles, and headings—short bodies of

FIGURE 9.8

Serifs, tails stemming from the ends of the strokes of a letter, make it easier for our eyes to follow a line of type.

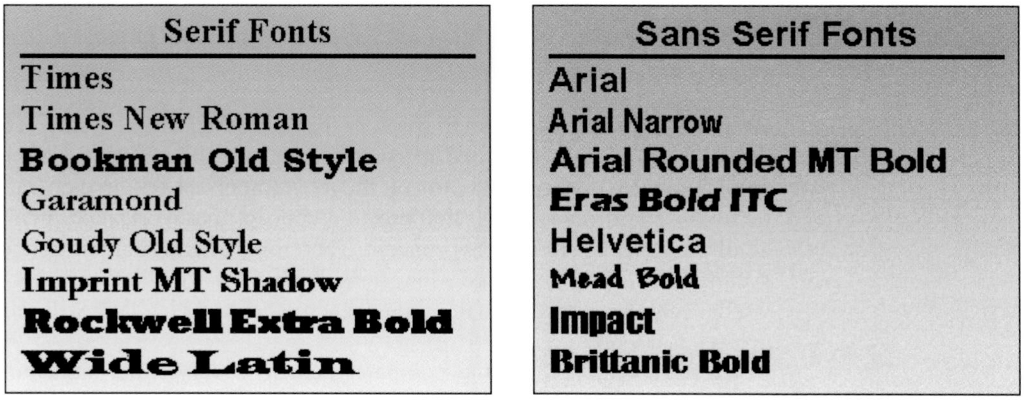

Serif Fonts	Sans Serif Fonts
Times	Arial
Times New Roman	Arial Narrow
Bookman Old Style	**Arial Rounded MT Bold**
Garamond	*Eras Bold ITC*
Goudy Old Style	Helvetica
Imprint MT Shadow	Mead Bold
Rockwell Extra Bold	Impact
Wide Latin	**Brittanic Bold**

FIGURE 9.9
Make sure your type contrasts with the background.

**Black text on a White background
offers the greatest contrast.**

It is easy to read
dark text on a light
background.

If there is enough contrast,
light text on a dark
background will work.

text, and use the serif font for large bodies of text. Along with the descenders and ascenders found in lowercase letters, **serifs** make text easier to read.

Balance text elements against the other elements on the screen. And make sure your type contrasts well with the background. If you want someone to notice what you've written, make it easy to read. Use a variety of sizes, but make sure the text is a readable size. Don't use tiny type that is very hard to read on a computer screen. In general, bigger is better. Type looks great in big point sizes.

When you are wrapping text around images, it is usually easier to read the text if it wraps around one side or underneath the image. Though you may want to wrap text at the top and bottom of an image or around both sides of the image to achieve a special effect, if readability is your goal, only wrap the text underneath the image or to one side.

Graphics

Graphics should be designed to speak to the nonverbal, intuitive side of the brain. They should also be designed to complement text and objects in a multimedia application. In a multimedia project, the most important design element is stylistic unity. The designer must first create a concept that works and then fine-tune all of the elements around this concept. Therefore, when using multiple images in a multimedia application, consider how the images will look together. In other words, consider how they will relate to each other and how they will relate to the project as a whole.

Creating graphics for the computer screen is very different from creating graphics for other mediums. Computer systems vary widely. Some have small screens, others have large screens. Some have greater color depth and higher resolution than others. Different operating systems even deal with color differently. On the Web, different browsers will display the colors and graphics differently. All of these issues make designing graphics for computers extremely challenging.

Here are some design tips to consider when using images in a multimedia project:

- Select images for their quality and compatibility with the project.

- Crop images to remove unnecessary objects and backgrounds.

- Check scanned images for dust and other marks; clean them up with an image editing program.

- Use a variety of image sizes to create visual interest.

- Use interesting borders to call attention to images or specific areas of an image.

- Create interesting special effects with filters and transitions.

- Create backgrounds that reinforce the appearance of the other graphic elements.

- When choosing colors for graphical images, you should generally design for the lowest common denominator of 216 colors. If possible, give users a choice between higher-color resolution and lower-color resolution depending on their system.

- Use white space within and outside the graphic. White space may be particularly helpful if text or graphics are included within another graphic. Providing enough open space is important if you don't want to overwhelm the viewer.

- Consider incorporating some analog or traditional pieces within your multimedia application. The traditional piece often takes the edge off and adds a human touch.

- Don't use big, slow graphics on Web-based multimedia applications. Delay is not acceptable. Nobody wants to wait, and nobody will wait!

Today's technology makes creating digitized graphical images for multimedia production possible for almost anyone. However, the technology is merely the tool. To create unique forms of art, the multimedia designer must create or select images that work together to communicate to an audience. After all, the future of communication relies on design that meets real needs.

Animation

Designed well and used effectively, animation can be cute and informative. On the other hand, if the animation is poorly designed and poorly incorporated into the environment, it can be annoying and downright detrimental to a multimedia application. The bottom line is that you must design animation that is appropriate to the application and geared toward the viewers and users of the program.

Animation must be appropriate to the project. Thoroughly examine the script and storyboard to determine where animation fits. Use these standards to help ensure that animation is effective, not annoying:

- Consider the purpose of the multimedia application and make sure the animation adds to the project by gaining the users' attention or creating a more thorough understanding of a concept. Animations should impact, not detract from the ideas presented.

- Make sure the animation is appropriate to the mood and content of the application.

- Determine how much animation to use, what objects should be animated, and how long the animation should run. These factors will vary depending on how the multimedia application will be used.

- Imagine where the animation will play. Will it be over the Internet on a computer screen or through a projection system onto a big screen?

- Realize that moving objects draw attention. Make sure you animate what you want your users to tune in to. If you animate something else, viewers will be distracted from the content you are really trying to stress.

- If you want to catch the attention of your audience quickly, give them what they expect in a different way, give them what they don't expect, or use exaggeration effects.

- Don't use too many animated objects per screen. If you use too much animation, viewers don't know where to focus. They might become overwhelmed or annoyed.

- Animation that does the same thing over and over and over is also annoying. If possible, keep the animation changing, or stop the animation by limiting the number of cycles it loops through.

- Use transitions and special effects that help communicate your message, but don't get overzealous and add too many.

- On the Web, make sure your animation loads quickly. The importance of a Web page that downloads quickly cannot be overstated. The bottom line: users won't wait! Your animation is completely wasted if your viewers never see it because they don't have the patience to wait for it to download.

Save Computer Resources:
- Limit the number of animations running at the same time. More animated objects require more memory.
- Keep animated objects to a relatively small size whether you are creating animation for CD-ROM or the Web. One way to minimize the file size is to keep the color depth low.
- To save computer resources, incorporate animation into as many applications as possible, keep the sequence of recorded images at a rate that is as low as possible, yet high enough to maintain the illusion of motion.

Sound

Sound is an important multimedia element. To help ensure its quality, incorporate sound that is high quality, appropriate, and consistent with the goals of the multimedia application.

Keep the sound quality consistent throughout the multimedia application. Don't include low-resolution sound and high-resolution sound of the same type together in the same multimedia application. For example, don't include an 8-bit voice-over and a 16-bit voice-over within the same application. If you do, the difference will be obvious and the 8-bit sound when compared with the 16-bit sound will seem very poor quality. It is possible, however, to include an 8-bit voice-over and a 16-bit symphony music sound within the same application.

Remember that even though 44 kHz, 16-bit sounds provide higher-quality sounds, they also require greater storage capacity and can slow down your multimedia application when they are played. Record at a rate and resolution appropriate to your multimedia application's method of delivery. If possible, consider using external sound files to keep your multimedia application files smaller and more efficient.

Here are some additional design tips that should help you create more effective multimedia sound files:

- If different music files are used, they should be the same style of music.

- If possible and appropriate, it is best to use the same voice for narration and voice-overs, but different voices for different characters. Once again, balance is important. Too few voices may bore your audience while too many may confuse them.

- If different characters are used within an application, the voices for each should be distinct.

FIGURE 9.10
Quality must be balanced with file size.

Sound quality	File size/second	Recommended uses
8-bit, 11 kHz, mono	11,000 bytes	Voice playback
8-bit, 22 kHz, mono	22,000 bytes	
8-bit, 44 kHz, mono	44,000 bytes	
8-bit, 11 kHz, stereo	22,000 bytes	
8-bit, 22 kHz, stereo	44,000 bytes	
8-bit, 44 kHz, stereo	88,000 bytes	
16-bit, 11 kHz, mono	22,000 bytes	
16-bit, 22 kHz, mono	44,000 bytes	Record voice, sound effects
16-bit, 44 kHz, mono	88,000 bytes	
16-bit, 11 kHz, stereo	44,000 bytes	
16-bit, 22 kHz, stereo	88,000 bytes	Special sound effects
16-bit, 44 kHz, stereo	176,000 bytes	Music
24-bit, 11 kHz, mono	33,000 bytes	
24-bit, 22 kHz, mono	66,000 bytes	
24-bit, 44 kHz, mono	132,000 bytes	
24-bit, 11 kHz, stereo	66,000 bytes	
24-bit, 22 kHz, stereo	132,000 bytes	
24-bit, 44 kHz, stereo	264,000 bytes	High quality music

■ Coordinate your sound files with the other graphic, animation, and video elements used in your multimedia application.

In Web-based multimedia applications, consider using MIDI files for background sounds and music. Their small file size makes them quick to download. Also, be sure to clearly label the size and type of audio files when you embed downloadable sound files on your Web pages. This way, users can determine whether or not they wish to wait for the sound files to download. By labeling files, you also enable users to choose only those files that are compatible with their system. Unfortunately, labeling your files doesn't guarantee that users won't have problems, but it does help.

Video

Video can stimulate emotions, convey messages, provide instructions, demonstrate techniques, and relate experiences. As always, balance is important. You should use video where it is appropriate. Because the inclusion of video in multimedia applications requires powerful processors and large amounts of storage, you should never use video if it does not add to the application.

Don't include sound files of the same type but recorded at different resolutions within the same multimedia application. For example, don't include both 8-bit voice-overs and 16-bit voice-overs within the same application. This is because the 8-bit sound when compared with the 16-bit sound will sound very low quality and you will lose consistency in your application.

If your computer system and processor are slow and sluggish when working with high-resolution video clips, work with lower-resolution clips. When you are ready to make the actual movie, revert to the higher-resolution video clips for output.

Because video is important to your multimedia application, it is worth your time and patience to design it properly to be high-quality, appropriate for the method of delivery, and consistent with the other media elements and goals of the application.

Video is important in multimedia applications. Record and capture clean, high-quality video. Always use the highest-quality video that the processor and storage medium can handle. However, remember that even small video files require powerful processors and large storage capacities.

Plan accordingly. Keep your audience and the method of delivery in mind when you design video for a multimedia application. Your time will be wasted if only a few people have the ability to benefit from what you've created because they don't have the equipment to use it. Keep your video files at an appropriate size so they can be stored and played on standard equipment if you plan to distribute your multimedia application to a wider audience.

Keep the video quality consistent throughout the multimedia application. Don't include poor-quality video footage and high-quality footage within the same multimedia application. Also, make sure the video is consistent with the other multimedia elements in the application.

Remember that in most cases, when the video from your application is displayed on the computer monitor, it will probably take up about one quarter of the computer screen. Appropriately adjust the recording and processing of your video based on this smaller screen size.

If possible, use video files that are external to your multimedia application. This will enable the application to run more efficiently. In doing so, however, store them in the same folder with the multimedia application so that the scripts that reference these files will be able to find them.

FIGURE 9.11

Video quality must be balanced with file size.

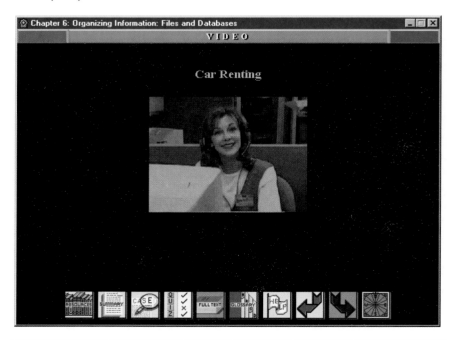

Not only should your video be consistent in quality with the other video in the application, it should also be consistent in content with the rest of the multimedia elements. In other words, stylistic unity should be created with the elements. They should work together to create a theme and enhance the content of the multimedia application. When you include video in your multimedia application, keep the following guidelines in mind:

- Make sure the sound or music and the video match or complement one another.
- Use high-quality video footage that lends credibility and a professional feel to your multimedia application.
- Use different characters to add interest to the application, but don't use so many that your users get lost.
- Coordinate your video files to complement the application and the other graphic, animation, and sound elements used in your multimedia application.
- Don't overuse transitions.
- Trim video clips of footage that is excessive, boring, or inconsistent with your application.
- Properly place and time video clips so that they are consistent with the content included in the other multimedia elements nearby.

Testing the Multimedia Application

Testing and revising the multimedia application is critical. There are several different groups that should test the multimedia application throughout the development process and upon completion. Among other items, the multimedia project team should evaluate the multimedia application's design, content, multimedia elements, programming code, user interface, method of navigation, and interactivity. Team members must also ensure that the goals and objectives of the multimedia application are being met, that the project is progressing as scheduled and budgeted, and that all legal considerations, such as copyright licenses and releases, have been obtained.

Throughout the development process, clients should also be included in the evaluation of the multimedia application. Keeping clients involved and informed will help guarantee the final approval and overall success of your multimedia application. If you don't involve your clients and incorporate their comments and suggestions in revising the multimedia application, they may choose to reject the final product.

As a multimedia developer or member of a multimedia project team you are too close to the application to test it properly. You have too much insight into its purpose and design. It's also much easier for you to overlook or work around potential trouble areas. Therefore, in addition to evaluating the application yourself and getting feedback from your clients, have a selected group from the audience of potential users give you recommendations and feedback about your application. Find out how the group feels about the overall program, the user interface, the way the program is executed, the multimedia elements, and the design. Ask for suggestions on features and changes in design that would improve the application. Get positive feedback as well. Find out what they really like about your multimedia application.

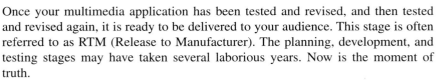

Delivering the Multimedia Application

Once your multimedia application has been tested and revised, and then tested and revised again, it is ready to be delivered to your audience. This stage is often referred to as RTM (Release to Manufacturer). The planning, development, and testing stages may have taken several laborious years. Now is the moment of truth.

Throughout the planning and development stages, the storage and distribution media for the final multimedia application should have been considered. Now is the time to store the multimedia application on magnetic tape, magnetic disks, magneto-optical disks, CD-ROM, DVD, laser disk, or a combination of these storage devices. The multimedia application may also be stored on a Web server.

After your multimedia application has been stored, it can be packaged and delivered. Packaging and delivery may involve the development of special boxes and containers to be shipped to retail stores, or it may simply involve adding a download link to a Web site. Regardless, the packaging and delivery must be professional and consistent with the application and the way it is stored. Don't forget to include details regarding licensing the product, documentation and instructions for setting it up, as well as phone numbers and contact information for technical support.

Copyright

Remember that many files are creative endeavors subject to copyright laws. Always obtain appropriate releases before including another artist's multimedia elements in your multimedia application.

All art forms, including electronic art forms, are subject to copyright laws. Therefore, if you wish to use a particular element within your multimedia application, don't take chances. Always get permission from the artist or publisher.

After obtaining a release to use a piece, be sure to read the agreement carefully. Though you can use some sounds royalty-free in any multimedia application you create, with others, you will need to pay the creator a royalty for each application in which you use the sound.

SUMMARY

A well-designed plan will lead to a well-designed and successful multimedia application. At the onset of the project, the multimedia team should discuss the intended audience of the application and clarify its purpose through the creation of a **storyboard, flowchart,** and **scripts.** A design strategy will assist in the development of an effective multimedia application.

In addition to the audience and the purpose of the multimedia application, the method of distribution must also be considered. Platforms have slight differences including the file formats they will display, the way they handle color, and their method of playing sound and video. If a multimedia application will be distributed via multiple platforms, it may need to be produced differently, and it will definitely need to be tested thoroughly on all potential distribution platforms.

In addition to the platform, the computer processor and memory must also be considered when designing the multimedia application. The processor and memory on the computer playing the multimedia application must be powerful enough and fast enough to effectively play back the multimedia elements included in the application. These minimum computer requirements should be stated when the application is distributed.

Different distribution methods offer different storage capacities. In designing multimedia applications, you must know how much space has been allotted for the media elements. **Bandwidth** also plays an important role if the multimedia application is Web-based. If files on Web-based multimedia applications take too long to download, users simply will not wait to see what you have created.

Putting together and designing the interface for the final multimedia application is crucial. The **user interface** is the foundation of the multimedia application and the means through which the user will navigate and interact with it.

Unless you are trying to achieve some special effect, all of the multimedia elements used within a multimedia application should be consistent. Users appreciate the help of a common metaphor, color scheme, and navigation method as they move from screen to screen.

Generally, multimedia applications created with a **monochromatic color scheme** look better. The idea is to use a color scheme that is appealing to your audience and conveys the desired mood. To keep your multimedia application from disappearing in all of the clutter, keep colors to a minimum.

Screens in multimedia applications should attempt to balance all of the elements including text, graphics, hypermedia, buttons, and icons; at the same time, the screen shouldn't bore the user. The goal is to grab the user's attention, while maintaining a balanced feel on the screen. One way to accomplish this is to incorporate different-sized elements on the screen. In addition to appearance, the layout must also be closely analyzed and programmed for **hypermedia** and **hotspots.**

The **navigation structure** of the multimedia application should be determined at the onset of the planning process. You must make it easy for users to find their way around your multimedia application without providing them with a complex set of instructions to help them navigate. Because navigability is a vital part of a multimedia application, keep it simple and intuitive for all users. In essence, if the multimedia application is well designed, the navigation structure should be transparent.

Transitions apply special effects as users move from slide to slide, scene to scene, or object to object. Transitions should be clean, smooth, and appropriate to the goals, theme, and mood of the multimedia application; they should not detract from the goals of the project, nor should they interfere with the smooth playback of the application.

The final multimedia application must be presented as a unified piece. All of the multimedia elements created for this application must come together and complement one another in the final application. **Timing** refers to the speed with which the sequential images will appear on the screen. Timing the sequence of activities is essential. The amount of time the multimedia elements remain on the screen depends on the interface, the navigation, the interactivity, the user, and the other elements including potential sound and music. All of the multimedia elements should be properly sequenced and synchronized to create a clean, smooth, unified application.

All of the multimedia elements should also be designed to work with one another and the entire multimedia application. Text is still an incredibly useful and viable component for conveying information in multimedia applications. At the same time, in a multimedia application, less text is usually better. Readability should also be considered. Avoid using all capital letters, tiny font sizes, more than two fonts, and sans serif fonts for large bodies of text. Balance text elements with the other elements on the screen. For easier reading when wrapping text around images, wrap them around one side or underneath the image.

Graphics should be designed to speak to the nonverbal, intuitive side of the brain and complement text and objects in a multimedia application. Because different monitors and platforms display images differently, it is important to design images with these considerations in mind. Generally, quality images should be created or selected to work together to communicate the purpose of the multimedia application to the audience.

Designed well and used effectively, animation can be cute and informative; poorly designed and poorly incorporated into the environment, it can be annoying and downright detrimental to a multimedia application. The bottom line is that you must design animation that is appropriate to the application and geared toward the viewers and users of the program.

Sound is an important multimedia element. To help ensure its quality, incorporate sound that is high quality, appropriate, and consistent with the goals of the multimedia application. In addition, the sound quality should be consistent throughout the multimedia application. In Web-based multimedia applications, sound files should be clearly labeled so that users can choose only those files that are compatible with their system.

Video can stimulate emotions, convey messages, provide instructions, demonstrate techniques, and relate experiences. As always, balance is important. Because the inclusion of video in multimedia applications requires powerful processors and large amounts of storage, you should use video only where it is appropriate. As is true with all multimedia elements, it is worth your time and patience to properly design video to be high-quality, appropriate for the method of delivery, and consistent with the other media elements and goals of the application.

All art forms, including electronic art forms, are subject to copyright laws. Therefore, if you wish to use a particular element within your multimedia application, don't take chances. Always get permission from the artist or publisher. After obtaining a release to use a piece, be sure to read the agreement carefully. Though you can use some elements royalty-free in any multimedia application you create, with others, you will need to pay the creator a royalty for each application in which you use the sound.

KEY TERMS

Storyboard	Hybrid CD	Bandwidth
Design strategy	Monochromatic color	Hypermedia
User interface	scheme	Transitions
Hotspots	Navigate	Serif
Unity	Timing	Copyright
Sans serif	Point size	
Flowchart	Script	

Matching Questions

a. bandwidth   **b.** user interface   **c.** monochromatic

d. hybrid   **e.** design   **f.** navigation structure

g. storyboards,   **h.** method of distribution   **i.** transitions
flowcharts, scripts

j. sans serif   **k.** hotspots   **l.** timing

_____ 1. Planning documents that provide the multimedia team with a perpetual reference guide.

_____ 2. Strategy that will help the multimedia team create an application that effectively achieves the purpose of the product for the intended audience.

_____ 3. The kind of hardware and software that will be used to store and play back the final product.

_____ 4. CD that will work on more than one platform.

_____ 5. Major consideration when designing an application for the Web.

_____ 6. The means by which the user will navigate and interact with a multimedia application.

_____ 7. Color scheme that should be used to create better-looking multimedia applications.

_____ 8. Triggers in a multimedia application.

_____ 9. Method by which users find their way around a multimedia application without a complex set of instructions.

_____10. Special effects that occur as users move from slide to slide, scene to scene, or object to object.

_____11. The speed with which sequential images appear on the screen.

_____12. Type of font that should be used with callouts, pull quotes, titles, and headings—short bodies of text.

Fill-In Questions

1. In a multimedia application, less _____ is usually better.

2. Reserve _____ _____ fonts for callouts, pull quotes, titles, headings, and short bodies of text, and use the _____ font for large bodies of text. Along with the descenders and ascenders found in lowercase letters, _____ make text easier to read.

3. _____ images to remove unnecessary objects and backgrounds.

4. Designed well and used effectively, _____ can be cute and informative. On the other hand, if the _____ is poorly designed and poorly incorporated into the environment, it can be annoying and downright detrimental to a multimedia application.

5. In Web-based multimedia applications, be sure to clearly _____ the size and type of audio files when you embed downloadable sound files on your Web pages. This way, users can determine whether or not they wish to wait for the sound files to download. By _____ files, you also enable users to choose only those files that are compatible with their computer system.

6. If possible, use video files that are _____ to your multimedia application. This will enable the application to run more efficiently.

7. All art forms, including electronic art forms, are subject to _____ laws. Therefore, if you wish to use a particular element within your multimedia application, don't take chances. Always get permission from the artist or publisher.

8. In addition to your audience and the purpose of the multimedia application, when creating and designing multimedia applications you must also consider the _____ __ _____.

9. Unless you are trying to achieve some special effect, all of the multimedia elements used within a multimedia application should be _____.

10. The _____ _____ should serve as a friendly helper to the user. Keep the _____ _____ simple, functional, and most importantly, consistent.

DISCUSSION QUESTIONS

1. What factors should be considered in developing a design strategy for a multimedia application?

2. What are some of the questions that should be answered when you are defining the purpose a multimedia application?

3. What are some of the questions that should be answered when you are defining the potential audience of your multimedia application?

4. What are some of the hardware limitations that should be considered when you are designing a multimedia application?

5. What are some important design factors that apply to text?

6. What are some important design factors that apply to graphics?

7. What are some important design factors that apply to animation?

8. What are some important design factors that apply to sound?

9. What are some important design factors that apply to video?

10. How do copyright laws apply to the elements used in a multimedia application?

HANDS-ON EXERCISES

1. Describe a multimedia application you would like to create. Clearly identify its purpose, the potential audience, and the method of distribution for your multimedia application.

2. Based on the multimedia application you described in Exercise 1, explain which type of navigation structure would be most appropriate for this application. Draw a navigation bar that would enable users to navigate transparently throughout your multimedia application.

3. Based on the multimedia application you described in Exercise 1, draw a sample background screen. Include the navigation bar, and a sample of the color scheme, buttons, icons, animation, and other elements that you might use in this multimedia application.

2D image object existing in two dimensions: width and height.

3D image object existing in three dimensions: width, height, and depth.

3D modeling programs software used to create or modify three-dimensional graphic images.

3D paint tools tools used to create paint shapes directly on the surface of an object.

3D sound sound that includes delays that attempt to simulate the time it would take for sound waves to reach the ears if the sound was happening live.

Access time the time it takes for data to be located.

Active matrix screens screens that use individual transistors for each crystal cell.

ActiveX software developed by Microsoft to extend object linking and embedding (OLE) on the Web.

Adobe After Effects a program used to create effects for Adobe Premiere and other video projects.

Adobe Premiere a non-linear video-editing program used to capture, edit, and incorporate video into multimedia applications.

AIFF or **AIF** Apple's Audio Interchange Format.

ALA AudioLink proprietary audio/video format.

Ambient light light that is uniform throughout a scene.

Amplitude the distance between the valley and the peak of a waveform.

Analog sound a continuous stream of sound waves.

Analog-to-digital converter (ADC) equipment used to convert impulses to numbers that can be stored, understood, and manipulated by a microprocessor.

Animated GIFs a special kind of GIF file known as GIF89a used to create animated 2D and 3D images for Web pages.

Animation a moving graphic image.

Animation engine compiler used to create animation from graphic images.

Animation specialist multimedia team member responsible for creating 2D or 3D animation.

Apple Cinepak a cross-platform compression scheme or CODEC that works well for CD-ROM video delivery.

Apple Video Player software that allows you to record and play QuickTime movies.

AppleScript another scripting language available with HyperCard.

Applets tiny little applications that are platform independent.

ARPANET foundation of the Internet that was started by the military in the 1960s to create a decentralized communication network.

Art director multimedia team member responsible for creating the artwork for a project.

ASFS   a proprietary audio compression algorithm from Eurodat that offers up to 130:1 compression.

Attributes   properties that modify HTML tags.

AU   a 16-bit compressed Sun Audio format developed by Sun Microsystems to be used on UNIX, NeXT and Sun Sparc workstations.

Audio   sound that has been digitized.

Audio board   an expansion card on a PC that is required for recording sound or playing sound through external speakers.

Audio specialist   multimedia team member responsible for ensuring that appropriate sound is delivered in real time. An audio specialist works with musical scores, sound effects, voice-overs, vocals, and transitional sounds and is responsible for recording, editing, and selecting voices and sounds.

AutoCAD   a vector-based graphics format used with CAD and drawing programs.

AVI   Microsoft Corporation's movie file format.

AV-Tuned Drives   hard drives specifically designed to work with audio and video.

Bandwidth   a measurement of the amount of data that can flow over a channel on a network in a given period of time.

Betacam SP   a high-quality, component video format used in professional video editing.

Bèzier curves   mathematically defined curves named after Pierre Bèzier that are used to fine tune a curve into almost any shape imaginable.

Bit resolution   measurement of the number of bits of stored information per pixel or how many tones or colors every pixel in a bitmap can have. This is also referred to as **bit depth**, **pixel depth,** or **color resolution.**

Bitmap   a grid similar to graph paper from which each small square will be directly mapped back onto the computer screen as a pixel.

Bitmap graphics editors   software used to create or edit bitmapped graphics. These programs are also called **paint programs.**

Blending   the process of creating a series of intermediate colors and shapes between two selected objects.

BMP   a graphic file format that has been adopted as the standard bitmapped format on the Windows platform.

Boolean text searching   feature where text can be searched using advanced "and" and "or" operators.

Browser   program that provides the front-end interface that translates and displays downloaded **hypertext markup language (HTML)** documents and the media files and **applets** that accompany these documents.

Buffer   a temporary storage area where data can be stored until the computer is ready to process it.

Bus   any line that transmits data between memory and input/output devices or between memory and the CPU.

Card-based authoring programs   multimedia authoring programs that use stacks of cards or pages as a metaphor.

Cast members   the basic elements of any Director movie.

Cast to Time   method of transitioning from one cast member to the next to create the illusion of animation.

Cast Window   the window in which cast members are made available.

CAV recording   format used for videodisks to create 30 minutes/side of freeze-frame video with stereo sound.

CD Plus   a CD-ROM format that permits the inclusion of multimedia on a regular audio CD. This format is also called **CD Extra** or **Enhanced CD.**

CD-ROM (Compact Disk–Read Only Memory)   an optical storage device that can hold about 680MB of data.

CD-ROM Multisession   format that permits the recording of a CD to occur in more than one session.

CD-ROM Recordables   drives that allow you to record CDs. Unfortunately, these drives only allow you to write to the CD one time.

CD-ROM Rewritable   drive that allows you to write to a CD up to 1,000 times.

CD-ROM XA   extended architecture CDs that can hold more audio than audio CDs; though they are fine for speech, they are not as consistent and reliable as regular CDs for music.

Cell-based animation   method of creating animation where key frames are created on cells or frames.

CGI (common gateway interface)   programs used to provide interactivity such as counters and online forms to HTML documents.

Channels   location used to represent different activities that will take place in an animated Director movie.

Charts   type of graphic used to illustrate data.

CISC (complex instruction set computing)   computers that have hundreds of commands in their instruction sets.

Clip art   commercially prepared drawings that come packaged with many application programs.

CLV recording   industry format used for videodisks that creates 60 minutes/side of video.

CODECs   compression/decompression algorithms used to compress data.

Color images   graphic images that contain anywhere from 4-bit color (16 colors) to 36-bit color (millions of colors).

Color palette channel   palette from which special colors such as metallic or pastels can be selected.

Combination   navigation method that combines linear, non-linear, or hierarchical navigation.

Commercial image providers   business that finds and sells the rights to images.

Compressed   reduced in size for storage and transfer.

Compression   a technique that mathematically reduces the size of a file.

Computational animation   method of animating an object by varying its x and y coordinates.

Computer programmer   person who creates the underlying software that runs a multimedia program and responds to the user's actions.

Computer-based training (CBT)   multimedia applications used by companies or educational institutions to teach skills and knowledge. This is also referred to as **computer-assisted instruction (CAI)** or **multimedia computer-assisted instruction (MCIA).**

Condenser microphones compact microphones that can be powered by low voltage batteries.

Content sounds sound in a multimedia application that furnishes information. Narration and dialog are content sounds.

Content specialist multimedia team member who is responsible for providing some measure of authenticity or accuracy to the information in an interactive project.

Converters programs that translate existing document formats into HTML.

Copyright ownership of rights to copy anything that is in a tangible medium.

Crop process of removing areas of a photograph.

Cross-platform the capability of computer software or hardware to be used on another computer system.

D1, D2, and **D3** common digital video standards.

Data transfer rate (dtr) the time it takes for the data to be transferred from the processor and displayed on the monitor.

DCR a cross-platform Macromedia "Shocked" Director Movie format that includes both audio and video.

Decibel the smallest variation in amplitude that can be detected by the human ear.

Deformers a powerful class of manipulation tools that enable you to twist and modify objects and groups of objects.

Desktop videoconferencing technology that enables video conversations to occur over telephone lines or networks.

Destructive processing methods that changes the original file.

DIB (device-independent bitmap) format used to transfer bitmaps from one device or process to another.

Digital audio sound that has been converted from analog to digital.

Digital audio tape (DAT) device used to store digital data.

Digital cameras cameras that store photographs in a digital format on magnetic disk or internal memory.

Digital sounds sounds that have been converted to numbers.

Digital video video that is in a number format that can be interpreted by the computer.

Digital video cameras video cameras used to capture full-motion images as digital data.

Digital-to-analog converter (DAC) device that converts digital sound to analog sound that can be played through speakers.

Digitized process of capturing or converting data to a series of 0's and 1's that can be interpreted by a computer.

Digitizing tablet a touch-sensitive board that converts points, lines, and curves drawn with a stylus or digitizer device to digital data.

Digizines print magazines translated into a digital format.

Disk cache section of memory that will be accessed first.

Dot pitch the distance between pixels.

Downloadable files that are stored before they are played.

Drawing programs art production and illustration tools for creating and editing vector-based graphics.

DV Sony's new **Digital Video** recording format that has been set as the standard by the major producers of video camera technologies.

DVD (digital versatile disk) optical storage device that holds from 4.7–17 GB of data.

DVI (Digital Video Interleave) Intel's proprietary compression technology.

Dynamic application or program that can be updated and changed at a moment's notice.

Editors multimedia team members responsible for providing a point of view and either originating or filtering information in a multimedia application.

Edutainment multimedia applications designed to educate as well as entertain.

Electronic agents application programs designed to automatically search for information.

Electronic cash (e-cash) method of electronically paying an online vendor through a third party.

EPS vector-based graphic file format popular for saving image files because it can be imported into nearly any kind of application.

Event handler set of instructions or program that determines what should occur when a certain event takes place.

Executive producer multimedia team member who is responsible for moving a project into and through production.

External casts libraries of commonly used cast elements that can be shared by more than one multimedia application.

Fair-use policy exclusionary right to use copyright images under certain circumstances such as research and instruction.

FAT (file allocation table) index or table of contents that the operating system uses to find data on a disk.

FC-AL (Fibre Channel–Arbitrated Loop) bus structure backed by Seagate, Hewlett-Packard and Quantum that offers simplified ports and cabling over SCSI.

FC-EL (Fibre Channel–Enhanced Loop) a bus structure that is a planned hybrid of SSA and FC-AL.

Film loops a Director cast member that consists of a series of animated frames looped to play over and over again.

Filters special effects applied to an image or part of an image.

Firewalls hardware and software that lie between the Intranet Web server and the Internet to monitor connections, encrypt and protect data, and generally maintain the security of the internal network.

FireWire (also known as **IEEE 1394**) a new high-speed connector used to transfer video and sound from digital video cameras to computers.

Flash RAM a relatively new type of fast, expensive memory generally found on PCI cards and other portable devices.

Flat panel displays flat computer screens that use **liquid crystal display (LCD)** or **gas plasma technology** to produce images on the screen.

Flat-bed scanner input hardware that is able to translate a graphic image into computer data so the image may be displayed and manipulated on a computer.

Flicker when the illusion of motion fails and the animation appears as a rapid sequence of still images.

Flipbook approach   method of creating animation where a sequence of slightly different visual images is compressed and then played back to convey a sense of motion.

Flowcharts   multimedia planning document that illustrates the decision-making process that results as users make choices.

Flowline   Authorware feature that organizes icons and determines the sequence in which they will be played in the multimedia application.

Fragmented   when data is stored in noncontiguous tracks and sectors.

Frame animation   method of creating animation where key frames are created on cells or frames.

Frame rate   the speed at which individual frames display.

Framework icon   built-in navigation controls in Authorware used for branching from different options.

Free form objects   a drawing tool that allows you to create any shape.

Frequency   the number of peaks that occur in one second of sound. The frequency of a waveform determines its pitch.

Full-duplex   mode of transmission in which data is transmitted in opposite directions at the same time.

Games   popular and varied entertainment product.

Geometric forms   wire frame models that serve as the basic building blocks in creating 3D objects.

GIF (graphics interchange format)   graphic file format created by CompuServe for use on the Web. The GIF format only supports up to 256 colors.

Gradient fill   a graduated blend between colors.

Graphic designer   multimedia team member responsible for creating and designing all of the graphic images for a project.

Graphics   2D and 3D images.

Graphics editors   software used to create or modify two-dimensional graphic images.

Graphics tablet   converts points, lines, and curves from a sketch, drawing, or photograph to digital impulses and transmits them to a computer; also contains unique characters and commands.

Grayscale   continuous tone image consisting only of black, white, and gray data.

Group   to piece together objects so that they become one image.

GSM or **GSD**   speech compression schemes originally devised for cellular phones that are used on the Internet for audio on demand and Internet telephony applications.

Handheld scanners   small roller device used to digitize images.

HDTV (high definition television)   video standard that supports a resolution of 1,200 horizontal lines with an aspect ratio (length:width) of 16:9.

Helper applications   tiny programs added to an application to extend its capabilities.

Hertz (Hz) or **Kilohertz (kHz)**   measurements used to determine frequency.

Hi-8   the highest quality videotape format found in the consumer market.

Hierarchical   method of navigation used to maneuver through a multimedia application following a logical, branching structure.

Hotword a link used to access a different multimedia screen, page, or topic.

Hybrid CD a CD that can be played on multiple platforms.

Hybrid Fiber Coax (HFC) cabling scheme that will permit transmission of 10 to 40 Mbps, about 26 times more than T1 lines and about 1,300 times more than standard modems.

Hyperaudio audio in a multimedia application that serves as a trigger to another screen, page, or topic.

Hypergraphic graphic in a multimedia application that serves as a trigger to another screen, page, or topic.

Hypermedia multimedia element in a multimedia application that serves as a trigger to another screen, page, or topic.

HyperTalk HyperCard's powerful, English-like scripting language.

Hypertext text in a multimedia application that serves as a trigger to another screen, page, or topic.

Hypervideo video in a multimedia application that serves as a trigger to another screen, page, or topic.

Image editing program software used to manipulate images using a variety of features that combine painting, editing, and other image composition tools.

Image maps graphics that contain more than one trigger or hypermedia element.

Image resolution the amount of information stored in each image; measured in pixels per inch (ppi).

Immersion virtual reality a type of 3D world that requires special equipment including a headset and gloves; most often encountered in electronic games and simulations.

In-Between an animation method that adds incremental sprites between a starting and ending sprite.

In-Between Linear an animation method to tween between locations in a straight line.

In-Between Special an animation method to tween between sprites that have been resized, squeezed, stretched or otherwise modified.

Indeo Intel's Indeo Video (IVI) compression scheme or codec for the PC and Mac.

Ink effect feature in Director that is used to give a sprite or range of sprites a particular appearance.

Instructional specialist multimedia team members who are experts in designing instructional projects for education or computer-based training.

Integrated Services Digital Network (ISDN) cabling scheme that can deliver almost four times greater performance than most modems.

Interaction icon Authorware feature used to define interactivity.

Interactive multimedia multimedia applications that allow users to respond directly to and control any or all of the media elements.

Interactive scriptwriter multimedia team member who is part traditional writer (film scriptwriter, novelist, or storybook writer) and part interactive designer. This person writes all of the scenarios for the different choices the user may make in an interactive multimedia application.

Interface designer multimedia team member responsible for the look of the multimedia user interface.

Interlaced GIF   file that appears blurry when first downloaded, and then gradually increases in detail until it becomes completely clear.

Internal casts   Director casts that are stored with the movie.

Internet audio e-mail   application that reads your e-mail messages.

Internet audioconferencing   tool that permits two-way, full-duplex audio conversations over the Web.

Internet Explorer   Web browser created by Microsoft Corporation.

Internet   a network of networks that connects millions of computers and people around the globe.

Internet telephony   tool that permits two-way, full-duplex audio conversations over the Web.

Internet voice mail   application that uses the Internet to store and transmit voice mail messages.

Intranets   private networks accessible only by the people within the organization or people with proper authorization to access the internal network.

Jaggies   the stair-step-shaped edges that result when you enlarge a bitmapped image too much.

Java applets   tiny application programs used to create animation and extend Web pages.

Java interpreter   technology capable of coping with the variations that are encountered on different platforms.

Java   non-platform specific programming language that is becoming more and more popular on the Web.

Javascript   Netscape's scripting language used to create animation and interactivity on the Web.

JPEG (Joint Photographic Experts Group)   graphic file format used to create very compact bitmapped file.

Kerning   the amount of horizontal space between characters.

Kiosks   interactive information stations usually installed in public places to answer customer or visitor questions.

Laser disks   read-only, optical storage technology that provide high-quality display of audio and video.

Layers   different levels in a document; often used in image editing programs to create special effects in graphic files.

LCC   waveform compression scheme from FastMan that offers from 20:1 to over 70:1 compression for music and other audio recorded at up to 16 bit, 44 kHz.

LCD projection panels   projection panels that use liquid crystal display (LCD) technology. These projectors are connected to the computer and then placed over a light source such as an overhead projector.

LCD projectors   self-contained projectors with a built-in light source.

Leading   the amount of vertical space between lines of text.

Line art   images that contain only black and white pixels.

Linear   sequential method of navigating through a multimedia application.

Linear media   application that starts at the beginning and progresses through a set sequence of events until it reaches the end.

Lingo   an object-oriented scripting language found in Macromedia Director.

Link map   a schematic that illustrates the interconnectivity of Web pages within and external to a Web site.

Live3D   virtual reality on the Web.

LiveCard   software used to share HyperCard projects over an Intranet or Internet Web site.

Lossless compression   mathematical algorithms that eliminate redundant data.

Lossy compression   compression scheme in which expendable data is removed.

MacPaint   graphic file format used by the Macintosh MacPaint program.

Macromedia Shockwave   plug-in that enables Director movies to be played in a Web browser.

Magnetic tape   media used to store digital data, generally used for backup.

Magneto-optical (M-O) disks   optical disks that can be rewritten through the use of a magnet that polarizes a different pattern of pits.

Mapping software   software used to create custom maps by geographic area, scale, and proposed perspective.

Markup tags   HTML codes that specify how the browser will display text and other multimedia elements.

Microphones   equipment used to translate analog signals into electrical impulses.

MIDI   an internationally accepted file format used to store Musical Instrument Digital Interface (MIDI) data, which are instructions on how to replay music.

MMX™   technology on Pentium processor instruction sets that offers a 50 to 100 percent improvement in the clarity and speed of audio, video, and speech.

Modeling   process used to create a 3D object or scene.

Modeling programs   software used to create and manipulate 3D images.

Modem (modulate/demodulate)   equipment used to convert a computer's digital signals to analog signals that can be transmitted along standard telephone lines.

Mono sounds   flat, unrealistic audio.

Morphing   special technique that uses frames to create the illusion of one object changing into another.

Mosaic   the first cross-platform Web browser that fully exploited the Web's hypermedia capability.

Moving coil microphones   rugged and reliable microphones that create an audio frequency by causing diaphragm coils to vibrate.

MPC1, MPC2, and **MPC3**   standards created to help consumers identify multimedia computer hardware devices.

MPEG and **MPEG2**   video compression formats established by the Motion Picture Experts Group that offer compression up to 14:1.

Multimedia   using more than one medium; integrating text, graphics, animation, sound, and video in an application.

Multimedia authoring software   application software used to incorporate different multimedia elements into one application.

Multimedia director   multimedia team member responsible for using multimedia authoring software to integrate all of the multimedia elements that have been created by the other media specialists. This person is also called the Multimedia architect.

Multimedia PC Marketing Council (MPC)   a special interest group of the **Software Publishers Association (SPA)** created to help sustain the organized expansion of multimedia in the home and workplace.

Navigate icon   icon that takes Authorware from one location to another location on the flowline.

Netscape Navigator   Web browser created by Netscape Corporation.

Non-destructive   method of processing sound or video that maintains the original file.

Non-linear   Navigation method with no prescribed or sequential path; users can navigate from one topic to another in any order they choose.

NTSC (National Television Standard Committee)   television and video standard in which video signals have a rate of 30 fps (29.97 to be exact) and a single frame of video consists of 525 horizontal lines.

Object-based authoring programs   software application that uses an object as a metaphor for creating professional-level multimedia applications.

OCR (optical character recognition)   software that translates bitmapped graphics of text images into editable text documents.

OLE (object linking and embedding)   term that describes a capability of software to import objects (embed) or maintain a path to an object or file (link).

One-way audio   applications that deliver sound on demand.

Onion skinning   animation technique that enables new images to be created by tracing over an existing image.

Online slide shows   presentations delivered using the computer and presentation graphics software.

Open architecture   software designed to be compatible with numerous programs, extensions, and file formats.

Open Media Framework (OMF)   file format created by Avid to enable media interchange in the high end of the digital video market.

OpenDML   file format standard that extends the AVI format making it more useful for the professional market.

Optical disks   storage devices read by lasers.

Page-fed   input hardware that is able to translate a graphic image into computer data so the image may be displayed and manipulated on a computer.

PAL (Phase Alternating Line)   television and video standard in which video signals have a frame rate of 25 fps and a single frame of video consists of 625 horizontal lines.

Pan envelopes   direction from which sound will be heard (from the left, right, back, or front) through a stereo system.

Parallel bus   structure that transmits eight bits of data at one time.

Passive matrix screens   screens that use only one transistor for each row and column.

Paste Special Relative   feature in Director that automatically positions a sequence of selected frames on the stage where the last sequence ended; a longer animation sequence is created by repeating a smaller sequence.

Path-based animation   type of animation that creates animated objects by following an object's transition over a line or vector; also called **vector animation** because it tracks the beginning, direction, and length that an object travels over a line or vector.

PCD (Photo CD)   Kodak's Photo CD graphic file format; bitmapped format that contains different image sizes for each photograph.

PCM WAV   audio player that comes installed with every off-the-shelf PC.

PCX   an earlier, low-end PC standard graphics format.

PDF (Portable Document Format)   cross-platform file format that requires a viewer to be displayed.

Photoshop Native   proprietary file format used with Adobe Photoshop.

PIC   graphics format used by the PC Paint program.

PICT/PICT2   graphic file formats for the Macintosh; these formats are generally used only for screen display.

Pixels   picture elements represented by each small square or lighted dot on a monitor. A pixel is the smallest section of an image that can be independently displayed on a computer monitor.

Playback rate   the number of images displayed per second when animation is being viewed.

Plot File   vector-based graphic format used with some computer-aided drafting (CAD) and drawing programs.

Plug-ins   tiny programs added to an application to extend its capabilities.

Portable Document Software   electronic publishing tools used to create, edit, and read Portable Document Format (PDF) files.

PowerPC   a RISC-based processor developed by Apple and manufactured by IBM and Motorola.

Presentation software   programs used to create basic multimedia applications that are usually displayed in a linear sequence.

Primitive objects   3D geometric figures such as cones, spheres, and cylinders.

Printer fonts   fonts that are specific to the printer or printers connected to the computer.

Production manager   multimedia team member who is responsible for forming a project, moving it into production, and overseeing its creation.

Public domain images   images that can be used at the user's discretion for no charge beyond the initial cost.

Push technology   technology that enables users to make advanced requests for specific information. As new information is available, the server automatically delivers the information to the user's computer.

QTVR (QuickTime VR)   virtual reality software that allows developers to create entire 3D interactive environments for the Web that include 3D objects and full panoramic views of objects and locations.

QuickTime   software-based video-delivery system by Apple that allows delivery of multimedia and video on the computer without using additional hardware.

QuickTime Movie   platform-neutral, convenient and powerful format for storing common digital media types such as audio and video.

RA (RealAudio)   popular format by Progressive Networks used for streaming audio on the Internet; offers good compression up to a factor of 18.

RAID (Redundant Array of Inexpensive Disks)   technology that takes two or more hard drives and treats them as one.

Rasterizing   process of converting a vector-based image to pixels or a bitmapped file format.

Rate   number of waveform samples per second; usually measured in kilohertz with 22 kHz and 44 kHz being the most common sampling rates.

Raw   video compression scheme used to transport Macintosh movies to the Windows platform. This compression scheme is also called **None** because it doesn't really offer much compression when a file is saved or captured.

RealAudio   player needed to play RealAudio formatted files.

Real-time Recording   Director process that permits the recording of movement.

Red Book   international storage standard for compact disc audio that allows audio segments on CDs to be addressed by minutes, seconds, and frames.

Refresh rate   process of redrawing the screen each time items on the screen change.

Removable hard disks   portable magnetic storage devices that hold from 100MB to over 2 GB.

Rendering   process of capturing a view of a 3D scene and saving it as a 2D image.

Resolution   the number of binary bits processed for each sound wave or the number of pixels per inch used to store each graphic file.

Response type   Authorware option box used to specify the type of interaction that the user will encounter.

Result icon   Authorware icon that provides feedback to the user's response.

RF condenser microphones   unique, sophisticated class of condenser microphones that are known for their high quality, accurate sound reproduction, durability, wide frequency response and extremely low self-noise.

RGB (red, green, and blue)   the primary additive colors used in computer monitors and image recorders.

RIFF (resource interchange file format)   format developed by Microsoft that can contain a variety of data types including digital audio and MIDI.

RISC (reduced instruction set computing)   chip technology that reduces the computer's instruction set to only those instructions that are most frequently used, allowing the computer to operate faster.

RLE   lossless data compression scheme useful for making animated movies from screen captures.

ROL   the Roll file format is a proprietary format developed by AdLib, Inc. for use with their sound cards.

Rotational delay   the time it takes for the data to rotate underneath the read/write head after it is positioned on the right track.

Sampling rate   the actual number of different images that are recorded per second.

Sans serif fonts   typefaces without serifs or perpendicular lines at the end of the character.

Scanner   equipment used to digitize images so that they can be interpreted by the computer.

Score   window in Director that allows developers to control the animation elements and tie them together.

Screen fonts   fonts that are dependent upon the monitor and may not appear the same from one computer to another.

Screen size   the number of picture elements, or lighted dots, the monitor can display.

Script Channels   channel in Director that contains the Lingo programming scripts that control the different cast members.

Script-based animation   animation created through programming languages.

Scripting language   programming language used in higher-end multimedia applications.

Scripts   complete blueprints that contain all of the text and narration for a multimedia application.

SCSI (small computer system interface)   bus structure that offers a top speed transmission of 40 MB per second. There are different types of SCSI including **Fast**, **Wide**, **Fast** and **Wide**, as well as **Ultra**.

SECAM (sequential color and memory)   television and video standard in which video signals have a rate 50 Hz with 625 horizontal lines per screen.

Seek time   the time it takes the head to move into position over the data.

Serial bus   bus structure that transmits one bit of data at one time.

Serif fonts   typefaces with serifs or perpendicular lines at the end of the character.

Shading   the process of assigning surface properties such as color, texture, and finish to an object.

Shockwave   a set of compression tools that enable graphics, sound, and animation to be converted into a format appropriate for delivery via the Web.

Site map   illustration of the relationship of the Web pages within a Web site.

Slide-based authoring programs   multimedia programs that use the slide-show as a metaphor to create linear presentations with limited interactivity.

SMC   codec often used to compress computer-graphic sequences.

SMP   audio file format developed by Turtle Beach Systems to be used with their audio recording and editing software.

SMPTE (Society of Motion Picture and Television Engineers)   industry-recognized timecode that measures video in hours, minutes, seconds, and frames; SMPTE is used to synchronize voice, music, and sound effects to the appropriate frames of video based on the frame rate.

Snappy Video Snapshot   device that connects directly to the computer through a parallel port; Snappy can be used to capture digital images from video without installing a video capture card inside the computer.

SND   sound file format developed by Apple; limited to a sampling rate of 8 bits.

Sound card   an expansion card on a PC that is required for recording sound or playing sound through external speakers.

Sound channels   Director channel that contains the sound effects, voice-overs, and music for a movie.

Sound engineer   multimedia team member who handles the equipment used to produce high-quality voice and music.

Sound sampling   process of converting analog sounds into numbers.

Space to Time   an animation technique in Director that creates smooth transitions between sprites.

Specific light   settings in 3D modeling programs that create effects based on several types of light settings including **distant**, **bulb**, and **spot**.

Speed of transfer   refers to the speed at which data is transferred from a CD to the computer processor or monitor.

Sprite   a cast member that has been placed in the score.

Sprite channels   displays all of the image cast members on the stage. Sprites can be bitmaps, buttons, text, or shapes.

SSA (Serial Storage Architecture)   bus structure backed by IBM and Conner that offers simplified ports and cabling over SCSI.

Stage   location in Director where the action of a movie takes place.

Staircasing   the stair-step-shaped edges that result when you enlarge a bitmapped image too much.

Step recording   method of creating animation in Director where the position of the sprite is recorded from one frame to the next.

Stereo sound   dynamic and lifelike sound files that require greater storage capacity than mono sound files.

Stock photography   collections of digital photographs available on CD-ROM or from the Internet.

Stock photography houses   businesses that find and sell the rights to images.

Stock video footage   video footage offered by third parties.

Storyboard   a diagram that describes the content and sequence of each screen in a multimedia application.

Streaming   process in which sound or video is played while it is being downloaded.

Surround sound   sound that includes delays that attempt to simulate the time it would take for sound waves to reach the ears if the sound was happening live.

S-VHS   a video editing format that offers higher quality video than VHS, but slightly lower quality than Hi-8.

T1   digital communications line that transmits 1.5 Mbps (megabits per second), which is approximately equal to the bandwidth delivery of 12 ISDN lines or 50 standard modems.

TARGA   an earlier, high-end PC standard graphic file format; it is not very common in working with graphics, but more popular with video editing.

Tempo Channel   Director channel for changing the movie tempo and inserting wait states.

Text objects   blocks of 2D or 3D type that are used as images.

Texture map   feature that allows 2D images to be applied to objects to create the illusion of texture and realism.

Textures   surfaces that are applied or mapped to models to give them shadows and provide special effects.

Thermal recalibration   when the drive temporarily interrupts what it's doing to measure the size of its platters and adjust them for expansion and contraction due to changes in temperature.

TIFF   most widely used cross-platform bitmapped file format used in image-editing applications, scanning software, illustration programs, page-layout programs, and even word processing programs.

Tiled   repeated over and over behind the other elements on a Web page or multimedia screen.

Time-based   architecture that supports multiple tracks, each containing different media that can be played for different periods of time.

Tool palette   box that contains electronic drawing tools such as pencils, paintbrushes, and erasers.

Trails effect   result that occurs if the previous image is not completely erased when the image in the next frame appears on the screen.

Transition channel   Director channel that contains the effects that occur as the movie progresses from frame to frame.

Transmission speed   the time it takes for the data to be sent from the server computer to the client computer; usually measured in **bits per second (bps).**

TrueMotion   third-party codec from **Horizons Technology**.

TrueType fonts   scalable fonts that are consistent from computer screen to computer screen and from printer to printer.

TSP   DSP's TrueSpeech format.

Tweeners   artists who create the frames between the key frames.

Tweening   process of filling in the frames between the key frames to make the animation appear fluid.

Ultra SCSI   doubles the theoretical maximum throughput of current Fast and Fast and Wide SCSI-2 to 20 and 40 MB per second, respectively.

Ungrouped   when a graphic image is separated into all of the individual pieces used to create it.

Universal Serial Bus (USB)   a low-cost, low-speed interconnect designed to connect PCs to keyboards, mice, joysticks, telephones, and low-end scanners using a daisy chain configuration.

Universe   the 3D workspace in Ray Dream Designer.

Vector-based graphics   images that are created and recreated from mathematical models or formulas.

Vector graphics editors   programs used to create and edit vector graphics.

VHS   lower-quality video format most often found in the consumer market; not really a usable format in video editing.

Video 1   the original video compressor for Video for Windows files; rarely used today because other compression schemes are superior for encoding video footage.

Video capture cards   expansion boards installed on the motherboard that convert analog video signals from camcorders, VCRs, and TVs to digital data that the computer can interpret.

Video files   photographic images played at speeds that make it appear as if the images are in full motion.

Video for Windows (VfW or AVI)   video file format created by Microsoft and supported on all PCs.

Video specialist   multimedia team member who may manage the entire process of shooting, capturing, and editing original video for use in interactive products.

Videographer   multimedia team member who creates and records appropriate, compelling, and high-quality video to be used with interactive technology.

Viewpoint   the position and orientation of a camera used to provide the perspective for rendering.

Virtual reality (VR)   when multimedia is used to create artificial environments complete with 3D images that can be explored and manipulated.

VMF   Vocaltec's Internet Wave format that can compress a WAV file up to 10 percent of the original size while still maintaining good quality.

VOC   a voice file format developed by Creative Labs for use with their Sound Blaster audio card.

VOX   a proprietary sound file format by Voxware for ToolVox.

VRML (Virtual Reality Modeling Language)   the programming language used to create and view 3D environments on the World Wide Web.

WAV   the Waveform sound file format developed by Microsoft and established as the most commonly used and supported format on the Windows platform.

Waveform   the graphic representation of sound showing time on the horizontal axis and amplitude or strength on the vertical axis; includes the frequency, the amplitude, and the harmonic content of the sound.

Wavetable   a list of numbers on a multimedia computer, which represents the waveshape of each sound.

Web master   multimedia team member responsible for creating and maintaining Internet Web pages.

Web page authoring programs   programs that use a GUI (graphical user interface) instead of HTML to create Web pages.

Web page editors   programs that use buttons and icons to insert common HTML tags.

Windows Metafile (WMF)   a metafile, bitmapped, and/or vector-based file created by Microsoft.

WordPerfect Graphics (WPG)   bitmapped files for WordPerfect graphics.

World Wide Web   a world-wide network of linked documents.

WORM (Write Once Read Many)   technology that can only be written to one time.

WPLANY   player used to play AU, WAV, AIFF, and other formats transparently.

Zine   a net-based document generally targeted to a very specific audience through e-mail.

INDEX

REFERENCES

Abernethy, Ken and Allen, Tim, *Beta Edition Exploring the Digital Domain, An Introduction to Computing with Multimedia,* (Boston, MA: PWS Publishing Company, 1998).

Allis, Les; Armstrong, Jay; Davis, Matt; Dillon, Rob; Tab, Julius; Keller, Kirk; Kerner, Matthew; Miller, David; and Silva, Raul, *Inside Macromedia Director 6 with Lingo,* (Indianapolis, IN: New Riders Publishing, 1997).

Ames, Patrick, *Adobe Web Development for the Designer, Web Design & Publishing Unleashed,* (Indianapolis, IN: Sams.net, Publishing, 1997).

Bain, Steve and Gray, Daniel, *Looking Good Online,* (Research Triangle Park, NC: Ventana Communication Group Inc., 1997).

Binder, Kate and Alspach, Ted, *Photoshop 4 Complete,* (Indianapolis, IN: Hayden Books, 1997).

Black, Roger, *Web Sites That Work,* (San Jose, CA: Adobe Systems Inc., 1997).

Bouton, Gary David, *Official Multimedia Publishing for Netscape: Make Your Web Pages Come Alive,* (Research Triangle Park, NC: Ventana Communication Group Inc., 1997).

Brandon, Charles, *Web Publishing with Microsoft Front Page 97,* (Research Triangle Park, NC: Ventana Communication Group Inc., 1997).

Carter, Sean and Branwyn, Gareth, *Internet Power Toolkit,* (Research Triangle Park, NC: Ventana Communication Group Inc., 1996).

Cohn, David S. and Higgins, Justin, *Web Designers Guide to Front Page 97,* (Indianapolis, IN: Hayden Books, 1997).

Davis, Steven R., *Learn Java Now,* (Redmond, WA: Microsoft Press, 1996).

Dream, Ray, *Ray Dream Design 4 The Leader in 3D Illustration,* (Mountain View, CA: Ray Dream Inc., 1993-1995).

Espeset, Tony, *Kick Ass Java,* (Scottsdale, AZ: Coriolis Group, Inc., 1996).

Fahey, Mary Jo, *Web Publisher's Design for Macintosh,* (New York, NY: The Coriolis Group, Inc., 1995).

Fluckiger, Francois, *Understanding Networked Multimedia Applications and Technology,* (Hemel Hempstead Herfordshire, HP2 7EZ: Prentice Hall International (UK) Limited, 1995).

Fromm, Ken, *Careers in Multimedia,* (Louisville, KY: Ziff-Davis Press, 1995).

Gray, Daniel, *Web Publishing with Adobe PageMill 2,* (Research Triangle Park, NC: Ventana Communication Group Inc., 1997).

Haskin, David, *Mews Junkies Internet 500,* (Research Triangle Park, NC: Ventana Communication Group Inc., 1996).

Helmstetter, Anthony, *Web Developer's Guide to Sound & Music,* (Scottsdale, AZ: Coriolis Group Books, 1996).

Heslop, Brent and Budnick, Larry, *HTML Publishing on the Internet,* (Research Triangle Park, NC: Ventana Communication Group Inc., 1995).

Hofstetter, Fred T., *Multimedia Literacy Second Edition,* (New York, NY: McGraw-Hill, 1997).

Honeycutt, Jerry and Brown, Mark R., *HTML 3.2 Starter Kit,* (Indianapolis, IN: Que Corporation, 1997).

Johnson, Nels, *Web Developer's Guide to Multimedia & Video,* (Scottsdale, AZ: Coriolis Group Books, 1996).

Lai, David and Simsic, Greg, *Photoshop 4 Type Magic 1,* (Indianapolis, IN: Hayden Books, 1997).

Lamb, Clarence and Keller, Kirk, *Multimedia Animation,* (Indianapolis, IN: Que Education and Training, 1997).

Lemay, Laura, *Teach Yourself Web Publishing with HTML 3.2 in a Week,* (Indianapolis, IN: Sams Net, Publishing, 1996).

Lemay, Laura; Robichaux, Kabriel A.; and Woolworth, Derrick T., *Net Objects Fusion 2,* (Indianapolis, IN: Sams.net, Publishing, 1997).

Lozano, Jose, *Multimedia Sound and Video,* (Indianapolis, IN: Que Education and Training, 1997).

Mansfield, Richard, *Visual Basic 5 the Comprehensive Guide,* (Research Triangle Park, NC: Ventana Communication Group Inc., 1997).

McGloughlin, Steven, *Multimedia on the Web,* (Indianapolis, IN: Que Education and Training, 1997).

McKinley, Tony, *From Paper to Web, How to Make Information Instantly Accessible,* (San Jose, CA: Adobe Systems Inc., 1997).

Meyer, Eric K., *Designing Infographics,* (Indianapolis, IN: Hayden Books, 1997).

Meyer, Marilyn and Barbar, Roberta, *Computers in Your Future,* Second Edition, (Indianapolis, IN: Que Education and Training, 1997).

Milbunn Ken and Warner, Janine, *Designing Web Pages with PageMill 2.0,* (Indianapolis, IN: New Riders Publishing, 1997).

Milburn, Ken, *Photoshop 4 The Professional Guide to Creating Advance Special Effects,* (Research Triangle Park, NC: Ventana Communication Group Inc., 1997).

Miller, Deborah M. and Miller, Michael D., *Macromedia Director 5 Power Toolkit, Adobe Illustrator 5.0,* (Research Triangle Park, NC: Ventana Communication Group Inc., 1996).

Millhollon, Mary; O'Loughlin, Luanne; and Zuccarini, Toni, *Microsoft Internet Explorer 3.0 Front Runner,* (Scottsdale, AZ: Coriolis Group Inc., 1996).

Mohler, James L., *How to Teach Yourself How to Become a Webmaster in 14 Days,* (Indianapolis, IN: SamsNet, Publishing, 1997).

Mortier, R Shamms and Steward, Winston, *Web Publishing with Macromedia Backstage Internet Studio 2,* (Research Triangle Park, NC: Ventana Communication Group Inc., 1997).

Muscians, Chuck and Kennedy, Bill, *HTML The Definitive Guide,* (Sebastopol, CA: O'Reilly & Associates, Inc., 1996).

Neiderst, Jennifer, *Getting Started in a New Medium. Designing for the Web,* (Sebastopol, CA: O'Reilly & Associates, Inc., 1996).

Neugass, Jonah, *Easy Web Publishing with HTML 3.2,* (Indianapolis, IN: Que Education and Training, 1997).

Oliver, Dick, *Teach Yourself HTML 3.2 in 24 Hours,* (Indianapolis, IN: SamsNet, Publishing, 1997).

Parker, Charles S., *Understanding Networking and the Internet,* (Orlando, FL: Dryden Press, Harcourt Brace College Publishers, 1998).

Parsons, June and Oja, Dan, *Computers, Technology, and Society,* (Cambridge, MA: Course Technology ITP, 1997).

Petrik, Paula and Dubrovsky, Ben, *Creating and Designing Multimedia with Director Version 5,* (Upper Saddle River, NJ: Prentice Hall, 1997).

Petroutsos, Evangelos, *Interactive Web Publishing with Microsoft Tools,* (Research Triangle Park, NC: Ventana Communication Group Inc., 1997).

Pfaffenberger, Bryan and Wall, David, *The 10 Secrets for Web Success,* (Research Triangle Park, NC: Ventana Communication Group Inc., 1996).

Plant, David, *Shockwave: Breathe New Life Into Your Web Pages,* (Research Triangle Park, NC: Ventana Communication Group Inc., 1997).

Poorman, Shepard, *Adobe Photoshop for Windows,* (Indianapolis, IN: Mac Millian Computer Publishing, 1997).

Raggett, Dave; Lann, Jenny; and Alexander, Ian, *HTML 3 Electronic Publishing on the World Wide Web,* (Edinburgh Gate, Harlow Essex, England: Addison, Wesley Longman Limited, 1996).

Richer, Mark and Richer, Julie, *Official Netscape Live Wire Book,* (Research Triangle Park, NC: Ventana Communication Group Inc., 1997).

Rosenzweig, Gary, *The Comprehensive Guide to Lingo,* (Research Triangle Park, NC: Ventana Communication Group Inc., 1997).

Sawyer, Ben, *The Ultimate Web Developers Sourcebook,* (New York, NY: The Coriolis Group, Inc., 1995).

Simpson, Alan, *Official Netscape Navigator Gold 3.0 Book,* (Research Triangle Park, NC: Ventana Communication Group Inc., 1996).

Steinhauer, Lauren, *Director 6 Studio Skills,* (Indianapolis, IN: Hayden Books, 1997).

Sullivan, David, *The New Computer User,* Second Edition, (Orlando, FL: Dryden Press, Harcourt Brace College Publishers, 1997).

Sullivan, Michael J., *Make Your Scanner a Great Design & Production Tool,* (Cincinnati, OH: North Light Books, F & W Publications Inc., 1995).

Tas, Jan and Van Hoey, Rudy, *An Introduction to Digital Scanning,* (Belgium: Agfa-Gevarert N.V., 1994).

Thomas, Susan Sayegh, *Photoshop—A Hands on Introduction Version 3.0,* (Albany, NY: Delmar Publishers, 1995).

Trujillo, Stan, *Cutting Edge Direct 3D Programming,* (Scottsdale, AZ: Coriolis Group Books, 1996).

Turlington, Shannon R., *Official Netscape Plug-In Book,* (Research Triangle Park, NC: Ventana Communication Group Inc., 1996).

Vasquez-Peterson, Anne-Rae and Chow, Paul, *Teach Yourself Great Web Design,* (Indianapolis, IN: Sams.net, Publishing, 1997).

Villamil-Casanova, John and Molina, Louis, *Multimedia an Introduction,* (Indianapolis, IN: Que Education and Training, 1997).

Villamil-Casanova, John and Fernandez-Elias, Leony, *Multimedia Graphics,* (Indianapolis, IN: Que Education and Training, 1997).

Villamil-Casanova, John and Molina, Louis, *An Interactive Guide to Multimedia,* (Indianapolis, IN: Que Education and Training, 1997).

Villamil-Casanova, John and Molina, Louis, *Multimedia Production, Planning and Delivery,* (Indianapolis, IN: Que Education and Training, 1997).

Weinman, Lynda, *Designing Web Graphics .2: How to Prepare Images and Media for the Web,* (Indianapolis, IN: New Riders Publishing, 1997).

Williams, Al, *Developing Active Web Controls,* (Scottsdale, AZ: Coriolis Group Books, 1996).

Wilson, Gloria and Bitter, Gary C., *Learning Media Design,* (Indianapolis, IN: Que Education and Training, 1997).

Wrona, Thomas and Parker, Elisabeth, *Build a Web Site in a Day,* (Research Triangle Park, NC: Ventana Communication Group Inc., 1997).

ABC	http://www.abc.com
Agfa Corporation	http://www.agfa.com
Alchemy Mindworks	http://www.mindworkshop.com
Apple Computer	http://www.apple.com
QuickTime	http://www.quicktime.apple.com
Audix	http://www.audixusa.com/useaudix.htm
Blender	http://www.blender.com
Blue Wolf Browseteria	http://www.bluewolfnet.com
Byte	http://www.byte.com
Caere Corporation	http://www.caere.com
Cakewalk Music Software	http://www.cakewalk.com
Cinemania	http://www.msn.com/Cinemania/Reviews/ReviewsHome.htm
Clipart Connection	http://www.ist.net/clipart
CNN	http://www.cnn.com
Computer Music Journal	ftp://mitpress.mit.edu/pub/Computer-Music-Journal/CMJ.html
Computer Shopper	http://www.computershopper.com
Connectix	http://www.connectix.com
Dataquest	http://www.dataquest.com
Dave Chalk's Computer Show	http://www.chalk.com
Digidesign	http://www.digidesign.com/
Digital Video (DV)	http://www.livedv.com
Doctor Audio Links	http://www.doctoraudio.com/links.html
Dolby	http://www.dolby.com/
Dreamshop	http://www.dreamshop.com
Educorp	http://www.educorp.com
Epson Corporation	http://www.epson.com
FOOTAGE.net	http://www.footage.net:2900
FutureNet - Music	http://www.futurenet.co.uk/music.html
Gartner Group	http://www.gartner.com
Gateway	http://www.gw2k.com
GIF Construction Set	http://www.mindworkshopcom/alchemy/alchemy.html
GIFBuilder	http://iawww.epfl.ch/Staff/Yves.Piguet/clip2gif-home/GifBuilder.html
GIFBuilder's FAQ	http://iawww.epfl.ch/Staff/Yves.Piguet/clip2gif-home/BifBuilde Doc/GifBuilder-FAQs.html
Harmony Central	http://www.harmony-central.com/Newp/
Hewlett-Packard	http://www.hp.com
Horizons Technology	http://www.horizons.com
I-Shop.IWorld	http://i-shop.iworld.com
IBM	http://www.ibm.com
Image Club	http://www.imageclub.com
Imaging	http://www.imaging.com
InFocus	http://www.infocus.com
Intel Corporation	http://www.intel.com
Internet growth charts	http://www2.mids.org/growth/internet
Internet Mall	http://internet-mall.com
Internet Phone	http://www.vocaltec.com
Internet Shopping Network (ISN)	http://www.isn.com
Internet Television Network	http://www.intv.net
Internet Underground Music Archive (IUMA)	http://www.iuma.com
Intersound	http://www.intersoundmusic.com

InVision Interactive	http://www.cybersound.com
Iomega	http://www.iomega.com
Kim Komando	http://www.komando.com
KITS	http://www.live105.com
Kodak	http://www.kodak.com
Logitech Corporation	http://www.logitech.com
m-Tropolis	http://www.mtropolis.com
Macromedia	http://www.macromedia.com
Macromedia - Shockwave	http://www.macromedia.com/shockwave/
Micron	http://www.micron.com
Microsoft Corporation	http://www.microsoft.com
MIDI	http://www.eeb.ele.tue.nl/midi/index.html
Miramax	http://www.miramax.com
Motorola	http://www.motorola.com
MPEG-1 Audio	http://www.crs4.it/~luigi/MPEG/mpeg1-a.html
MPEG-2 Audio	http://www.crs4.it/~luigi/MPEG/mpeg2.html
Multi-Media Music	http://www.wavenet.com/~axgrindr/quimby.html
Music Previews Network	http://www.mpmusic.com/
NBC	http://www.nbc.com
Netscape	http://www.netscape.com
NetSpeak	http://www.netspeak.com
New Media	http://www.newmedia.com
New York Times	http://www.nytimes.com
NuReality	http://nureality.com
Opcode	http://www.opcode.com
Oracle	http://www.oracle.com
PointCast Network (PCN)	http://www.pointcast.com
Power Computing	http://www.powercomputing.com
Power Computer	http://powercc.com
Progressive Networks	http://www.realaudio.com
QSound	http://www.qsound.ca
QuickTime City	http://quicktime.apple.com/qt-city
Royal Frazier's awesome site	http://member.aol.com/roalef/gifanim.htm
Rykodisc	http://www.rykodisc.com
Seagate	http://www.seagate.com
Sennheiser	http://www.sennheiser.ca/english/mics.htm
Simpson's Page	http://www.wantree.com.au/~richmond/simpsons.htm
Snappy	http://www.play.com
Software Publishers Association (SPA)	http://www.spa.org
Sony Pictures	http://www.spe.sony.com/Pictures/SonyMovies/index.html
Sun Microsystems	http://www.sun.com
Supercard	http://www.supercard.com
Syquest	http://www.syquest.com
The Classical MIDI Archives	http://www.prs.net/midi.html#index
The Dave Chalk Computer Show	http://www.chalk.com
The Digital Audio Directory	http://www.westworld.com/~wizard/dad.html
The Sound Page	http://www.ucsalf.ac.uk/pa/soundp/sphome.htm
The Web Multimedia Tour	http://ftp.digital.com/webmm/fbegin.html
Toshiba	http://www.toshiba.com
US Robotics	http://www.usr.com
US West Dex	http://yp.uswest.com
USA Today	http://www.usatoday.com
VDOnet	http://www.vdolive.com
Wal-Mart	http://www.wal-mart.com
ZD Net	http://www.zdnet.com

CREDITS

Chapter Five

All screen shots from Macromedia's Director, SoundEdit 16, and Authorware courtesy of Macromedia.

pg. 140   Figure 5.6   Courtesy of Sierra On-Line, Inc.

pg. 141   Figure 5.7   Courtesy of Sierra On-Line, Inc.

pg. 158   Figure 5.23 Courtesy of Hewlett Packard Company

pg. 160   Figure 5.25 Courtesy of Microsoft Corporation

Chapter Six

All screen shots from Adobe Premier courtesy of Adobe.

pg. 172   Figure 6.3   Courtesy of Sony Electronics Inc.

pg. 173   Figure 6.4   Courtesy of Sony Electronics Inc.

pg. 175   Figure 6.6   Courtesy of Sony Electronics Inc.

pg. 182   Figure 6.14 Courtesy of International Business Machines

pg. 190   Figure 6.19 Courtesy of International Business Machines

pg. 193   Figure 6.23 © Index Stock Photography and Matthew Borkoski 1998

Chapter Seven

All screen shots from Macromedia's Director, SoundEdit 16, and Authorware courtesy of Macromedia. All screen shots from Adobe PageMill courtesy of Adobe Systems.

Chapter Eight

pg. 258   Figure 8.28 Copyright Power Production Software, www.powerproduction.com